Healing Cultures

Healing Cultures

Art and Religion as Curative Practices in the Caribbean and Its Diaspora

Edited by
Margarite Fernández Olmos
and Lizabeth Paravisini-Gebert

palgrave

Figures 3.1–3.5 printed courtesy of the artist, Héctor Delgado.
Figure 13.1 and 13.2 printed courtesy of the artist, LeRoy Clarke.
"Archipelago" (from *Douens*) and "My Work is Obeah" reprinted courtesy of LeRoy Clarke.
"Ethnomedical (Folk) Healing in the Caribbean" is reprinted with the permission of the author, Brian M. du Toit.
"Los negros curanderos," (translated here as "Black Arts: African Folk Wisdom and Popular Medicine in Cuba") and citation from *El monte* reprinted with the permission of Isabel Castellanos.
"Afro-Caribbean Healing: A Haitian Case Study" is reprinted with the permission of the author, Karen McCarthy Brown.

First published 2001 by
PALGRAVE™
175 Fifth Avenue, New York, N.Y.10010 and
Houndmills, Basingstoke, Hampshire RG21 6XS.
Companies and representatives throughout the world

PALGRAVE is the new global publishing imprint of St. Martin 's Press LLC Scholarly and Reference Division and Palgrave Publishers Ltd (formerly Macmillan Press Ltd).

ISBN 0-312-21898-2 hardback

Library of Congress Cataloging-in-Publication Data
Healing cultures : art and religion as curative practices in the Caribbean and its diaspora /
edited by Margarite Fernández Olmos and Lizabeth Paravisini-Gebert.
    p.   cm.
    Includes bibliographical references.
    ISBN 0-312-21898-2
    1. Traditional medicine—Caribbean Area.   2. Blacks—Caribbean Area—Religion.   3. Healing—Religious aspects.   4. Medicine and art—Caribbean Area.   5. Caribbean Area—Social life and customs.   I. Fernández Olmos, Margarite.   II. Paravisini-Gebert, Lizabeth.
GR120.H43   2001
398'.353'09729—dc21

                                                    00–059148

A catalogue record for this book is available
from the British Library.

Design by Letra Libre, Inc.

First edition: March 2001
10 9 8 7 6 5 4 3 2 1

Printed in the United States of America.

To the memory of my father,
Peter Fernández,
who knew and practiced the healing power of love.
[MFO]
and
To the memory of my dear friends,
Carlos Yorio and Gil Watson,
cherished lives lost to AIDS.
[LPG]

Contents

II
ARTISTIC HEALING

List of Illustrations

Archipelago

For Lynette Wilson

1
This geography opened with a fan of macaw tails,
Flung her vertebral necklace wide with frond and fin
To show her flowering pulp that leapt from the bark
With her breasts full of panthers' eyes . . .

Clear seasons, the taste of soft clouds and curling salt
Recur around her waist; kisses of round clouds descend sweet;
The ears among her sands blossomed, quivered, caught
In pubescence the first draught of alcohol from conquering
          beards . . .

Beyond her plumed forehead, beyond her fine objects of fine earth
They plunged with prow and anchor, with cannon, with flag
Into her navel of revolving waters.
O Mayas, skies of saffron, of living gold. Crushed anthill!

Witness their caged Ibises. Flocks of ghosts on the edge
          of a scarlet cloud.
Reduced to history and entertainment, their lost hieroglyphs,
          an only cluster
Of fossilled bird-feet Arawak and Carib, the simplest traces
          of mnemonic bush,
Heads without their Gods, spilled suns wear their fire like mud.

The diarist thumbs the log, unfurls the surrounding sea,
          calculates . . .
Each fallen star, each sweet island . . .

. . . Fallen trees, gardens left agape; scorched
Earth, smoke; alligators, gnarled breasts with feathers;

Cracked bells; temples vacated by their gods; stampedes;
Lice-shredded nights; days to come more numerous than sand.

2
Sterner west, the musketeers held no remorse.
Long lost were his fine art of wife grazing sheep on the Lee.
Waste no time to enter pleas where the ear sours.
Each tide crashed with a taste of broken bronze . . .

And then, its waiting ports, its whips, its scales, its chains.
Choice died. Denial became privilege. Promise was prayer
With wayward wings. And so with backward-turned feet
He entered his landscape laughing with each his deaths.

History pretends amnesia here, though faces smile
From rocks their careful etchings of defeat. A last
House slave, tuxed'n spats, glares from hooded eyes,
circumspec', jokes under a crisp Sunday's unwaning architecture.

3
The first look I had of these islands
Was one green morning in Dada's spacy grin
We chased whales over de whole "ocean-sea"
From de Bahamas to out dey in de Gulf
Coming up through de Serpent's Mouth.

A rainbow opened with his wings, and a child heard
Seagulls dive down his eyes, the silent plash
Of bittersweet between beak and fin, the salt
Falling backwards, the gentle fleeting curve

From wave to sky-droning kites.
Putting me down, he stood into his full height.
The whole ocean laughed from his shoulders, now
Fish were leaping from his one hand to the other!
Grouper, shark, barracuda, mackerel, leaping

Carite, moonshine, power and cro-cro;
Saparte, red snapper and pampadores . . . O Sauteurs!
He held the rainbow, this Vincentian fisher, casting
Its net. From his stories the ports rose baptised
Like sails of starched winds.

The real Cuba, with its iguanas, its khaki, stitched
By their own hands, their guitars and the burning

Fingers of Guillén and Macandal, the real Cuba
With a sword in a peg-legged buccaneer's
Throat, that fisher saw a bird on the stern . . .

Saw the sea-swell, stirred by his own oar
In a mighty womb, the quick shudder of a harpooned whale
The barracuda in his retreat, the white clouds
Of water, the spurt of red from the nostril he carved
Of flesh and salt and wind and current . . .

Their bodies writhed black and wet like his catch. Haiti,
Clamour of gongs, and drums in the groundswell
Of dethroned Gods, around that citadel where starved dogs
Of our soul eat their tails. Under the Dawn, bespectacled Houngans
Lift their glasses of clairin to a string of corpses . . . feet first!

Puerto Rico, Barbados and de Bahamas
Proliferate of rape and gamble . . .
Candles, incense, spices burn in breasts
Of St. Vincent, St Kitts, St Lucia . . .
From Cesaire's lice-poxed Martinique of maidens
The lizards cast shadows on water of blue, bluer
Than blue and mist-congealing infinite green
Where Antigua-Grenada weeps, the children weep:
Sauteurs, again, Sauteurs!

To the furthest leaf South, the Atlantic windfall of sailors
Drunk on the main drags . . . bastard oil . . .
Bastard cane . . . bastard banana, bastard me,
You, Guyana, Guatemala
And their own mother too!

Crumpled rainbow
From Haiti to Trinidad and Tobago . . .

To my task of broken mirrors,
My archipelago!

4
Those were the days, father said,
When the hunter sat to rest on snakes
That were huge tree trunks that devoured cattle, whole . . .
And those waves he swam were taller
Than the tales that washed away the sins against him.

How clearly I see him among the vast currents
Alone, above the undertow, for he was a good swimmer;
The early voyager sees Mountains, steady above the crest;
Sees the stark beach thin its thread to a lost heartbeat.

He embraces the bay, the smallest laughter of spilled surf,
And those little friends,
'Who had not even missed me!'
Cavorting among the sand.

A good swimmer knows how to float
And how to go against the current, and, he said:
That is why I am alive to tell the tale today.

LeRoy Clarke, Douens (1981)

Acknowledgments

Grateful thanks to the Professional Staff Congress of the City University of New York for a research grant that greatly facilitated the completion of this project; to Robert Scott for his gracious assistance and encouragement; to Santiago Nieves for taking time from his New York Latino radio program to share ideas; and to my patient and understanding family, Enrique and Gabriela.

[MFO]

The Faculty Research Program at Vassar College generously supported the completion of this project. To the members of the award committee, and to my gifted and most resourceful research assistants, Malian Lahey and Jennifer Romero, my deepest gratitude. And to my two Gordons—husband and son—all my love.

[LPG]

❊   ❊   ❊

Photographs in figures 3.1–3.5 were reprinted courtesy of the artist, Héctor Delgado.

Illustrations in figures 13.1 and 13.2 were reprinted courtesy of the artist, LeRoy Clarke.

The poem, "Archipelago" from *Douens . . .* , and the interview "My Work is Obeah" were reprinted courtesy of LeRoy Clarke.

"Ethnomedical (Folk) Healing in the Caribbean" is reprinted with the permission of the author, Brian M. du Toit.

The essay "Los negros curanderos," originally chapter vii of *La medicina popular de Cuba,* and translated and reprinted here as "Black Arts: African Folk Wisdom and Popular Medicine in Cuba," as well as citation from *El monte* were reprinted with the permission of Isabel Castellanos.

Chapter 4, titled Afro-Caribbean Healing: A Haitian Case Study, a version of which was originally printed in *Healing and Restoring: Health and Medicine in the World's Religious Traditions,* is reprinted here with the permission of the author, Karen McCarthy Brown.

Preface

The Spanish expression *la cultura cura* (culture heals) is understood, in the context of Caribbean culture, as an affirmation of the potential healing power of a variety of cultural practices—religion, art, music, literature, folklore, the vernacular language—that together constitute the ethos of the various peoples of the region. What happens, however, when cultures themselves are in jeopardy? What occurs when cultural practices come under siege as they enter the debate over national identity in colonial and postcolonial societies? What are the antidotes for an ailing culture?

Healing Cultures examines a broad range of belief systems—among them Haitian Vodou,[1] Cuban Santería, Puerto Rican Espiritismo, Jamaican Obeah—from a variety of disciplines—anthropology, literature, film, cultural and religion studies—addressing these far-reaching questions via scholarly research and personal interviews in an attempt to bring to life the various cultural practices that have sustained the peoples of the Caribbean through colonialism, the impact of slavery and its concomitant racial and class hierarchies, economic underdevelopment, and the Caribbean diaspora to various metropolitan centers. Powerful repositories of inner strength and cultural affirmation, the Caribbean's African-derived syncretic religious and healing practices have penetrated to the very core of cultural development in the region, leaving deep imprints on every cultural manifestation of significance.

This collection arises from a previous volume, *Sacred Possessions: Vodou, Santería, Obeah, and the Caribbean,* which we published in 1997. As a result of the research undertaken for *Sacred Possessions,* it became clear to us that more attention needed to be paid to the healing aspect of these important religious systems and their impact on the "well-being" of cultures. Among the broader aims of this work, therefore, is an in-depth exploration of the types of knowledge and spectrum of healing practices in the region and their contribution to the development of Caribbean societies. *Healing Cultures* is divided into two broadly defined areas: the curative practices derived from Caribbean religious traditions and the "healing" arts, including the survival through art and literature of cultural healing practices in the Caribbean diaspora. With the exception of Espiritismo (which originated in European Spiritualism), the religious systems from which these practices derive are the Caribbean "diasporan religions"—as Joseph Murphy has coined them—that share a common West African or Central African heritage, and gods, rituals, and theologies easily traced to common roots. These are, their similarities notwithstanding, dynamic practices that differ from each other in significant ways.

Vodou, the oldest and perhaps least understood of all Afro-Caribbean belief systems, was born in the Dahomean, Congolese, and Nigerian regions of West Africa and filtered through Roman Catholic symbolism and liturgical traditions. The deities of Vodou, the *loa* (or *mystères*), are generally divided into two main rites, or "nations": the *Rada* pantheon of Dahomean or Yoruban origin, and the *Petro,* Creole loa originating principally in Haiti. A complex practice of myths and rituals linking the devotees to the divine entities and to the community, the cornerstone of the Vodou belief system is the possession of believers by the loa.

The syncretic nature of *Vodou* (and other belief systems of the region) originated in the demand, during the colonial period, that slaves relinquish their gods for those of their masters. When Catholic missionaries displayed lithographs displaying the symbolism associated with the lives of the Christian saints, slaves linked this iconography to the representation of their own gods. Thus Erzulie, the beautiful water goddess of love in Dahomey became the Virgin Mary, and Legba, the guardian of the gates of the underworld, Saint Peter. Syncretism is the outcome, therefore, of a process of accommodation, preservation, and cultural resistance.

Cuban Santería, also known as *la Regla de Ocha,* or the belief system of the *orichas,* is the consequence of a similar process: the convergence of Yoruban rituals and practices honoring the orichas, or deities, with the obligation to worship Roman Catholic saints (*santos*). In like fashion, true membership in the Santería spiritual community involves unconditional dedication, rigorous discipline, and lifelong commitment to a particular deity or spirit.

In the English-speaking Caribbean, Obeah, defined by George Simpson as a Jamaican conjuring practice closely linked to witchcraft, differs from Vodou and Santería in that its beliefs and rituals are not centered on the participation of the community but involve secret individualized consultations aimed at fostering specific ends.[2] The term "Obeah" (from the Ashanti word for witch or wizard, *obayifo*) can be traced to the Ashanti tribes from the African Gold Coast, heavily represented in the slave populations of the British colonies. The practice involves the "putting on" and "taking off" of "duppies" or "jumbees" (ghosts or spirits of the dead) for good or evil purposes. Obeah is analogous to Vodou and Santería, however, in the vital cultural role it has played throughout the English-speaking Caribbean as a repository of the African folk's cultural heritage.

Despite important differences, the diverse practices examined in *Healing Cultures* can be said to coincide perfectly in two significant respects: their promotion of a union of humankind with the spirit world (a commonality they share with Espiritismo) and the notion of "service." As observed by Joseph Murphy, the reciprocity between community and spirit is expressed in music, word, and movement to summon the spirit, who in turn empowers the congregation. "Diasporan ceremonies are thus services *for* the spirit, actions of sacrifice and praise to please the spirit. And they are services *of* the spirit, actions undertaken by the spirits to inspire the congregation. . . . It is 'service,' in all its elegant multiple meanings, that shows the active quality of the spirituality of the African diaspora."[3]

The service Murphy refers to encompasses a variety of cultural elements. In Haitian Vodou, for example, it comprises individual practices and creeds, a structure for community justice, a fertile oral tradition, a rich iconography that has nourished Haitian art, a wealth of metaphors of political affirmation, as well as a complex system of folk medicine. Cuban Santería has similarly inspired a rich tradition in literature and the arts and in healing; herbalism and ritual cures are fundamental components of practices that have sustained their communities for centuries despite vilification and condemnation by the dominant culture. It should be recalled that Vodou, Santería, Obeah and the other religions discussed here were repressed and persecuted partly as a result of their practitioners' reputed skills in the preparation of spells and cures.

Healing Cultures argues for a different focus: the beneficial aspects of these practices as seen from within the communities in question. With the reevaluation of traditional curative practices taking place worldwide, we would appeal for a reconsideration of the healing methods used by peoples accustomed to adaptation and reinvention; alternative and integrative strategies have been the tools of survival in these creative Caribbean societies, as the following essays will demonstrate.

These essays also attest to the importance of the discourse of illness and healing in addressing issues of colonialism and dependency in the Caribbean region. Beginning in the nineteenth century, illness, as a metaphor for the Caribbean islands' condition of colonial inferiority, becomes a central concept for both pro- and anticolonial groups. The symbolic representation of Caribbean colonies/natives as diseased bodies—inferior in race, deficient in intellect, indolent in body, insalubrious in climate—presupposes the need for superior, industrious, rational European colonizers whose influence can be brought to bear in seeking to ameliorate these geography- and race-bound conditions. The discourse of illness, in its many forms, seeks to justify colonial control. Adopted by Creole elites of European extraction, it also serves to uphold racialist class structures imposed by slavery and the plantation.

Nowhere is this clearer than in the many examples derived from nineteenth-century Caribbean literature that posit illness as endemic to native peoples and culture—and miscegenation as contributing to racial "weakness" and propensity to disease—in which the European-educated white Creole doctor emerges as the cultural hero working to achieve some degree of health. Among these, the most salient example, that of Puerto Rican Naturalist writer Manuel Zeno Gandía, author of a series of novels intended as a *Crónica de un mundo enfermo* (*Chronicle of a Sick World*), reveals the degree to which the representation of disease as symbolic of Caribbean colonial and racial realities had taken hold in the literary imagination. Zeno Gandía can write thus about the Puerto Rican peasant as weakened by racial mixture, deprived through ignorance, hunger, and predisposition of the faculty to reason and develop intellectually, in need of the wisdom of the white planter and doctor to survive. His analysis, characteristic of the paternalistic approach to the examination of society and culture of the liberal Puerto Rican elite of the end of the nineteenth century, will find its way eventually to Antonio S. Pedreira's more conservative view of the Puerto Rican mulatto population as a collective body weakened and degraded by miscegenation. Pedreira's *Insularismo* (1934) will seek to articulate, using biology and illness as points of departure, how the negative aspects of mixed racial inheritance and an insalubrious environment, together with what he describes as a sad lack of direction in their spiritual culture, have left Puerto Ricans adrift, requiring "white" guidance.

Not surprisingly, Caribbean writers and intellectuals, faced with a discourse of illness stemming from the most conservative defenders of the colonial and postcolonial status quo, have turned to the discourse of healing—particularly that of healing through African-derived religious and cultural practices—to articulate a contestatory discourse of cultural and political liberation. The healing metaphor—as a counterargument to the metaphor of illness—has become perhaps the most frequent and most effectively deployed weapon against colonial discourse. One has only to recall the names of the many authors whose work relies on a representation of the individual's power to heal his/herself through an affirmation of belonging to the Afro-Caribbean folk and the acceptance of African-derived folk wisdom—Simone Schwarz-Bart's *Pluie et vent sur Telumée Miracle,* Erna Brodber's *Myal,* Ana Lydia Vega's "Otra maldad de Pateco," Mayra Montero's *Como un mensajero tuyo,* the poetry of Derek Walcott and Edward Kamau Brathwaite—to be conscious of the importance of the healing discourse to the development of Caribbean thought.

The healing metaphor, as some of the essays in this book suggest, has gained considerable strength as a tool of literary and essayistic representation among Caribbean writers and artists in the Caribbean diaspora, where it has indeed emerged, in the last two decades, as a most salient theme. Caribbean migrants living in formerly colonial metropolitan centers have shared common ills: in the threat to the strong bonds of family; the discovery of the racial self in the eyes of the Euro-American "Other"; the debilitating loss of culture and the concomitant forfeit of identity; rootlessness and urban decay; violence as a test of manhood for ghetto youth; early death and prison stays; and generational clashes and conflicts over gender roles that have been the product of migration. Essential in the representation of these concerns have been the recurring metaphors of illness and healing. Nervous breakdowns, madness leading to suicide, deadly infections caused by treacherous Caribbean *microbios,* evil possessions, insidious cases of diabetes with roots in miscegenation, drug addiction as lingering self-destruction, and AIDS are all called upon to attest to the destructive aspects of Caribbean migration and acculturation in the United States, Canada, England, or France, as the case may be. They become the embodiments of the threat to psyche, body, and culture posed by assimilation, and spawn a converse metaphor, that of healing as the recovery of self and culture, of the reclaiming of memory as the remedy for rootlessness, of the elaboration of myth as a cure for history-lessness at the core of these emerging diasporan cultures. Readers of diaspora writers like Jamaica Kincaid, Edwige Danticat, Oscar Hijuelos, Pedro Juan Soto, Julia Alvarez—to name only a salient few—have come to associate healing as a central response to alienation.

🔲 🔲 🔲

The essays collected in this book seek to engage the many ways—and the many disciplines—through which the theme and process of healing have become of central importance to Caribbean peoples. We should note here our gratitude to the artists and scholars who so generously and enthusiastically contributed their talent to creating this work. Some indeed discovered that sharing their vision of these healing cultures—the creative process itself—became for them a healing modality. We hope that the antidotal effects will be shared by our readers.

Chapter 1 ▨

La Botánica Cultural:
Ars Medica, Ars Poetica

Margarite Fernández Olmos

In the Latino barrios of many U.S. metropolitan centers, there are establishments that bewilder the inexperienced passerby: botánicas. Fascinated (or disconcerted) by the term—is this, perhaps, some sort of garden shop?—and the colorful and eclectic shop windows—a seemingly unfathomable melange of books, statues, herbs, candles, soaps, powders, spiritual lithographs and leaflets—few are aware of their cultural and functional diversity and complexity. A glance inside and the mystery increases, as one is confronted with the copious pharmacopoeia of traditional folk and ritual healing: shelves of multicolored "solutions" in a variety of forms claiming power to effect important changes in one's life—from a remedy for a problematic love life to the cure for a serious illness or relief from distress. With time the mesmerized onlooker soon discovers, however, that the botánica is a multifaceted reality. Part herb shop and folk clinic, more than a "poor man's pharmacy," the botánica is a curative promise. With a pluralistic and eclectic worldview, botánicas are a community enterprise, a heritage, and a symbol of Caribbean cultural healing, a palpable representation of medical *mestizaje,* or syncretism. *La botánica cultural* is our metaphor, then, for the diverse range of holistic/artistic and spiritual remedies that Caribbean peoples have drawn upon for centuries whenever the need has arisen for individual and/or communal healing.

I

CAFÉ
Besides being delicious, coffee is medicinal. It provides warmth. The green
leaves, in gargles, soothe a toothache. The green berry is a laxative. The root, cut
into three and boiled, lowers a fever. In spiritual offerings to the dead the cup of
coffee they once enjoyed in life is always present. Greatly manipulated in sorcery,
one should take care where it is drunk.[1]

CHEST PAINS
Scorpion oil. Much used by the people, one would see vials filled with scorpi-
ons for public consumption in pharmacies. It was as much in demand as boa oil.
Scorpion oil is an ancient remedy utilized in sixteenth-century Spain.

The keen interest in alternative approaches to healing and the reevaluation
of the Western biomedical model in recent years was stimulated in the mid-
1970s by critiques of institutional medicine—as exemplified by the works of
Michel Foucault and Ivan Illich among others[2]—as well as the analytical
perspectives of feminists, anthropologists, and those with competing claims
of knowledge, such as nontraditional healers. Within the field of anthropology, the quest for a reconceptualization of health, healing, and human experience has led to a proliferation of studies in the fields of medical and
psychological research, and their concomitant cross-cultural and transcultural therapies. But medical anthropology has expanded beyond these limited parameters; it is now also a prominent site for the analysis of power and
domination, "a site for joining debate of critical social, political, existential,
and epistemological issues."[3] The language of medicine, according to Byron
J. Good, is more than a reflection of the empirical world: "It is a rich *cul-*
tural language, linked to a highly specialized version of reality and system of
social relations, and when employed in medical care, it joins deep moral
concerns with its more obvious technical functions."[4] And while the exotic
"other" of non-Western cultures was initially the exclusive object of ethnomedicine and ethnopsychiatry, there has been an increased realization that
the dominant biomedical model is not just a product of Western, industri-
alized culture but a culture in itself, and as such it too is subject to anthropological analysis.

> There is, then, no essential medicine. No medicine that is independent of his-
> torical context. . . . So much variety, indeed, is apparent even within the same
> society that to talk of "traditional healing," or for that matter "biomedicine,"
> as if the term denotes a homogeneous social reality would be a serious misap-
> prehension of ethnographic descriptions. . . .
>   Medicine, then, like religion, ethnicity and other key social institutions,
> is a medium through which the pluralities of social life are expressed and
> recreated.[5]

Caribbean healing systems have frequently been the object of such scrutiny from varying perspectives, based largely on distinctions described as "emic" (inner) and "etic" (outer). Among emic Caribbean scholars, Lydia Cabrera (Cuba) and Michel Laguerre (Haiti) are ideal examples of authors writing from "within"; their works demonstrate a respect and an appreciation for folk practices and "syncretic medical traditions" not usually present in research anchored in exclusively Western scientific conceptual categories.[6] Such researchers have been able to examine and elucidate their world with tolerance, compassion, empirical knowledge, cultural sensitivity, and creativity; that is, with the ideal attributes of a healer.

PREVENTIVE MEDICINE

To purify the body of evil influences and avoid or cure illnesses, baths are taken with the herb that corresponds to the person's patron spirit, or with that of the orisha indicated by a healer. Rainwater baths are medicinal. These waters are stored. The rains gathered on Easter Saturday are holy.

To avoid apoplexy it is good to always have on hand a white-painted coconut in the house. Greet Olofi every morning, at 6 A.M. and at noon, and roll the coconut. If this can be done on a hill, even better.

Healing practices originated in spiritual practices. The Judeo-Christian tradition ministered to body and spirit, as exemplified in the Jewish spiritual healing practice of anointing an individual with oil and then purifying and expelling the disease and/or evil spirit through prayer, a pattern of healing recorded in the New Testament in the miracle cures performed by Christ. (The practice was later codified into a sacrament of the Roman Catholic Church for the dying and today exists as part of the healing ministries, a continuation of the earlier tradition of healing through the laying on of hands and prayer.)[7] For centuries the institutional care of the sick was church related. Gradually, however, boundaries began to be erected between scientific medicine (symbolized by the germ theory of disease) and the supernatural. By the nineteenth century the process of desacralization of medicine appeared to be complete; in truth, however, it was not.

Faith healing, a traditional component of the Pentecostal religion (which is increasingly displacing Roman Catholicism in Latin America and the Caribbean) as well as of other religious practices that consider faith a more effective cure than biomedicine, experienced a revival in the 1980s as part of an ever-growing search for guidance in matters of life and death and for spiritual approaches to wellness: "It was Hippocrates who first banished spirits from the healing arts, and for the past 2,500 years the faithful have struggled to force them back in."[8]

In the Caribbean the spirits never left. They were an intrinsic part of the Amerindian world that later blended with the saints of the Roman Catholic colonist and the *orishas* and *loas* of the African slave to form the syncretic Caribbean culture examined by Michel Laguerre in *Afro-Caribbean Folk Medicine* (1987). The healing system Laguerre describes has survived with the strategies of transculturation—adaptation and renewal, tradition and experimentation—and is inclusive, pluralistic, local, anonymous, and, in many cases, magical. What at first glance may indeed appear by mainstream standards to be bizarre practices and beliefs can be better understood by taking into account the region's historical and cultural context; in the Caribbean that context is fundamentally the institution of slavery. Laguerre reminds us that slaves were obliged to recur to distant memories of home to attempt to reconstruct African medicinal knowledge, an often lonely and frustrating task given the initial language barriers among people of differing cultural groups, the psychological complexities of the selective memory process, and the "structural and ecological limitations" slaves encountered: locating familiar medicinal plants was difficult to do in the unfamiliar New World physical environment, and the structure of plantation life left little free time for curing practices, much of which were conducted in secrecy to avoid the slave owner's hostility. Clandestine healing rituals thus became a form of resistance and self-preservation.[9] "Slave medical culture" evolved from this harsh reality, but also "out of the slaves' ability to remember past African medical traditions and to borrow from the medical experiences of the Europeans and Amerindians."[10]

Present-day folk healing modalities in the region are varied and complex; migrations within the Caribbean and throughout the world have created new medical syncretisms.[11] But two things remain constant: Caribbean folk healing continues to be marginalized and rejected by mainstream culture even as it remains a cultural recourse and resource for Caribbean peoples, an example of the struggle for democratization of healing knowledge. "[T]he existence of Afro-Caribbean folk medicine must be seen within the political context of western science, where political power is a key to legitimacy. If Afro-Caribbean folk medicine is marginal, it is because its adherents are powerless."[12] And the other constant of Caribbean folk healing is that the elements most rejected by mainstream culture—those that cannot withstand the scrutiny of scientific empirical investigation—are precisely those that claim the most tenacious hold on the Caribbean cultural imagination, namely the magical/spiritual/religious methodologies of Vodou, Santería, Obeah, Espiritismo, and the myriad other spiritual practices in the region and its diaspora ("root" and "hoodoo" doctors studied by Zora Neale Hurston and others in the southeastern United States are an example of the herbal/magical ethnomedical practices transplanted to the area from the

Caribbean).[13] Numerous illustrations of the insistent grip of this powerful cultural force in Caribbean society can be found in language, music, dance, art, literature, and film,[14] expanding beyond narrow definitions of what constitutes a "curative" practice, a fact early recognized by the Cuban ethnographer Lydia Cabrera, whose magnificent work *El monte: Igbo-Finda; Ewe Orisha, Vititi Nfinda. Notas sobre las religiones, la magia, las supersticiones y el folklore de los negros criollos y del pueblo de Cuba* (*The Sacred Wild: Igbo-Finda; Ewe Orisha, Vititi Nfinda. Notes on the Religions, the Magic, the Superstitions and the Folklore of Creole Blacks and the Cuban People*, 1954) embodies the concept of curative transcultural Caribbeanness.

Acclaimed for her literary contributions to Caribbean and Latin American letters in her collections of short stories based on Afro-Cuban folklore, Cabrera also amassed a significant body of ethnographic material, elucidating the practices of the various Afro-Cuban religious traditions on the island, and linguistic research (classifications of popular sayings and compilations of diverse African dialects spoken by certain sectors of the Cuban population). Of her nonfictional work, *El monte* is considered her most valuable, compared by one critic to the Judeo-Christian Bible and the Mayan *Popol-Vuh*.[15] *El monte* transcribes the belief systems of New World African peoples in Cuba—their gods, their rituals, and their miracles. Cabrera claimed only one methodology and purpose: to allow Afro-Cuban people to express their spirituality in their own words, "they are truly the authors,"[16] permitting lapses, repetitions, omissions, and errors, as well as the occasional journey into genuinely artistic creativity. The first half of the nearly 600-page work is organized according to several themes, including initiation rituals, the magical causes of illness, the utilization of herbs and specific prayers in spiritual healing, legends regarding religious and natural symbols, descriptions of secret societies, the African deities, and the traditions associated with the diverse *reglas,* or religious systems, in Cuba. This part of the book has attracted the most interest, as it sheds light on practices considered taboo for centuries and therefore secretive; it has also become a useful tool for deciphering Cabrera's fiction as well as that of other Cuban writers.

The second half of *El monte,* however, is illustrative for our purposes. In it Cabrera presents an extensive list of medicinal plants utilized by *curanderos* (folk healers), the format of which generally follows a pattern. The plant is classified alphabetically according to its local, colloquial name in Cuba, with the official Latin botanical nomenclature stated on the same line. The next category is spiritual: whenever possible Cabrera includes the Lucumí-Yoruba name ("L.") used by followers of the Santería, or Regla de Ocha, religion as well as its classification in the Congo, or Palo Monte, tradition ("C."). Succeeding these are the plant's *dueño,* or lord, i.e., the deity associated with it. After this initial information the entries vary widely. Some are brief with several lines describing their medicinal use, alternative names, and suggested medicinal recommendations, followed by a popular expression or anecdotal story related to the plant in quotations, indicating that the source is derived from an informant, occasionally contradicting a previous source and thus presenting an alternative or "second opinion."

Other entries are much more detailed. Several pages may be required to present more complex curative and ritual uses, historical background, and, on occasion, extensive and elaborate narrations (the entry for "Cotton," for example, is fourteen pages long), akin to literary short stories with characters, plot, dialogue, and climax. The stories are at times the retelling of *patakís,* the Santería narratives that correspond to the Yoruba divination system of Ifá, a "vast information-retrieval system that preserves, accesses, and processes the texts of mythological, naturalist, medicinal, and spiritual knowledge,"[17] or they may be details surrounding the experiences of an informant—his/her problems, the outcome of a religious sacrifice, etc. The following entries for sweet and bitter oranges (*naranja* and *naranja agria*) illustrate the briefer categories:

NARANJA.
   L. [Lucumí names]:   Orolocun, Orómbo, Olómbo, Osán, Obburuku, Osaeyímbo, Esá.
   C. [Congo names]:   Bolo mámba, Máamba, Mbelia kala, Mbefo malala, Nkiánkián.
   Dueño [deity]: Oshún [Oshún is the Yoruba orisha associated with love and female sensuality, often portrayed as a fair-skinned mulatto].

It is the fruit that Yéyé [nickname for Oshún] demands when she comes down to dance with her *omós* [spiritual child of an orisha] and her adorers.
   "*Chí chí olómbo kini mó guase olómbo yéyé,* says the mulatto Saint."
   "Yalodde likes nothing more than finding a lovely basket of oranges along the banks of the river."
   After a bath, the goddess always savors with delight the sweet golden fruit, "as sweet as she."
   Oranges have many applications for a healer: with the crumbled dry leaves, cigarettes are prepared, considered useful to eliminate hoarseness and alleviate bronchitis. A decoction of the flowers is given to children who suffer acidosis, of the leaves is indicated for colds, and, after meals, an infusion of the orange peel helps in digestion.
   "Very often the skin of *obiri oloñú* (pregnant women) becomes discolored. When they give birth these spots are removed with the baby's first feces which is applied for a long while and later washed with orange and coffee leaves."
   Orange, oil, and salt also cure indigestion.
   For hiccups, an infusion of orange blossom: "for flatulence and the irritation that forms in the stomach, give a gentle massage with orange blossom pomade and sip the tea."

NARANJA AGRIA. Citrus aurantium, Lin.
L: Korosán.
For erysipelas: "I stop it with bitter orange leaves. After three full days, it's over, I bless myself, and say a prayer."[18]

Cabrera's brand of ethnobotany is neither the traditional format found in conventional botanical references nor that encountered in popular New Age herbal manuals. Although she initiates the data with systematic botanical terminology (citing whenever possible the standardized Latin name and the source of the nomenclature—"Lin." for the Swedish botanist and originator of modern scientific taxonomy, Carolus Linnaeus, for example), she quickly shifts the focus beyond official scientific language; established Western authoritative codes and hierarchies fuse in a fantastic synthesis and on equal ranking with popular belief, personal anecdote, religion, spirituality, indigenous and folk healing traditions, official and oral history, testimony, fiction and fantasy (Cabrera's preface to the work acknowledges informants who tried to "trick and confuse me. They did it with style and their mythifications were no less interesting or fantastic").[19] Not limited to one religion or knowledge tradition, Cabrera presents several (Lucumí-Yoruba, Palo Monte, Abakuá-ñáñigo and derivations of the same)[20] from within the Afro-Cuban context that complement rather than compete with the Euro-Western elements of Cuban culture. In most cases no attempt is made to interpret data or to translate African words or religious names used by sectors of the Cuban population, thus privileging a local, initiated reader and providing an authentic tone and flavor while conveying a sense of community.[21] But others are not discouraged; occasionally Cabrera will relate an African deity or belief to a Christian/Western counterpart, even extending to cultures beyond the Cuban historical tradition—"in Cuba, [the orisha] Changó 'is born in the palm tree' (like Brahma in the Vedic tradition of India is born in the lotus)."[22] The artistry of Cuban spiritual practices recalls other art forms and expressions; a description of the music and dance of an Abakuá or ñáñigo liturgical procession, for example, inspires the following comments:

> It is an incredible spectacle—disconcerting and deplorable for many who consider *ñáñigismo* a national disgrace—those parades of shabby-looking whites and blacks in which an African drum appears alongside a crucified Christ, the pagan head of a decapitated goat and an old earthen jar. Primitive and barbarous in nature, one need not stress its extraordinary interest to observers.
>
> The gait, the rigorously stylized gestures—each one is a statement—of the *ñáñigos* dressed as devils representing initiates of the distant past, the immemorial mask, in its religious function and beyond, transform them into abstractions, sacred and unreal beings; their mime and dance contemplated in the light of a magical Cuban evening is a spectacle of strange beauty, so out of

time, so remote and mysterious that it cannot help but fascinate anyone who watches it.

I remember the terror that the Iremes [figures dressed as devils representing spirits] with their white cyclops eyes, inspired in Federico García Lorca, and the delirious poetic description he made for me the day after having witnessed a celebration.

If a Diaghilev had been born on this island, he undoubtedly would have paraded these *ñáñigo* devils throughout Europe's stages.[23]

This type of observation, however, is infrequent; *El monte* is indisputably local and Cuban, only universalized when deemed essential to render its localized reality more human.

El monte, then, is a work that, like so much of Caribbean literature, must be read differently. Helpful hints for arriving at wellness (many of which are based on valid, empirical, time-honored folk remedies that are currently being rediscovered)[24] blend with magic and folklore. Cabrera offers no authoritative medical claims, nor in fact is a disclaimer required; she professes only to present the vox populi. Healing constructs should not be entirely dismissed, however. Anticipating many contemporary strategies, Cabrera crosses diverse boundaries to effect a genuine transformation of sorts: her work contributes to the constantly shifting, unfinished creation of social and cultural Caribbean identity,[25] providing an inclusive, holistic, more all-encompassing vision of Cubanness. *El monte* incorporates the disempowered and alienated into the social corpus, guiding it toward a sustaining wholeness and well-being, creating a flavorful and nourishing postdisciplinary, postmodern, and postcolonial *ajiaco "levantamuertos"*[26] to be savored by all.

II

From Dolores Prida, *Botánica*

ACT ONE
(As the lights go up DOÑA GENO is waiting on a customer.)

LUISA: I don't think it's another woman, Doña Geno. He doesn't have the time. The poor man is working two jobs. At first, I thought it was because of the hair, you know . . .

GENO: What hair?

LUISA: My hair. In the last few months it's been falling out, it's become dull, flat. And I had such a beautiful head of hair! But I saw on TV, in "Five Minutes with Mirta de Perales,"[27] that a woman wrote a letter telling Mirta how her husband had stopped even looking at her because her hair was so ugly. Mirta recommended she use Mirta Lotion and, Bam!, her hair became gorgeous and her husband fell in love with her all over again. I bought the same lotion, but nothing happened. Arturo doesn't even look at me. What would you recommend, Doña Geno?

GENO: Sábila. The americanos call it "aloe vera." I have it in liquid, gelatin, and capsules.

LUISA: For hair?

GENO: Child, it's been proven that aloe vera has medicinal properties for the treatment of arthritis, high blood pressure, asthma, vaginitis, bed wetting, warts, hemorrhoids, athlete's foot, boils, colitis, diarrhea, constipation, flu, apoplexy, dandruff, toothache and . . . baldness! But that's not all. Aloe vera is also a cleansing, refreshing and moisturizing nutrient for the skin. It stimulates the pancreas, repels insects, and eliminates foot odor; it helps you lose weight, it's a hair conditioner, and a powerful sexual stimulant.

LUISA: Heavens! Give me six bottles of the liquid, six jars of the gelatin and four bottles of capsules!

GENO: Just in case, I suggest that you burn this "Perpetual Help" incense several times a day, and put a few drops of this "Come with Me" essence in your bath water. I prepare it myself. Also, jot down this spiritual prescription to bring good luck to your home. Listen carefully. Take an egg, tie a piece of white and a piece of blue ribbon around it, put a few drops of your regular lotion . . .

LUISA: Mirta.

GENO: . . . place the egg on a dish and light up a red candle. Say three Lord's Prayers and blow the candle out. Place the egg at the foot of your bed all night. Next day, pick it up and throw it into the river.

LUISA: Which river?

GENO: Either one.

LUISA: I think I'll throw it into the Hudson.

GENO: The Hudson is OK, but throw it downtown. Uptown it's getting overloaded by the *dominicanos*. [. . .]

Insider jokes abound in Dolores Prida's Botánica[28], a place where an "emic" audience is privileged in more than one respect. The East Coast Latino will grasp New York City references to the predominance of residents from the Dominican Republic in upper Manhattan, and those who watch Spanish-language television are familiar with the flamboyant claims of local beauty products. From the perspective of language, Prida—like Lydia Cabrera in *El monte*—presumes that her bilingual and bicultural audience will "get it," i.e., they will have no need for translation. Written in Spanish with English words and phrases interspersed throughout, the occasional religious terms associated with Santería and Espiritismo also remain unexplained. Some will chuckle (uneasily) at the references to the "cures" suggested by the botánica proprietor Doña Geno (a woman who hails from a Puerto Rican town, Guayama, known for its sorcerers)—a mix of Espiritismo, Santería, traditional and New Age herbalism, folk psychology, and common sense. These are familiar experiences that many in the audience know either firsthand or indirectly; it is difficult to encounter anyone from the Caribbean who has not heard stories of unusual spiritual spells and cures.

But Prida's play is more than a humorous and compassionate look at several generations of Puerto Rican women in New York's Hispanic barrio with the characteristic ethnic identity and intergenerational conflicts of the type frequently found in U.S. Latino writing. The search for a personal identity that can be reconciled with the mainstream society without the loss of one's unique and valuable cultural heritage, an oft-repeated theme, is only one of the questions explored in *Botánica;* its poignant gender issues are the elements of the play that concern us here. The fact, for example, that the proprietor and unofficial "therapist" of Prida's store/"temple"[29] is female, as are many of those who enter in search of such medical/folk/spiritual advice and "ritual" therapy (men, of course, are not entirely absent), is authentic representation. Having played an important role in folk/spiritual healing for centuries, it is not unusual to encounter women running or presiding over such establishments or in comparable healing venues.[30] Unfortunately, they have endured an unequal share of the vilification and victimization traditionally associated with such practices.

Curanderismo ("folk healing," from the Spanish verb *curar*) is perhaps the best-known of these practices. Although usually associated with Mexicans and Mexican-American culture, curanderismo is in fact a complex cultural healing system with roots common to healing modalities found in the Caribbean and throughout Latin America. It combines—in varying degrees—Hippocratic humoral (hot-cold) theories of disease[31] with Amerindian herbal medicine and diverse spiritual traditions, ranging from African-based systems to the nine-teenth-century spiritualist/spiritist philosophy of Allan Kardec, which inspired the creation of spiritual healing centers throughout Mexico and the Caribbean.[32] It is the "integrative" medical resource of the people, sanctioned by the community. Commonly thought to be the ultimate recourse of the poor and marginal, curanderismo has proved itself highly resilient; even those with access to orthodox medical care may recur to its methodology.

> *Curanderismo* has not disappeared. It continues to exist, thrive, and even evolve creative new forms of dealing with health and misfortune, side by side with modern medicine, and in (often silent) partnership with it. . . . [C]*uran-derismo* resist[s] total assimilation because it satisfies basic psychological, spiritual, and health needs of the Mexican American communities.[33]

Nonorthodox medicine, like its religious counterpart, has been more accessible to women; there they can claim an authority denied them in mainstream institutions and are more at liberty to utilize female traditions of caretaking to alleviate their suffering communities. Several recent studies observe women's growing importance in maintaining Caribbean healing/spiritual practices both in the region and in its diaspora. Mercedes Cros Sandoval traces the curative role of Santería in Cuba and in its "exodus" to Puerto Rico and such major U.S. cities as Miami, New York, and Los Angeles, where it has been forced to "adapt to new ecosystems, the new needs of its followers, and to new followers."[34] Outside of Cuba, Santería has become a "viable mental health delivery system,"[35] particularly for those suffering from the alienation and lack of control that often accompany the experience of exile and immigration, perhaps fascinated by its diversity and inclusiveness:

> The attraction is in part due to the fact that Santería has borrowed heavily from Kardecian spiritism and curanderismo which are also widely known in Latin America. Many spiritist practices and beliefs have been adopted by Santería; the wide usage of herbal remedies and esoteric magical practices in curanderismo make it quite akin to Santería. The prevalence of beliefs in the interference of the souls of the deceased in human affairs is also a common denominator, as well as a subjugation orientation towards nature and the supernatural.[36]

With practitioners from outside the Cuban community, including Puerto Ricans, Dominicans, Venezuelans, Mexicans, and other Latin Americans, as well as African Americans, Santería is evolving into a "Third World religious complex" in which women are playing an increasingly important role, taking advantage of the opportunities the religion provides as "an avenue for social and economic mobility via a populist priesthood."[37]

Similar observations have been made regarding women in the field of ethnopsychiatry in rural Louisiana, practicing a combination of African and Christian cosmologies, in a "realm of care where female practitioners predominate,"[38] as well as in the U.S. Haitian community, where a Vodou priestess/healer must draw upon a variety of resources to serve her spiritual "family":

> Mama Lola, as Alourdes is sometimes called, ministers to the many needs of a substantial immigrant community of taxi drivers, dishwashers, gas station attendants, nurses' aides, telephone operators, and the chronically underemployed. She reads cards, practices herbal medicine, manufactures charms and talismans, and uses her considerable intuitive powers ("the gift of eyes") and the well-honed empathy of a strong woman of fifty who is now a homeowner and head of a sizable household yet spent the first half of her life in Haiti, where at times she was driven to prostitute herself to feed her children. In addition to her personal skills and strengths, Mama Lola also provides her healing clients with access to the wisdom and power of the Vodou spirits . . . through dreams and through possession-trance, which is central in Vodou. In treatment sessions, she will frequently "call" the spirits for diagnosis, insight, or specific instructions as to what is to be done about healing.[39]

How might Mama Lola's diagnoses vary from those of an orthodox practitioner? What indeed might be the expectations of a woman suffering from the stresses of immigration and powerlessness, for example, if she were to enter Dolores Prida's fictional *Botánica* in search of advice and solace? Much would depend on the value system of the person behind the counter.

If on a given day the unfortunate woman should encounter Doña Geno's granddaughter Millie (née Milagros), and describe her excitable outbursts and other such erratic behavior, Millie would undoubtedly suggest psychotherapy, having heard of such "culture-bound" illnesses[40] in her college psychology class, where, when referring to Puerto Rican women and their *ataques de nervios* ("nervous attacks") at "inappropriate" times, the behavior would have been assigned the unlikely name of "Puerto Rican Syndrome." An actual diagnosis in the 1950s through the 1980s, Puerto Rican Syndrome is a malady that varies in its description depending on one's medical/anthropological/political perspective and/or agenda. First reported in the 1950s and 1960s among Puerto Rican male patients in U.S. veterans hospitals on the island, their sudden hostile outbursts and partial loss of consciousness, among other symptoms, were attributed in Freudian analyses to an inability to adapt to the "highly competitive culture" of the U.S. military and, among other things, to inadequate child-rearing practices that created "personality deficits" in Puerto Rican men.[41] In the 1970s and early 1980s, Latino mental health professionals began to describe *ataques* as a social phenomenon, a culturally sanctioned response to stressful situations, a coping mechanism of Latino communities. Among medical anthropologists, connections were drawn during the same period that linked family conflicts, the *ataque* response, and Puerto Rican spiritual beliefs in Espiritismo. From a female perspective, the *ataques* were considered a reaction to *machismo,* "the idiom by which further male violence is prevented or by which women attempt to extricate themselves from untenable situations and gain caring attention."[42] And within a wider framework that includes other U.S. Latinos, *ataques de nervios* have been viewed as a symptom of colonialism and dependence:

> It is our premise that the triggering of ataques, the behaviors manifested in them, and the impact they have on others is understood through socioeconomic circumstances of colonialism experienced by *ataques* sufferers. *Ataques de nervios* provide Puerto Rican and other Latinos opportunities for displacement of anger, secondary gains, and direct rebellion against repressive conditions. An examination of the living conditions of Puerto Ricans in their own territory and in the United States reveals how these social and economic problems relate to *ataques*. . . . Our view is that *ataques* should be studied holistically and analyzed by situating the *ataque* in the broader context of economic, ideological, and social struggle . . . cultural expressions of colonized classes for Latinos in the United States and in their home countries.[43]

None of this would be entirely lost on an empathetic folk healer. She/he has seen people from a variety of Caribbean and Latin American cultures and knows that these symptoms are not exclusive to any one particular group; the source of the problems may in fact be any or all of the above. Ironically, the imaginary woman who enters Doña Geno's botánica and is referred by Millie to a mental health professional may actually wind up back where she started. Having ascertained her belief system (Espiritismo, Santería, Vodou, etc.), a progressive and empathetic cross-cultural therapist may direct her once again, full circle, to Doña Geno in a respectful and collaborative relationship with the folk healer to relieve the patient's anxieties, valorizing the cultural resource in Doña Geno and the others like her, understanding that "since non-pharmacological psychotherapy depends heavily for its efficacy on the words, acts, and rituals of the participants, spiritist therapy has the particular merit of allowing both healer and sufferer to deal with the latter's problems within a shared symbolic framework."[44] Being "culture bound" need not lead to illness; it can constitute an integral component of health.

After the final act, some members of the *Botánica* audience will have experienced a cultural catharsis; the play is *un remedio,* spiritually therapeutic for those who have never seen their cultural values validated on the stage of a U.S. metropolitan theater. Having been told for decades that they are victims of "cultural schizophrenia" (a term often used to describe colonized peoples)[45] and other culture conflicts described in a medicalized discourse, art becomes a palliative, a reassurance, and a remedy, concepts embodied by poet/physician William Carlos Williams, who, when asked how he had continued an equal interest in medicine and poetry replied that to him they amounted to nearly the same thing.

In 1956, around the same time that Puerto Rican Syndrome was becoming a psychiatric diagnosis, William Carlos Williams, at the invitation of the president of the University of Puerto Rico, was revisiting the island of his mother's birth. Born into a family with deep Caribbean roots (Williams' father was an English-born Caribbean islander who spoke perfect Spanish), Williams was raised in a bilingual, multicultural home. Julio Marzán's fascinating study demonstrates the significance of these previously unexplored cultural influences on the poet's artistry, in particular those of his mother, Raquel Helene Rose Hoheb. While other critics have focused on Williams as the "outsider" from various perspectives ("to his fellow poets because he was a doctor . . . to his fellow townspeople because he was a poet . . . to poetry because he was an American and the literature of the time was European even if written by American expatriates"),[46] Marzán discerns an additional and equally important conflict in the author between his North American persona—the Anglo "Bill"—and Williams' ambivalent sentiments toward his Latino "Carlos" identity. Both inform the American vision of his poetry.

Among the sources of this ambivalence were Williams' attitudes toward his mother Elena's practice of Espiritismo. Although, as Marzán notes, the poet's father, William George, was also a believer in spiritualism/spiritism, and his English grandmother, Emily Dickinson Wellcome, was a medium like his mother, Williams' discussions of spiritualism focus on her:

> This was because she was the person in whom Williams saw himself, and as medium of a foreignizing practice she also foreignized him from "normal" American culture. His reaction therefore had to be normal, making him one with his reader, whose popular reflex was to ascribe to such activities "from the islands" some stigmatizing, racially dark seed. . . . Williams' fear of Elena's spiritualist trances is quite understandable, as they were both an unusual phenomenon and a powerful symbol of so much that he needed to reject. For, in Williams' defense, his Bill persona was an expression of a deeply rooted tradition in U.S. history, the American persona of every child of an immigrant or marginal culture, on whom the culture imposes the challenges of having to earn acceptance.[47]

Ironically, not long after his death in 1963, this denigrated aspect of his maternal culture—feared, resented, and misconstrued—began to be reexamined by a more enlightened cross-cultural scientific community, assigning to it an authority and a therapeutic validity that undoubtedly would have appealed to William Carlos Williams' poetic sensibility as well as his medical persona, and perhaps have eliminated one source of his inner conflicts. In his efforts to tolerate or alleviate pain and anxiety and effect an inner balance and harmony through art (in his poem "The Cure," for example, Williams writes: "For when I cannot write I'm a sick man and want to die. The cause is plain"), fusing the dynamic forces of ars medica and ars poetica, Williams did what artists have always done and will always continue to do. Happily for the rest of us, their artistic remedies transcend; the healing transformation of their cultural botánicas sustains and restores us as well.

Part I

Healing Arts

Chapter 2 ▨

Ethnomedical (Folk) Healing in the Caribbean

Brian M. du Toit

Introduction

Academic interest and knowledge of folk healing have come a long way in the half century since Erwin Ackerknecht described "primitive medicine" as "primarily magico-religious, utilizing a few rational elements."[1] Through the studies of anthropologists, pharmacologists, health-related professionals, and a range of informed researchers, we today acknowledge the positive value of much traditional, folk, and alternative healing. Some of this healing exists in the realm of health and trust. Some involves the stimulation of endorphins. Some depends on biodynamic chemical properties of certain plants. These properties have long been acknowledged by pharmacological companies and university colleges of pharmacy, as the history of such vegetable drugs as digitalis, quinine, and curare illustrate.

Every healing tradition reflects a disease theory that explains causality. Thus folk etiologies may be based on supernatural causation (personalistic) or natural causes (naturalistic), such as the "hot/cold" dichotomy, or a combination of both. Given a particular ethno-etiological account, people will know what steps to take to restore health. It is this rich but diverse background that forms the basis of traditional medicine in the Caribbean.

Background

The Caribbean offers one of the most complex ethnological reservoirs of folk beliefs. An original subsystem can be traced to Arawak and Carib, but it unfortunately has almost completely disappeared except in Dominica.[2]

European colonists of different national, cultural, and linguistic backgrounds occupied the islands and concluded they needed slaves for plantation and other work. Thus came the African slaves[3] and East Indian indentured laborers[4] with their cultural traditions and personal experiences. Whether the hot/cold dichotomy was indigenous to South and Central America (including the Caribbean), as suggested by López Austin, Colson, and others, or introduced by colonists from the Old World, as argued by Foster, is an intriguing question.[5]

"The port cities of the islands," says Rogozinski, "provided a meeting place for the diseases endemic to three continents."[6] A high mortality rate resulted among all ethnic groups during the early decades of residence. These conditions also produced a variety of coping methods involving supernatural, ritual, pharmacological, and other strategies. People coped with ailments by relying on some nativistic beliefs transferred from their birthplaces in Africa or India and as a result of contact with other settlers and innovations empirically tested in the new ecological setting, with its new plant species. Slaves had originated in areas with well-developed horticulture, and they had excellent knowledge of plant usage,[7] which may have been responsible for parallel treatment of plants in Africa and the Caribbean.[8]

Ethnopharmacology

Pharmacology normally refers to the study of the products of plants and other natural substances employed in the pursuit of health. The prefix "ethno" suggests actions outside the cosmopolitan health system. We should be reminded that plants or plant products may be used not only for medicine but also for a variety of other reasons.[9] It is also important that unlike the popular information shared by mothers and grandmothers, specialized knowledge regarding plants and other organic products is frequently restricted to herbalists and other indigenous healers. Yet there is no such universal entity as "the traditional healer."[10] Knowledge of growing and fertilizing useful plants may also be restricted, while plant fertilization may be accomplished by magical means.[11]

In the mid-1980s a number of detailed studies about ethnopharmacology were published: Edward Anyesu discussed medicinal plants of the West Indies, D. Pedersen and V. Baruffati wrote about traditional medicine cultures in Latin America and the Caribbean, and Michel Laguerre produced a most valuable study of Afro-Caribbean folk medicine.[12] More recently, B. Weniger discussed pharmacopoeias in the Caribbean.[13] The present review does not cover the same material. Instead, it deals primarily, though not exclusively, with works published more recently.

Cuba is one of the regions in which a great deal of ethnographic and eth-nobotanical research has been conducted. A useful study by Lydia Cabrera investigates the religious and healing role of indigenous medicinal plants, while José Gallo produced a 900-page compendium as well as a more recent study of medicinal folklore.[14] The earlier work reports on interviews with health specialists—*el yerbero* (the herbalist), *el curandero* (the curer), *el santero* (the religious healer), and *el conocedor* (the botanist)—and on the fact that 92 percent of the illnesses reported were associated with specific curing methods. In the 1993 study, Gallo explained that some of these folk remedies were screened pharmacologically. Among 31 plant species prescribed as bronchodilators, only *Datura candida* was effective, most likely the result of the presence of scopolamine and atropine in the leaves.[15] One of the most popular medicinal plants, lemongrass, or *caña de limón,* used for its hypotensive and anti-inflammatory effects, has been found to be "relatively safe" but without major value in the areas mentioned.[16]

Jamaica has witnessed a number of studies of its African heritage. Cannabis has long played an important role in traditional healing in Jamaica, "either in the form of infusions of poultices, or as an important ingredient in 'tonics' and 'bush baths.'"[17] In fact, for Rastafarians, it "is considered a panacea."[18] Joseph Long was first to give detailed attention to the Jamaican balm system and balmyards.[19] Balmism, Long suggests, constitutes a collection of herbalistic and magical practices. Yet empirical knowledge was vague, and classification "of anatomical parts, symptoms, diseases, and remedies was . . . highly individualistic."[20] Jamaicans distinguish between interpersonal and nonpersonal diseases: folk healers are preferred for the former and biomedical physicians for the latter. More recently Elisa Sobo has studied ideas held by rural Jamaicans concerning embodied health and sickness.[21] She discusses abortifacients[22] (e.g., teas brewed from senna leaves, concoctions of basil, nutmeg, and guava buds, and a variety of purgatives), potency boosters (e.g., the "Chiney brush" or Obeah—"black magic"—oils and other accouterments), as well as thyme tea and castor oil to speed delivery of babies. Broomweed (*Corchorus siliquosus*) tea is said to induce quick delivery of the placenta. General health is assured by the use of a "roots tonic" supplied by a "roots man." According to Sobo, effectiveness and bitterness are directly correlated;[23] Cerasee (*Momordica charantia*) is favored as a morning drink, and tea from ground bissy (*Cola acuminata*) is used to purify the blood. As is frequently the case, health and health-care decisions may depend on the availability of conventional biomedical services. Thus clinical facilities in urban and especially upper-economic neighborhoods may be used more frequently than those in rural districts.[24] Combined with poverty, a preference for "traditional birth attendants and community midwives,"[25] and "glorified indigenous medicine,"[26] the result is continued choice of traditional delivery and postnatal care. Judith Gussler cites a very similar situation on St. Kitts, complete with bush teas of maiden apple (*Momordica charantia*) or French sticky thyme (*Plectranthus amboinicus*) and herbal baths for babies.[27]

There is even greater use of folk medicine in rural Haiti. Here the ailment must first be classified and labeled as either supernatural or natural in origin. If it is the former, the family must seek supernatural help. If the ailment is ascribed to natural causes, they may visit the leaf doctor[28] or employ home remedies. Weniger and associates found widespread use of medicinal plants, and in most of the 38 common diseases surveyed, home remedies were the first avenues of treatment.[29] Epilepsy and tuberculosis were exceptions. Another team surveyed 161 species of plants used as medicine in the same region, namely the Thomonde area of central Haiti.[30] Not only are these products collected, but medicinal materials are also traded in the markets of Haiti.[31] The contrast between urban and rural Haiti is significant due in part to differences in their worldviews and in part to availability of services. In a study of oral rehydration therapy, Coreil and Genece found, for example, an urban compliance twice as high as that among rural mothers.[32] It may thus be assumed that the latter prefer to use folk diagnosis and healing strategies. In fact the authors note that "traditional humoral beliefs regarding contraindications and proscribed behavior related to vaccines persist among some women. Injections are considered 'hot' by nature and therefore may exert too strong an opposing effect on a 'cold' illness such as an acute respiratory infection."[33] The use of traditional techniques alongside biomedical interventions may also point to the very common practice of medical pluralism common in the Caribbean and the Third World generally.

Occupying the southern rim of the Caribbean are the Ndjuka Maroons. "The fact that [the Afro-American health-care system's] closest cultural counterpart appears to be Haitian medicine," says Diane Vernon, "which like that of the Maroons also stopped receiving a constant input of Western medical theory during the [late] 18th century, would seem to suggest a chronological cultural continuum for Afro-American health care systems."[34] There are supernatural agents and spirits, particularly *obia*. This is a system that combines Mother Earth, white clay, and plants into a medicine. A single plant used in healing is not *obia*, and yet the single medicinal herb, though devalued, persists as "first-aid medication for minor physical problems."

Walter Edwards presents a valuable listing of 200 different words for plants, animals, and materials derived from Arekuna, Arawak, and other native languages used in treatment of ailments in Guyana.[35] There exists a "rich folklore of indigenous medicine," and most plants are supplied with a botanical identification.[36] In addition, medicine men "are also believed to have the power to summon spirits which cause disease. . . ."[37]

Though not an example of ethnopharmacological healing, the practice of creating zombies does entail a great deal of knowledge.[38] This *includes* the use of the hallucinogens *Datura metel* and *Datura stramonium* (known to contain scopolamine and atropine, both of which cause amnesia), the psychoactive agent from the toad species *Bufo marinus,* and a variety of other botanical and zoological products. It seems reasonable to conclude that if Haitians can concoct such effective drugs, they can employ a range of healing products from the same sources.

In Trinidad and Tobago we find not only the influence of Africa but also healing traditions that derive from India. Roland Littlewood explains the rural medical practices, known as bush medicine, among Creoles of African descent.[39] Most residents know and use flowers, leaves, barks, shoots, and roots that are often combined with commercial oils, waxes, or essences. Many of these plants are grown in gardens or close to the homes. "Men are believed to know more about bush than women, and they treat themselves when working in the bush."[40] Recent attempts to cope with ill health have included use of herbal preparations that follow the Chinese method of application.[41] Discussing the Indians of Trinidad and Tobago, Noor Mahabir covers a wide range of medicinal and edible plants.[42] Poor, rural populations, he states, still rely on herbal medicines for most of their health care. We also find the age-old practice of massage of pregnant women. This same practice is found among Haitian midwives and leaf doctors and the massage curers in Puerto Rico.[43]

Other island communities employing plants for healing have been superficially discussed in the literature, for example, Martinique, Dominican Republic, Carriacou, and the Bahamas.[44] These island communities await further detailed research.

Spirits, Mind, and Body

Under this rubric we find a wealth of information deriving from traditional beliefs, contact with other groups, missionary teachings, and syncretism. We should then expect faith or sacred ritual[45] to accompany these treatments. In fact, Jane Beck faults Laguerre for his narrow interpretation of faith healing.[46] She insists that "faith healing must be extended beyond a religious phenomenon to incorporate the whole realm of the supernatural."[47]

In Haiti, voodoo (Vodoun) ritual pervades the daily life of a majority of the population, accompanied by the lighting of candles, the pouring of libations on family altars, or festivities marking events in the annual calendar. Health problems determined to come from some "supernatural" cause must be treated in the voodoo. A "supernatural" problem implies that it was caused by the spirits and is considered to be within the province of the spirits' curative powers.

"Health problems that have a history of being resistant to scientific medical treatment often end up in the Vodou temple."[48] Herbalists and midwives also recognize an invisible spiritual entity called guardian spirit—*anj gadyen*.[49] The nature of a patient's problem is frequently established by divination. Divinatory rituals include pouring alcohol on a human skull and reading the pattern made by the flow of the liquid or by employing cards that are prayed over while a candle is lit. "Diagnoses point to disruptions in relations . . . with the spirits themselves. Broken promises, lax or insufficient offering . . ."[50] Such an impersonal diagnosis also carries over into philosophies of child care. De Santis studied immigrant Haitian and Cuban mothers, and found on one hand that among Haitian mothers there was a lack of biomedical preventive health care resulting from a fatalistic view of life.[51] On the other hand, Cuban mothers practiced preventive health care, active intervention, and stimulation of desired behavior—they actively "loved" the child through infancy and childhood.

In Jamaica, the balm system may be associated with different cults, and the balmyards may involve medicinal herbs. The yards may also be "more directly associated with Obeah in providing rituals whereby the disturbing influence of duppies [ghosts] may be removed from ill persons."[52] This may involve church-related healers, chanting of the Eighteenth Psalm, smoke fumigation, or sweeping out the evil Obeah and malicious ghosts. Ritual acts serve to forcefully restore faith, calm, and health. Most balm healers are women who establish almost a maternal relationship with their patients. William Wedenoja suggests that the emphasis on mothering in balm reflects "the strong degree of maternal dependency in Jamaican society, which is encouraged by a high rate of father-absence and a general lack of involvement by men in child rearing."[53]

The Shango cult among those of African descent in Trinidad and Grenada also serves in the context of ritual healing practices. Healing and conjuring are considered inseparable parts of Shango "works." Thus virtually "every Shango leader (*amombo*) and every head of a Shouter group, and . . . some spiritual Baptist churches . . . engage in healing."[54] George Simpson also lists a rich array of plants employed in healing and conjuring, cross listing his information with Robert Williams."[55] Laguerre points to the extensive geographical distribution: "Conjurers were found on various plantations in the New World and were known as hoodoo doctors in the United States, myal and obeah men in the Anglophone Caribbean, Voodoo priests in Haiti, and *quimboiseurs* or magicians in the French Antilles."[56] Angelina Pollak-Eltz suggests that much of the healing regimen of the Spiritual Baptists was adopted from the Shango cult: initiation rites (Shango), baptism (Baptists), faith healing, exorcism, holy water, and purification rituals.[57] What is said of people of African descent, however, applies equally to those from India.

The openness of Hinduism facilitated the incorporation of *jumbies* (spirits) and the belief in Obeah (sorcery). "The Indians have been an insecure minority group during most of their history in Trinidad, and one of the methods for increasing security was to adopt supernatural beliefs which were already a part of the total cultural environment."[58] Also featured is the power of the evil eye, a traditional belief reinforced by local contacts, as well as the ability to "send sickness" in the form of contagious magic. Sending sickness is also encountered in Haiti, where it is believed voodoo practitioners can send tuberculosis to an enemy. Now such practitioners are considered able to send AIDS.[59] As noted earlier, however, tuberculosis is one of the two diseases not treated with herbs in Haiti.

Psychotherapy and religious healing are not that far apart, though the former rests more on allopathic principles, and spiritism relies more on homeopathic principles. In Puerto Rico the traditional healer roles of *curanderos* (curers), *sobadores* (massage curers), and *comadronas* (midwives) were early on attacked by the Catholic Church. The curer role was taken over by the Espiritistas—mediums and believers who tend to religious *centros*. "Healing can occur when the spirit medium assists the sufferer to come into harmony with the spirit world so as to change his or her physical condition, emotions, way of life, or destiny."[60] The *comadronas* have now become traditional birth attendants, as have the *nanas* in Jamaica.[61] Because of the realm in which Espiritistas operate, it is understandable that negative effects or conditions may also be ascribed to them, often leading to accusations that they are *brujas* (witches).[62] But because they deal with health and healing, Espiritistas are attacked from pulpits and by some medical doctors. "Fear of legal sanctions seems to have motivated the division of labor by spiritists into *causa material* and *causa espiritual,* and the consistent referral of the material cases to medical doctors."[63] This author also points to the common aim of psychotherapy and spiritist healing, namely to reduce anxiety, to permit the patient to acknowledge socially unacceptable emotions by catharsis, to permit regressive types of behavior such as dependency to deal with nonverbalized guilt, and to encourage the confession of feelings that may be hidden even to the sufferer.[64]

A great deal of healing is performed in what we may call healing cults. These include Espiritismo, Rastafari, and Santería but are certainly not restricted to these formal groups. Nuñez Molina states that "*Espiritismo* functions as a religion for some Puerto Ricans, as a healing system used in moments of crisis for others, and as a 'philosophy' and 'science' for those who are academically oriented."[65] The belief system conceptualizes a spirit world that is constantly interacting with the material world (*mundo material*). Healers actively bring about improvement in the condition of their patients through direct advice and medication such as herbs and baths. Since they attribute mental illness to external sources, the client is relieved of guilt feelings. Rastafarians teach that physical illnesses have spiritual causes but that mankind is so important that there is no disease for which God has not provided a cure.

The influences of Native Baptists and 1860s Revivalism—fanned by the teachings of Allan Kardec—have left their mark on Jamaican Rastafarians and Cuban Santería. Like Espiritistas, Rastafarians hold that spiritual power is greater than the material and that many illnesses may require a Revival, or folk, healer. Folk healing is a charismatic gift and involves ritual in the form of a "bath, psalmody, or amulets and charms."[66] Cuban Santería contains a strong element of spiritism, particularly in the eastern city of Santiago, but first and foremost "all santeros are herbalists."[67] In some cases though, especially when the patient is a child, the santero uses a curative system known as *santiguo,* meaning "to bless" or "to heal by blessing."[68] A santero or santera may recommend that a patient receive outside medical service such as surgery, but first the patient will receive *omiero,* a "magical herbal infusion," and often "miracle cures" result.[69]

Expressed to a greater or lesser extent, and interwoven with all that has been discussed, is the theme of faith healing. Harry Ramnath, against the background of Hinduism, discusses the use of holy mantras to cure or relieve ailments in Trinidad.[70] In the same context Shango followers believe in healing by faith. In Jamaica, folk healing is "a charismatic gift, and the healer's diagnosis is by divination rather than by inquiry, as a physician would [employ]."[71] The Obeah proper works by way of contagious magic and is seen by Chevannes in the same context as that of a Revival leader using supernatural assistance. "Revival Zion leaders heal publicly in regular or special church services and in private; obeah men practice privately."[72] Cannabis has also gained a prominent position in the rituals, religion, and healing of a number of Afro-Jamaican religious groups, including Rastafarians. Cannabis is defined as having "therapeutic effects." Santería would be included in this context, though recent literature does not mention the healing aspects of this religion.

Earlier anthropological literature contains numerous references to physiological and psychological pressures experienced by people undergoing acculturation, or subject to programs of planned change. Frequently such individuals suffered nervous strains, mental conditions, or high blood pressure. Dressler et al. slightly rephrased this to highlight the social class of the group under study. These researchers found a positive correlation between religiosity and low blood pressure, especially among the lower class. This may be due to the fact that "a system of meaning" is intact for these people and that "traditional culture per se" is protective.[73] Traditional culture in this case includes folk models of explanation and folk models of coping and healing.

The conceptual distance between body and mind, between physical and spiritual healing, or between health beliefs and their consequences is not very great. Thus the actions of practitioners of voodoo (conjurers) or Shango (a blending of African deities and Christian saints) and Espiritistas are shades of each other, as are the Hindu Kali cult and local healing responses to folk illnesses.

Culture Specific Illnesses

Through the years anthropologists have described a large number of folk illnesses or culture-specific syndromes. These range from Arctic hysteria and *susto* to *latah* and *windigo*. The value of these studies is that they are specific to the communities where the illnesses occur. Lee Pachter, in fact, suggests that the "categorization of a folk illness within biomedical noso-logical categories serves no purpose in itself."[74] Only if the patient enters the biomedical diagnostic and treatment program will such comparisons be useful.[75]

Though Guyana—with a considerable East Indian population—is mar-ginal to the Caribbean, it is included due to the strong presence of East In-dians and the Kali cult in Trinidad and Tobago. Phillip Singer worked with an East Indian Kali healer and psychiatrist in the former British Guiana.[76] Normally these healers relieve symptoms through public or private rituals, and they do not use herbal medicines. In the ritual there is a transference to mother Kali, guilt is turned inward, and the family is encouraged to partic-ipate in fasting, among other behaviors.[77] Increasingly the role of these heal-ers is changing from folk psychotherapists to agents who deal in mundane complaints and living problems.[78]

A syndrome frequently seen in people of the Spanish-speaking regions in the Caribbean (e.g., Cuba, Puerto Rico, Dominican Republic) has to do with "nerves" and is frequently expressed as *ataques de nervios*.[79] *Nervios* es-sentially refers to temperament and emotions that disturb or prevent tran-quillity. Symptoms may vary from auditory hallucinations and sleeplessness to falling to the floor and even attempted suicide. Peter Guarnaccia prefers to speak of "popular illness" and looks at its expression in Puerto Rico fol-lowing the 1985 floods and mudslides.[80] Since this is a culturally sanctioned form of illness, it persists as an avenue of expression even among Puerto Ri-cans who have left the island and reside elsewhere.[81]

Folk illnesses may also be physical. Some years ago Murray described *pedisyon* as a Haitian culture-bound syndrome.[82] Merrill Singer et al. see it as only part of a larger complex of interrelated reproductive illnesses, including *matris deplasé* (displaced uterus), *lamne tonbé* (fallen uterus), and *grann chale* (vaginal burning).[83] Herbal healers and midwives can treat certain cases of *pedisyon,* but others must be treated by the spiritual healers—especially when the voodoo practitioner diagnoses the case.

Conclusion

The practice of traditional ethnomedicine in the Caribbean is receiving a great deal of attention by researchers. It is essential that the inquiry continue, as regards both endangered flora and specialists who have useful knowledge that may disappear upon their deaths and the inevitable influence of "modern" biomedicine. This is a vital topic on which different kinds of conservationists can cooperate.

Medical pluralism is an inevitable consequence of the meeting between traditional beliefs and practices and biomedical interventions. In some cases economic factors or the nonavailability of services may be causal factors. In all cases studies should ascertain the medical value and possibility of perpetuating the traditional practice. Such studies should also establish what real needs exist for biomedical interventions and low-cost ways of making such introductions.

Greater communication among persons from different, and sometimes distant, academic disciplines is needed. One example is the case discussed above concerning the cooperation between the psychiatrist-director of the mental hospital in British Guiana and the East Indian Kali healers. Their cooperation and communication in diagnosis and therapy was facilitated by the anthropologist. Each had to perform the triple role of healer-social worker, peer therapist, and mediator-interpreter. This is an example of applying traditional healing within the modern scientific context and learning from and adapting folk healing for practical use to benefit patient and healer alike.

Chapter 3 ▨

Black Arts: African Folk Wisdom and Popular Medicine in Cuba

A translation of Lydia Cabrera
by Margarite Fernández Olmos

Born at the turn of the twentieth century in Havana, Cuba, Lydia Cabrera enjoyed the privileges of a Cuban upper-class life—travel, culture, and the company of artists and intellectuals, as well as a household of black servants. The latter became Cabrera's entrée to the complex world of Afro-Cuban culture, an interest she would pursue as an ethnographer, oral historian, artist, and folklorist. *El monte* (*The Sacred Wild*, 1954), her first major study (discussed in Chapter 1, "La Botánica Cultural"), is considered a fundamental text on Santería and other African-based Cuban religious traditions.

Often compared to the U.S. scholar/artist Zora Neale Hurston for her dogged defiance of gender and color prejudice in the pursuit of knowledge of underestimated cultures, Cabrera amassed a significant body of work during her lifetime, including a 1984 study on the diverse historical and contemporary medical and folk traditions comprised by Cuban healing: *La medicina popular en Cuba* (*Popular Medicine in Cuba*). The following translation is an excerpt from chapter 4, "Los negros curanderos" ("Black Folk Healers"), which is fittingly illustrated with the contemporary images of Cuban photographer Héctor Delgado. Delgado's 1998 photos (part of an extensive photoessay) document the resilience of belief/healing practices that have survived and continue to thrive despite enormous social changes on the island in recent decades. The subject of Delgado's photoessay is *ebbó*, a ritual cleansing consisting of herbs, blessing, and other "workings" utilizing sacred figures and spells to remedy the subject's problems; the ebbó, Cabrera reminds us, is "the inevitable rite that inspires confidence in the patient . . . basic to all cures (and undertakings)." Cabrera's caveat to *La medicina popular en Cuba* could appropriately be added here for our readers as well: "I wish to make clear that in no way am I responsible if a reader should follow the advice, treatments or remedies that I have gathered from the lips of the people."

Black Folk Healers

Lydia Cabrera

In colonial times, in the home of the aristocratic white slave owner as in that of the masses of the people, black male and female *curanderos* [folk healers] rivaled the medical doctor. Their clientele was numerous; their wisdom, or better yet, their natural ability, their "gift," sparked more faith than the awe-inspiring science of the university graduate.

The above can be explained by taking into account the daily interactions between masters and their domestic slaves, who were so often regarded as if members of the family. The African slave, if well treated, placed his knowledge at his master's disposal . . . and cured successfully. Blacks, as we have learned from some former masters, knew quite well which herbs, massages, ointments, and decoctions would ease pain. When young daughters or sons fell ill and burned with fever, the black nanny, who in those days never left her charges' bedside, would stretch out on her straw mat like a loyal guardian, watching over their sleep and lowering their temperature with the infusions she prepared.

Of many it was said in praise that they could set a broken leg or arm by applications of sheep lard, causing less pain than any Western-trained professional. Some thirty years ago a Cuban lady, the aunt of one of Havana's most notable doctors, had her fractured leg treated by an old black servant, preferring his ministrations to her nephew's: "He knows more about bones than you do," she told him. The medications and cures of African slaves and their descendants were often supplemented by other secret methods and practices of which their masters were fully aware, and which they accepted and even solicited at trying moments of their lives when they were deemed potentially beneficial.

Among black curanderos in Cuban cities there were—we are told—many literate ones who added to their ancestral knowledge of medicine what they had learned from published compendiums. . . . But these were the exception, and those curanderos who could not read were convinced, as were the masses of the people, not without reason, that they could not learn anything on the subject from whites. . . .

Curanderos would seem to be the perpetuation of the white physician of centuries past. But the difference between them is a religious one: our black curanderos are priests and conjurers. They belong to the cult of the *orichas* that extends throughout the western part of Cuba—the *oloricha* [initiate], the *iyalocha* [priestess] and the *babalawo* [high priest], the *odosain* [herbalist], the *onichogún* [healer]—as they all were called in the *cabildos* and former slave barracks; to the *bokono* and the *vodunsi* of the *Arará* [Fon] cult of Dahomey; and to the *nganga* [consecrated receptacle], the father and mother *nganga* [priest and priestess] of the Congos.[1]

The curanderos of the Regla de Ocha are called *santeros,* understood by the people as those who, having been *asentados*[2] or initiated, into the Yoruba or Lucumí religious tradition, which honors deities identified by the Yorubas with our own Catholic saints, are chosen and endowed with the capacity to carry out the functions of a priest and with the power and knowledge to cure with the assistance of the orichas (saints). Their cures are of body and soul. The reader should not imagine, however, that these privileged doctors ever had any vague notion of physiology. . . . They did not need it. Their divinely inspired science was limited to fulfilling the required sacrifices—*ebbó*—and administering remedies to cure a malady. The origin of the problem would be determined after the oricha had taken possession of the oloricha or of the iyalocha (differentiating them from the babalawo, who does not fall into trance, "whom the saint does not mount"), or after the *babalocha* (priest) and the iyalocha had questioned their shells, or the babalawo his *okpelé* (metal chain with eight corozo seeds, fragments of hicotee shell, disks of metal, ivory, or gold stretching out like the beads of a rosary) and his *iki* [cola nuts)].

If the sick person consults a curandero of the Congo tradition, a father or a mother nganga, it is a *fumbi*—the spirit of a deceased person—or a *mpungu*—a supernatural force—who will "mount" or "climb" (as they name, in the spiritual language of both traditions those who fall into trance) and who will speak and diagnose. In the Lucumí, or Yoruba, tradition there are cases in which a dead ancestor, friend, or acquaintance of the consultant manifests a desire to address him or her in order to advise or warn. The trances often take place at the fiestas—*bembé*—offered to the orichas who descend to dance and speak with their "children."

The nganga father, or *mayombero* (Palo Monte priest/sorcerer), generally uses a mirror for divining, a *vititi-mensu* or *lumuene*. He also augurs by placing before the *fundamento* [items such as stones, shells, etc., believed to embody spiritual forces], a sacred object, a pot or cauldron, and small sticks of gunpowder that he lights with the tip of his cigar; he responds to questions with a "yes" or "no" according to the number of sticks that explode.

A long-held belief among our people was that curanderos were predestined individuals, like twins who as children are capable of calming sharp lower back pains by sitting on the afflicted area, or of easing any other pain by contact, and who as adults become notable santeros. But there are also some who possess "healing hands," as a midwife tells us, hands that, while not those of twins, relieve pain upon touching the body. . . .

The fact of being "seated," of "making saint," that is, of having been initiated into the cult of the orichas, does not qualify all the *iyawó* [the initiated, wives or husbands of the oricha] to practice the priesthood. Some will worship for their personal protection but will not consecrate other believers; they will not become fathers or mothers of saints—which is what should be understood when it is said of a devotee or believer that "he has made saint" but cannot "give birth to saints"—nor *registrar* [give consultations]. They can only consult the *dilogún,* the divining cowrie shells, for their own benefit. The oricha designates the beloved *omó* [spiritual child of the oricha], the one whose life it has saved or for whom a service has been rendered, and by whom in payment and in gratitude it wishes to be adored until death; the omó chosen for the priesthood, on the other hand, should predict, advise, and perform the sacrifices and rituals of the cult in order to help mankind.

Anyone who has been around practitioners of the African religions in Cuba can appreciate the fact that sickness and death are not always attributed to natural causes. The concept of death held by the ancient Africans, their present-day descendants, and the masses of the Cuban people takes us back millennia in human history. Life and death "come from the hand of God." One dies, according to an old santero priest, "to make room so that Olodumare [the Creator] can send other beings to earth . . . and so, being born and dying, some come and some go." But if indeed God wills one's birth, one's death does not always occur at the hour He has willed; a curse can cut our lives short, as can the ire of an oricha when carelessness, disobedience, or unfulfilled promises incur its anger. Neglecting the deceased is yet another cause for suffering and death.

The saints are touchy, susceptible, we are warned, even more than the creator Olodumare, and many diseases are the result of a slight or of an omó or devotee's incorrect behavior. If the oricha's attitude is unforgiving because the error has been grave, "if its back is turned" and it refuses to gratify the mediator who pleads for indulgence and irrevocably carries out the punishment, there is no escape for the guilty party. This explains the helplessness of the babalocha when confronted with an incurable illness for which there is neither ebbó nor natural herbs: it is the result of inflexible divine rage. We can cite the following example told to us by an old and respected iyalocha from Matanzas: "Yewá refused to forgive her! The saint withered her away and killed her little by little," she assured us. She was referring to her goddaughter, who had not only forgotten to fulfill a promise, but had also offended the oricha on a daily basis by living licentiously (she was the daughter of Yewá, the severe goddess of death who demands chastity and absolute abstinence of her omós and devotees, which is why her priestesses are always older women). Note that this is not far removed from Western theological concepts, which for centuries perceived in diseases and terrible epidemics the consequence of divine ire and retribution. . . .

Despite their severity, the orichas ultimately come to the aid of their children and the faithful who beg them and offer gifts. A generous and timely ebbó will appease them. They forgive the offense and the patient recovers his health or is saved from the jaws of death. The inevitable rite that inspires confidence in the patient and in those who find themselves in difficult circumstances, as we know, is the ebbó, basic to all cures (and undertakings). It would be impossible to separate the role of healer from the cult of the babá (or that of the iyá),[3] comparable to that of the priest in the ancient world.

The therapeutics of santeros and mayomberos is based essentially on plants used in decoctions, infusions, inhalations, aromatics, unguents and baths that cleanse (expel) an evil spell, clearly discernible by the presence of an unusual, indefinable substance like a ball of hair, fibers, herbs, feathers (see figures 3.1 and 3.2). Thus, with a sort of white hoof with two imbedded eyes tied on one side into a small tail, a certain woman I met who had undergone treatment with a santero was able to prove that she had been the victim of a harmful spell. In some cases, according to the location of the *bilongo* [harmful spell], the *brujo* [sorcerer], in a state of trance, can extricate it with his mouth. Performing, as disbelievers might suppose, a fabulous trick, . . . a mean-spirited mayombero confessed to having swallowed a bilongo, any of those creatures used by the evil sorcerer—a toad, snake, lizard, spider—and, after sucking on the sick man's limb, spitting it out alive onto a white dish with a lit candle placed next to it . . . A woman friend of Omí Tomí[4] was sprayed with the dust of a tarantula that drove her mad. Happily she was cured by the famous sorcerer Bokú, who took her into his home and freed her from the madness that was simply due to the spider that was later shown to her. Only a spirit or an oricha is capable of "removing witchcraft" by mouth. But the mayombero or *ngangulero* possessed by the fumbi who performs these extractions should not do it without a helper or someone with sufficient experience. Thus there was the case, some time around the year 1948, of the mournful death of a kind mayombero who paid for the healing of a Canary Islander with his own life. Alone with the patient, without an assistant knowledgeable in guiding and dominating the spirit, a nganga father in a trance state set his mouth to the thigh of a bewitched individual, yanking out the harmful spell, which consisted of a pile of straight pins, a cartridge, a bullet, a scorpion, and a spider. He had not followed the precaution of preparing the magic design properly, of placing a lit candle next to the white plate where the spell would be cast. The spirit, working through the sorcerer without guidance, instead of spitting out the bilongo, began to chew it furiously "because they want to eat the harm," and, upon

Figure 3.1   Herbs are prepared with sprays of alcohol. Photograph by Héctor Delgado.

swallowing it, the bullet lodged in his throat, causing his death. No one can save the victim of these spells.

> Okují was so evil that back in Africa the king of his land ordered him killed. He gathered together his few belongings and ran away to the coast, selling himself to the slavers. He managed to bring to Cuba his "thing" (amulet). One of the overseers of the Francia family, strongly feared by the blacks, had it in for Okují, who wound up on our sugar plantation. That overseer, Don Pedro Aguérrebere, punished him with the stocks for three days and three nights. There he swore to finish off Don Pedro. When they removed him and revived him with massages, he swore a curse on Don Pedro that was overheard by several blacks, and three days later Don Pedro fell ill. He suffered horribly for exactly three years. La China, a good-looking mulatto girl who was the overseer's lover, gathered together all the gold jewelry he had given her and offered it to Okují to forgive him and restore his health. The black man replied that he no longer was able to do anything. It was impossible to lift the curse! He advised her to save her jewelry and her money for the future. Don Pedro died and his torment lasted three days. . . . Okují had spent three days in the stocks!

They buried Don Pedro in the plantation cemetery, and a black man who was close to me, Estebabé, referring to Okují, said that "although we're not in the same bunch," that is, though his magic was not of the evil sort used by Okují, he nevertheless cared for and respected him.

Figure 3.2 Tobacco smoke makes ready the plants used in the cleansing. Photograph by Héctor Delgado.

A serious healer, in order for his honesty to be undoubted, proceeds in the following manner to extract the harm from an injured organism. The mouth is not used.

> If the witchcraft is in an arm or leg, a spot that can be tied up, I fasten it with a consecrated necklace so that it won't escape, limiting the affected area. If it is in a part of the body that cannot be tied, I close it in by drawing crosses. The spot is slashed with a knife or blade, I take a small hollow jar, and, placing alcohol inside, it serves like a cupping glass and I extract the harm. None can say that I perform tricks. . . . My work is clean.

There are spells—*murumbas,* bilongos, *wembas*—so powerful, performed with such force, that another sorcerer cannot undo them without risking his own life. Victims of these curses can find none to save them. "A doctor's errors are of this earth," the saying goes. "Those of a curandero lie in his failure to confront one more powerful."

In initiation rites the neophyte, who should enter the sacred room—that of the "saints" (*igbodu*)—in an immaculate state, is bathed with herbs . . . all of which possess forces that can indeterminately be used for good or for harm. An informant from a town in Matanzas remarked axiomatically, not without cause: "If the santero is good, his work will be for the good." The reader should be aware that in the Lucumí religion witchcraft can also be found; the *aye* or *ochono,* the "evil sorcerer," is as feared as the worst of the evil mayomberos. Nor should it be thought that the babalocha and the babalawo, as is believed, only defend themselves, or abstain from attacking if the occasion should present itself. . . .

❊ ❊ ❊

The herbalist is another important and very popular and useful individual who has a specialized knowledge of plants. He is the "pharmacist" who searches for plants in the wild, selling them in the market or delivering them to santeros, distinguishing himself from the latter in that herbalists are not usually santeros, although they are at times confused with them as they too prescribe and cure; they can advise which *ewe* [plant] can soothe or heal and which can drive away evil spirits or attract good ones and good fortune (see figure 3.3).

All plants serve the curandero; God provides an herb for everything. A magical power, a healing quality resides in all herbs . . . and he who knows how to harvest and work them can use the same plant to save a life or to kill or harm. The good or evil performed with them depends on the intentions of those who make use of their power. The curandero's role as herbalist, a role that assures him a numerous clientele, is deployed in those cases in

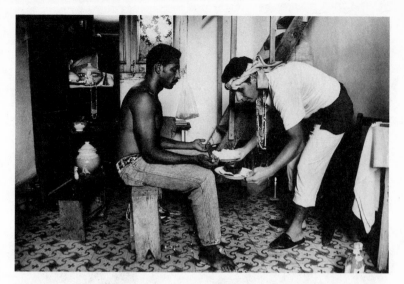

Figure 3.3   Prayers to Obbatalá and a dish of healing objects. Photograph by Héctor Delgado.

which one finds it absolutely necessary to consult the oracles and undergo such important and costly rituals as the "exchange of heads." No less terrible than the punishment of an oricha is the harm caused by the evil arts of a sorcerer who avails himself of sinister spirits to sicken or kill; if another sorcerer fails to discover and bind the evil in a timely manner, the organism of the victim is defenseless.

We have heard of the mayombero seated on the floor next to the patient administering the brew he has prepared to "extract the witchcraft," and of the latter who drinks it and vomits feathers, stones, and hair. At that moment the sorcerer "switches lives" [*cambia vida*]: he uses chalk, twine, a doll, or the stump of a plantain tree. He measures the patient and ties the doll or the stump with seven knots. With this procedure the evil that attacks the patient is transferred by the curandero onto the doll or stump, which is given the sick person's name, and thus death is tricked into believing that the buried stump or doll is the patient's cadaver. The following morning the nganga demands an herb: "One pays for the use of the herb that is needed, it is peeled, the juice extracted, strained and bottled. During the entire day the sick person drinks the amount he needs and the harm ends." (See figures 3.4 and 3.5.)

A doll, we are told, properly baptized, is placed to sleep beside the sick person in his bed. The following day it is placed in a box, as if dead, and buried. The patient is cleansed three times with a rooster that is passed over

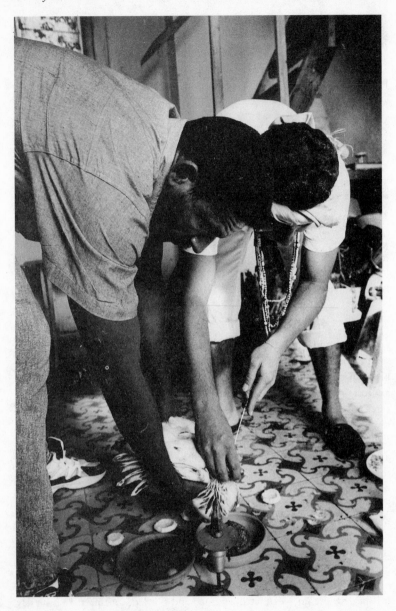

Figure 3.4   A hen is sacrificed and the blood offered to the oricha warriors. Photograph by Héctor Delgado.

Figure 3.5   The receiving of the oricha warriors. Photograph by Héctor Delgado.

the entire body. The rooster dies because it has absorbed the illness and is taken to a crossroad. The patient then rests and undergoes a treatment of infusions. A mayombero who "switches lives" with chickens describes his procedure:

> When they call me for a healing, first I spiritually consult, I inquire, and if my nganga tells me to go, I go. I gather up the patient's bedding and cleanse him with a chicken that dies if the man or woman is going to be cured. Having purified the body I take him or her to my home, to my nganga. The chicken's gizzard is extracted and the membrane surrounding it is roasted and then boiled with coffee. The patient is ordered to drink the tea of a tree bark. I take what remains of the chicken with the bedsheets, calling out the patient's name, to a ceiba tree and leave them there with a coin and a candlestick. I give the patient the broth made of the gizzard membrane and the bark, and later a cup of purple or white hamelia tea. A pole is placed over a basin, the patient is seated on the pole covered with a sheet, and with very hot water I bathe his feet. When he begins to perspire, the illness or the witchcraft that is in his body or his home departs, and while I have him in this steam I sing:

> > Cambia cuerpo Nganga
> > Va mono con é
> > lé la ngangara
> > yo pué con é . . .
> > Dié cun dié cundié . . . etc.

After the baths he is put to bed, and later has another bath of ceiba or of the herb that I am directed to use. When he is cured, my nganga gets paid with a goat or a rooster, and I with money.

Let us recall that many years back this ceremony took place in the Colón Cemetery of Havana, costing a desperate father, the relative of a high-ranking government figure, several thousand pesos. Trading logic for faith and the desperate hope of saving his young son ill with leukemia, a doll was buried that symbolized the boy and was meant to confuse *Ikú* [Death] and remove the illness from the child for whom science had given up all hope . . .

In order to retard the arrival of Ikú, "to block and entangle the way," her hunger is appeased with an important sacrifice so that "the appetite becomes heavy and she forgets whom she was coming for." To alienate Ikú is the most important function of the santero-healer; the authority to decree any changes is held by the babalawo, minister of *Ifá*[5] whom, we are told, forced a pact with Ikú binding her to respect Ifá's godchildren and proteges. She would not take them without warning before their appointed time in Oru and he would correspond with what is legitimately her due. They have fulfilled this pact, and thus in serious cases one must take into account the advice of the babalawo, who, according to some experts, had won the war he had waged with Death, and, according to others, returned to Death the scythe that her cohort and messenger Eleguá had wrenched from her hands, giving it to Ifá. Without a scythe, Ikú "had been disarmed."

In the markets of Havana, in the old and bygone Plaza del Vapor, in the Mercado Unico, where for three cents one could drink the best coffee in the world, in the cities and towns of the Island, one would always find the herbalist active at his post, a small sacred forest in miniature, not only in the cool early morning hours but at any time of the day, serving humanity. This man, with his knowledge of nature and awareness of the god Osain, the deity of plants, who smelled of earth and of cut branches, would listen to those who came to him to speak of their ailments or their little problems in life, and resolve them with his knowledge and experience without the intervention of babalochas or babalawos.

"A toothache? Here, have some prickle weed leaves . . . Some gargling mixture made of marigold or violet vine."

"A sore throat? Sweet peppers, rosemary, but nothing better than pumpkin gourd. Let's see, for a cold? Infusions . . . spiderwort, mastic, scabiosa, devil's-bit, plum tree, trumpetwood, castor-oil plant, violets, milk thistle . . ."

I recall this dialogue:

"Belén, how are you, dear?"

"Selling raffle tickets . . ."

"Are you walking a lot? Do your feet hurt?"

"Oh, honey, yes, they hurt, that's why I'm here!"

"Take some dropseed. Do they itch?"

"That too."

"Rattlebox."

A young mulatto girl with feverish eyes stays home from work: she woke up constipated and with a headache. The herbalist shouts out his suggestion of a heavy infusion of bridal bouquet, a whiff of incense, or a compress of aloe vera or amomum leaves, or of prophet-eye. Another client feels nervous, "everything is jumpy inside," and she hasn't got an herb garden or even a pot to grow an herb in. She needs jasmine flowers, marjoram, white lily, orange blossom, chaste-tree leaves, sweetsop or sarsaparilla, and when they bloom in our tepid winter and the old women's hearts flutter a bit, the herbalist provides poinsettias to calm them. If it has been rainy, "rheumatism is all stirred up," and bones are sore, the herbalist has jimson weed, gentian, rosemary, or mountain damson to place into cane alcohol with a piece of camphor for your massages and a drink, and decoctions of borage; and for those who suffer digestive problems there is always licorice, reseda, orange tree, cedron, anise, lemon balm, grama grass, purple basil. The customer who approaches in shirtsleeves and sandals has been told by his white doctor that his blood pressure is high and has been prescribed medicine, humm!, but it might be better to help the medicine along, the herbalist tells him, with decoctions of fescue, canary grass, or parsley that really do lower blood pressure, and to swallow a clove of garlic every morning before breakfast.

Others are better informed, and whisper requests for leaves, roots, or reeds for their pains that the herbalist does not always have on hand, like the crab reed that a devotee of the Virgin of Regla/Yemayá orders for her hemorrhages, and remedies for other afflictions, preventive ones or those having to do with good luck; in these things too our herbalist is equally well supplied. If he does not have it on hand he will search for what is advisable. Luckily, nature provides many good talismans like the jack bean, oxeye, peony, liana; stones, the ones from Cobre,[6] loadstone, the stony mass they say is imbedded in the boa's head—like the cobra of Indian mythology—and in that of the very difficult to obtain, very expensive but insuperable turkey buzzard, hidden in the nest of Kolé-Kole or Mayimbe, the sacred vulture, with virtues comparable to those of the famous eagle. . . . Could some of these stones, or at least their fame, have arrived in Cuba on a contraband ship and, as there are no eagles on the island, been substituted for that of the vulture, bird of prey and of such soaring flight it can carry messages to the heavens and is highly venerated by black people?

🜲   🜲   🜲

As we have observed, there is little difference between the therapeutics of the practitioners of the Lucumí or Yoruba religious systems and that of the Regla Conga or Mayombe traditions. Their remedies are located in the same pharmacy: nature. Illness is attributed to the same causes in both: spells, divine retribution, the ominous influence of the dead and of jinxers, and the dangerous "evil eye," worse than that of witchcraft, to which we are all vulnerable, especially children.

For this reason, in order to conserve one's health, it is indispensable, they insist, and I repeat word for word, "to behave well to the saints and the dead; have a spiritual reading from time to time, a cleansing of oneself and one's home with purifying waters and incense, defend one's door with a magical 'working,' obtain a good protection [talisman]." Don't violate the prohibitions dictated by the deities. Avoid sleeping with the old or the infirm, as they unconsciously deplete health, stripping the young and the healthy of their life force.

This is the basis of what we might refer to as the preventive medicine of *iworos* and *aborichas* [those who venerate the orichas]. As the saying goes, forewarned is forearmed, and many maladies could be avoided with a timely forewarning. Guided by the gods or by the fumbi who diagnose, the therapeutics are the concern of the babá, the iyá, or the nganga, who will discover, with the approval of the supernatural forces they serve or control, the appropriate remedy for each misfortune.

These forces put them in contact with their environment. They felt affection for plant life. "Felling so many trees to grow sugarcane is a crime because of all that is lost for our health, which is worth more than money," an old curandero lamented. If we can believe him, then our forests stored treasured remedies that were often infallible, miraculous, many of which are no longer available to contemporary curanderos because species have become extinct and "their very names forgotten."

Chapter 4 ▨

Afro-Caribbean Healing:
A Haitian Case Study[1]

Karen McCarthy Brown

"Moun fèt pou mouri" (People are born to die), Haitians are fond of saying with a shrug of the shoulders. This proverb comments on the suffering and death that are commonplace occurrences in poverty-stricken Haiti and shows the stoic acceptance that, on one level at least, characterizes the Haitian attitude toward such a life. Haitians have no vision of heaven in their religion,[2] no ideology of progress shaping their understanding of history, and virtually no experience of upward mobility in their lives or the lives of their children. Suffering is an expected, recurrent condition. It is not an exaggeration to say that problem-free periods in life are pervaded with an anxiety that anticipates crisis just around the corner. Life as a whole is thus characterized by cycles of luck and the absence of luck. The clever, faithful, and/or powerful person is one who manages by a juggling of scarce resources to give generously to the living, the dead, and the spirits. The resulting network of dependents who are obliged to serve and of elders or social superiors who are obliged to give sustenance and protection—even though subject to the inherent unpredictability of personal relationships—provides the only means any Haitian has of controlling his or her "luck." At the very least, the obligations created by these gifts construct the safety net that is essential for survival, given the uncertainties of life in Haiti.

Haiti occupies the western third of Hispaniola, an island it shares with the Dominican Republic. It is a small country—about the size of the state of Maryland—that is home to 5.5 to 6 million people. Haiti is still largely an agricultural country, although much of its land has been rendered nearly useless by short-range farming techniques and soil erosion caused by cutting trees to produce the charcoal most people still use to cook their food. Diseases such as tuberculosis, malaria, yaws, syphilis, and elephantiasis, which have been virtually eliminated in most of the Western Hemisphere, afflict the population in Haiti still. In parts of Haiti the infant mortality rate is above 50 percent, and anyone reaching the age of fifty-five or sixty is considered among the fortunate. The majority of children show some signs of malnutrition: spindly arms and legs; swollen bellies; reddish, brittle hair. Social disease is also rampant in Haiti, a country that has survived a succession of brutal dictators who have increased their personal wealth at the expense of the people and maintained their power through random violence and intimidation. It is estimated that 80 percent of the population is illiterate and that the average annual income for a Haitian is somewhere between $200 and $300. When the considerable wealth of the 8 to 9 percent of the population known as the elite is taken into account, it appears that most persons in Haiti get by on little more than $100 a year—and yet a chicken purchased in Port-au-Prince can cost as much as $5.

"Mizè mennen parespè," the Haitians say, meaning, If you show you are suffering, people lose respect for you. *Mizè* (literally, "misery") is an interesting word choice here, for while it can be used to refer to suffering in general, it is used most often to refer to poverty, with all its attendant pains and indignities. There are many beggars in Haiti. One sees them everywhere, but most often in markets, cemeteries, and churchyards. In spite of their numbers, there is a special shame associated with begging. This becomes apparent in the way begging is used within the Vodou system. When the spirits want to teach a lesson in humility to a devotee, they command that person to don the ritual version of rags and go to the market and beg. The ignominy of begging comes largely from the fact that beggars are seen as isolated individuals whose activity announces to the world that they have been abandoned by the extended kin group and now must forage on their own. Even if the family was lost through death rather than discord, the person who must beg can easily be seen as someone who was not clever enough or respectful enough or sufficiently hardworking to find a place as adopted kin in another family.

The Centrality of Family

For the slaves taken from Africa, the loss of extended family was so great that they apparently made efforts to re-create that family before they had even set foot on the shores of the New World. It is reported that some slaves recognized an incest prohibition as existing between males and females who had undergone the Middle Passage on the same ship. We know almost nothing about the interactions among slaves in the early part of the eighteenth century, when large numbers of them arrived in Haiti to work the plantations. However, knowledge of the crucial role of the extended family throughout West Africa easily leads to the conclusion that whatever blending among Fon, Yoruba, and Kongo cultures took place during that period must have been compelled in large part by the need for family. In the early stages this need would have been met through fictive kinship structures in which putative "mothers" and "fathers," "aunts" and "uncles," and "cousins" provided the individual with both identity (a place in society) and protection. Since the contributing African cultures defined family as including the ancestors and the spirits, the need for family was both a social and a spiritual need.

The slaves' loss of access to family land in Africa was as great as their loss of the African family itself. Indeed, from one perspective family and land were inseparable. Prevented from visiting family graves and from leaving food offerings and pouring libations at ancestral shrines, the enslaved African had also been denied the means of ensuring the spiritual blessing and protection of the ancestors. Thus when slaves could bring no other possessions with them, some nevertheless managed to carry away small sacks of the soil of their motherland. This connection of family, land, and religion persists in rural Haiti today.

Unlike most of the other Caribbean nations, Haiti is predominantly a country of peasant farmers, many of whom own their own land. Where the social structures have not been decimated by the combined pressures of overpopulation, depleted soil, and corrupt politics, rural people in Haiti tend to live in large, patriarchal, extended families. Even moderately successful men in the countryside may enter into multiple *plasaj,* or common-law, unions with women. Each of these women is set up in a house of her own in which she raises the children born of their union. Thus a multigenerational extended family can swell to considerable size even when counting only the blood kin. Such families, however, are not defined solely by blood ties. Large rural families invariably include adopted "godmothers," "godfathers," and "cousins," as well as a number of "maids" and other workers who exchange their labor for a place to sleep and for meager rations. Included in this latter group are the *restavèk* (literally, the "stay-withs"), children whose parents could not afford to feed them and so either sold them or gave them away to slightly more prosperous families. Social hierarchy is relentless in Haiti. There is always someone poorer than oneself. Even the most minimal rural household with only one or two able-bodied adults to work an unproductive square of earth manages to have a servant.

The patriarch of the extended family functions as the *oungan,* or priest, when that family serves the spirits. He is often the one who treats family members when they become ill, although an outsider may be called in for such treatments if there is someone in the vicinity who has a reputation as one who "knows leaves." However, it is necessarily the patriarch who presides at the *gwo sèvis,* the big dancing and drumming events that include animal sacrifice. These ceremonies are held annually if family resources permit. More commonly they are held at longer intervals and then only in response to crises within the group. The purpose of the elaborate ritualizing is to honor, entertain, and feed the ancestors and the Vodou spirits that those ancestors served.

The family dead are buried on the family land, and the cemetery is a major center for religious activity. In addition, a cult house for the ritual objects of the family is often built on a small, separate plot of land. Thus, to inherit land is also to inherit the bones of the ancestors and the duty to honor those ancestors as well as to serve the spirits represented in the cult house. Conversely, to be separated from the land is also to risk one's access to the power and protection that these spirit entities provide.

Separation from land and family is, however, an increasingly frequent experience for the younger generations of Haiti's rural poor. Inheritance laws in Haiti work to divide the land into smaller and smaller plots. This pressure, combined with that of the multiple problems cited earlier, has pushed large numbers of young people off the land and toward the elusive promise of a better life in the cities.

For young men urban life is often cruel. In the countryside they are reared to the expectations of male privilege and power. (Even the female-headed households that are prevalent in the cities perpetuate this ideology to a degree.) Yet some experts estimate unemployment among young urban males at 60 percent, and others argue that the figure should be much higher. Women fare somewhat better in the urban environment. Most of the factory jobs available are of the piecework variety, and European and American employers seem to favor women for these repetitive tasks. Urban women also have a market tradition bequeathed to them by their rural sisters. In the country it is the women who take the excess produce to market, along with bread, candy, herbal teas, baskets, and other things they make with their own hands. The urban woman spun away from the rural extended family frequently ends up not only in charge of her house and her children—as she might well have been in the country—but also solely responsible for their financial support. In the countryside her market money would have been the "rainy-day savings" for times of drought and hunger or the means to fulfill a private dream for herself or her children. In the cities she must rely on the old market skills more centrally. The poor urban woman is constantly engaged in small-scale commerce, often in several such enterprises simultaneously. For example, even if she has a regular job, she may sell peanut candy at the door of her home or work as a seamstress or beautician in the evenings and on weekends.

Both men and women who no longer live with their extended families feel the loss acutely. In fact, this sense of loss can persist for generations. In the cities, it is the Vodou temple and the fictive kinship network it provides that compensates for the missing large rural family. The head of the temple is called "mother" or "father," and the initiates are known as "children of the house." The Vodou initiate owes service and loyalty to his or her Vodou parent after the pattern of filial piety owed all parents by their children in Haiti. In turn, Vodou parents, like actual ones, owe their children protection, care, and help in times of trouble. In certain circumstances this help is of a very tangible sort: food, a place to sleep, assistance in finding work. The urban Vodou temples are currently the closest thing to a social welfare system that exists in Haiti.

The differences between men's and women's lives in the cities have also left their mark on the practice of urban Vodou. While in some parts of rural Haiti women can gain recognition and prestige as *manbo* (priestesses), herbalists, or *fanm saj* (midwives), nowhere in the countryside do they effectively challenge the spiritual hegemony of the male. This is not the case in the cities, where there are probably as many women as men in positions of religious leadership.

The urban Vodou temples run by men tend to mimic the patriarchal structure of the rural extended families. The urban oungan is notorious for fathering many children and recruiting desirable young women to be among his *ounsi,* brides of the gods, the ritual chorus and general workforce of a Vodou temple.[3] He thus creates a highly visible father role, which he then operates out of in relation to all those who serve the spirits under his tutelage. While the female manbo who heads a temple is not necessarily more democratic in all of her relationships with those that serve the spirits in her house, she does tend to be so in the ways that a mother's role is normally less authoritarian than that of a father. For example, many temples headed by women function as day-care centers for the working mothers associated with them. In sum, the woman-headed temple tends to reiterate the tone and atmosphere inside the home, a place where women have usually been in charge. This is an atmosphere that allows for more flexibility in human relationships than is found in the male-headed temple, which recalls the more public and therefore more rigid social rules of the entire extended family. This shift toward greater authority for women in urban Vodou has undoubtedly had an effect on the nature of the care given to individuals who turn to traditional religion to solve the many problems that urban life in Haiti can bring.

Whether the temple is headed by a man or a woman, it is clear that its appeal to the urban population is rooted in its ability to re-create family. A song sung at the beginning of Vodou ceremonies in Port-au-Prince illustrates this:

Lafanmi semble,
Semble nan.
Se Kreyòl nou yè,
Pa genyen Gine enkò.

The family is assembled,
Gathered in.
We are Creoles,
Who have Africa no longer.

The Vodou View of Person

In Vodou, persons are said to possess several "souls." In fact, there is no generic term in the Haitian Creole language that includes all of these spiritual entities or energies, even though each possesses some of the characteristics of what Westerners call soul. Furthermore, the word *nam,* derived from the French word for soul, is only one of the complex of forces that constitute a person. A person's nam is usually understood as the animating force of the body. The most immediate effect of death is the departure of the nam, which is sometimes said to linger for a short period of time around the corpse or grave. The nam is an evanescent thing that disappears soon after death.

By contrast the *gwo bonanj,* the big guardian angel, is capable of sustained existence apart from the body it inhabits. One of the situations in which the person is separated from his or her gwo bonanj occurs during the possession trance, which is central to Vodou ritualizing. The struggle that marks the onset of possession is understood as a struggle between a person's gwo bonanj and the Vodou *lwa* (spirit), who desires to "ride" that person and to use his or her body and voice to communicate with the faithful. One who is thus ridden by the spirit is known as a *chwal* (horse) of the spirit. Those who are possessed report that they lose consciousness after this initial struggle. The loss of consciousness and the resulting amnesia about what the spirit said and did while riding the chwal is explained as due to the departure of the gwo bonanj.

Similarly, it is the gwo bonanj that wanders from the body during sleep, even into the land of the dead, thus allowing deceased persons or those living at a great distance to appear in dreams. The wanderings of the big guardian angel during sleep are sometimes useful for information gathering. For example, a mother in Haiti said she learned from a dream that her daughter in New York had met with an accident and broken her arm. In like fashion, when a person is uneasy, she may say that her gwo bonanj is agitated. This is an undesirable state mainly because it robs the person of sound sleep and therefore of dreams, which are an important vehicle for communication with the dispersed family, the ancestors, and the spirits.

Finally, it is the gwo bonanj that must be ritually removed "from the head" of a person shortly after death. The big guardian angel is then sent "under the water" to dwell for a period of time until it (now referred to as a *mò*, one of the dead) is "called up from the water," installed in a clay pot known as a *govi*, and placed on the family altar. The Vodou ceremony known as *rele mò nan dlo*, "calling the dead from the water," calls them from Gine, Africa, a watery land said to exist below the earth. The ceremony ideally takes place a year and a day following the death. Because it is an elaborate and expensive ceremony, however, in practice families wait until there are several of their dead whom they may retrieve at once. As a result the dead frequently emerge complaining of cold, dampness, and neglect. In this ceremony, the dead speak through a kind of ventriloquism possession and genuinely sound as if they come from both far away and underwater. Their identity is confirmed by the intimate knowledge of family life that they display. The spirits called up from the waters of Africa inquire about family members and comment on problems within the group. Given these various understandings of the nature and activity of the gwo bonanj, it seems fair to conclude that this dimension of soul is both the consciousness and the essential personality of the individual.

The *ti bonanj* (little guardian angel), which each person also possesses, is much more difficult to define. One urban manbo, or priestess, gave me two interesting responses to questions about the nature of the ti bonanj. "When you look at your shadow," she said, "you will see that sometimes it has a dark center. That is the gwo bonanj, but the paler shadow around the dark center is the ti bonanj." When asked what the little guardian angel does, she gave another concrete illustration: "When you are walking a long way or carrying something very heavy and feel so tired that you know you are not going to make it, it is the ti bonanj that takes over so you can do what you have to do." The ti bonanj is thus perhaps best described as a spiritual reserve tank. It is an energy or presence within the person that is dimmer or deeper than consciousness, but it is nevertheless there to be called upon in situations of stress and depletion.

Much less routinely, Vodou oungan and manbo speak of another dimension of the person called the *zetwal,* or star. This is not an inner presence so much as it is a kind of celestial parallel self. The concept of the zetwal is rooted in the belief that each person is born with his or her fate already foreknown and unchangeable. The regular movements of the stars and their recurring patterns mimic, perhaps even direct, the larger contours of life in the human community. Whatever control an individual has over his or her life thus comes in specific moments and short-run situations. *Mizè* (suffering) may be held at bay only for a short time, and *chans* (luck) only marginally enhanced. The overall shape and direction of a life are determined by fate.

The nam, the gwo bonanj, the ti bonanj, and the zetwal are the constitutive parts of a Haitian view of personhood that is clearly derivative of what ethnographers call the "multiple-soul complex" in West Africa. The fact that Vodou contains European elements as well as African is also hinted at in this formulation. In addition to its Catholicism, the French planter class of Haiti was known for its participation in a variety of forms of marginal spirituality, including Freemasonry and spiritualism. It seems likely that the astrological flavor of the zetwal concept also owes its parentage to this line of influence, even though the notion that individual persons are born with their fate already cast by the gods was a belief held by the Fon and to some extent also by the Yoruba.[4]

While Vodou devotees understand the dead body (*kòr kadav*) of a person to be a material substance separable from these various animating spiritual entities and therefore subject to decay and ultimate dissolution, the body/soul or material/spiritual split is not central to their understanding of personhood. As an indication of this it is worth noting that there is no division within the Vodou view of person between drives or appetites that come from the body—for example, hunger and sexuality—and those that come from the spirit or mind. In fact, sexuality is perhaps the central animating force in all of life. Much of Vodou ritualizing suggests that sexual and spiritual energy come from the same source.

What complicates the understanding of personhood is the realization that individuals are not comprehensible apart from the Vodou spirits associated with them. It is easiest to discuss this in the urban setting, which I know best. Here, each person is said to have a *mèt tèt*, master of the head. This is the main spirit served by that person, and if the person is one who serves as a "horse" of the spirits, it will be the mèt tèt who most often possesses that person. To a certain extent the personality of the individual human being mirrors that of his or her mèt tèt. For example, a man who has Ogou as his mèt tèt will be expected to exhibit some of the warrior spirit's anger, strictness, and perseverance in his everyday behavior. Yet he will also have been told that Ogou is "too hot" to be served alone. The spirit of war and anger must be balanced by others, for example, by a strong "sweet" spirit such as the ancient and venerable snake spirit, Dambala.

In addition to a mèt tèt, each individual has a smaller number of other spirits, usually two or three, from whom he or she receives special protection. This complex of spirits, which may consist of some that are known only in that family and others that are recognized throughout Haiti, differs from individual to individual. It is partly because of this that Vodou, though centrally concerned with morality, could never produce a codified moral law that would apply equally to all persons. In Vodou, an individual lives a moral life by faithfully serving the particular configuration of spirits that "love" or "protect" that person. This includes following their advice, advice that will be consistent with the personalities of the spirits. Thus it might be said that the Vodou ethic is an intensely contextual one.

It is the urban devotee's particular grouping of protective spirits that determines the nature of ritual as well as moral obligations. Furthermore, it is important to note that the choice of this penumbra of protective spirits is not for "the living" to make; Vodou devotees insist that it is the spirits who choose the persons they love or protect. Yet, priests and priestesses do determine the choices the spirits have made, often through divination.

A question may well be raised as to whether the Vodou spirits are truly distinct and separate from the persons who serve them. This question is answered in paradoxical ways within Vodou ritualizing. Beliefs surrounding possession trance and the struggle of the gwo bonanj with the possessing spirit, as well as the insistence that the person is chosen by the spirit and not vice versa, point to a clear distinction between spirit and person. However, from the perspective of certain rituals such as those that occur during initiation and after death, the individual person cannot be separated from the spirits that reside "in the head" or "on" the person, these being equally common expressions among Vodou devotees. Initiation rituals simultaneously "feed the spirits in the head" and establish a repository for them outside the person. This repository is called a *pò tèt* (head pot). After initiation it is placed on the Vodou family altar and becomes the focus of rituals designed to cool, soothe, and strengthen the person. Furthermore, when the spirit is removed from a person's head at death, this spirit is sometimes treated as if it were the gwo bonanj and sometimes as if it were the lwa, the Vodou spirit who was the mèt tèt of the dead person. Similarly, when the ancestor is called up from the waters and established on the family altar, the spirit is called both by the name of the ancestor and by the name of the lwa. For example, reference may be made to "Marie's Ogou" or to "Pierre's Dambala." Thus there is also a sense in which at least the head spirit is identified with the gwo bonanj, if not with the individual in a larger sense.

In fifteen years of work on Haitian traditional religion, I have learned that paradoxes of this sort are to be cherished rather than resolved, for it is invariably such paradoxical statements that provide the greatest insight into the religious system we call Vodou. If it is understood that within the Vodou worldview the individual is both a separate self and an inseparable part of a family, then it can be grasped how the spirits who are part of that extended family can be *both* other than and merged with those who serve them.

Rituals of Haitian Vodou

For some individuals, coexistence with their spirits presents no problems; life flows more or less smoothly. It may be the case that someone within their family serves the spirits and this is sufficient to fill the hungry bellies, slake the dry throats, and stroke the wounded pride of the ancestors and the lwa. However, if one is not so fortunate and life is not going well—and it often is not in a country such as Haiti—then more is required. Vodou offers a series of ritual steps that escalate the intensity of the individual's involvement with the spirits. Each of these ritual steps is based on an exchange. The person commits to service of one sort or another; in return the spirits proffer relief and protection.

Some problems can be handled with a onetime or at least a short-term commitment to the spirits. This type of commitment could be something as simple as lighting a candle before the image of a spirit, or it could be an elaborate and expensive feast for several spirits, which would include dancing, drumming, and animal sacrifice. Other problems require a more routinized and long-term relationship with one or more spirits. Such lifetime commitments vary from "marriage" to a spirit to the decision to become a priest or priestess.[5]

In the process of escalating their commitments to the Vodou spirits, devotees accomplish two related things. First, they gradually increase the strength and stability of their own gwo bonanj. For those who move to the upper levels of initiation, this means mastering the art of possession trance, which is the art of both letting go of the gwo bonanj and bringing it back. Second, devotees gradually increase their control over the Vodou spirits as well. Men and women who advance to the grade of oungan and manbo do so through a ceremony in which they "take the *asson*."[6] The asson is a small, hollow gourd covered with a mesh of glass beads and snake vertebrae. This rattle, which is the emblem of the Vodou priesthood, is not used to make music but to signal key changes in the drum rhythms in a Vodou service, as well as to summon and send away the lwa. When a lwa tries to seat itself on an inexperienced horse, the struggle between the gwo bonanj and the spirit can become violent and even harmful to the horse. It is in situations such as these that the spirit must be sent away. Thus, within limits, Vodou priests and priestesses have power over the spirits. As one Vodou priest put it: "The spirits don't like the asson, but they give it to us anyway so we can work with them."

Although it is clear that overall the spirits have far greater powers than do the living, the relationship between devotees and spirits is nevertheless characterized by reciprocity and mutual dependence. The lwa, like the ancestors, depend on the living to feed them. Hungry spirits are troublesome and destructive. The living, in turn, depend on the protection and luck that only the spirits can guarantee. This relationship is not unlike the one that exists between parents and children. While the greater power and authority of the parents is unquestioned, parental care in Haiti is not purely altruistic. In the rural areas children work from a young age, and their work soon becomes essential to the ongoing family enterprise. Play for children four or five years old often consists of small fetching and carrying tasks; and all over Haiti, the childless person is pitied mainly because there will be no one to take care of that individual in old age. For those reared in monotheistic religious traditions, the notion that the spirits are dependent on their devotees is an especially difficult one to grasp. Yet comprehending this principle is essential, for without understanding that the spirits need the living, it is all too easy to attribute the problems, illnesses, and general harassment that the spirits at times dole out to the living as due to their temperamental, or worse, evil nature.

Vodou is a blend of various African traditions with Catholicism. Although it can be argued that Catholicism has been Africanized in Vodou and that this is a far truer statement than its reverse, this does not mean that the Catholic Church has no role in the life of the 85 to 90 percent of Haitians who serve the spirits. Pilgrimages to various churches and attendance at Mass are integrated into many complicated Vodou rituals. In addition, the church has taken over the major ceremonies of the life cycle. Birth, where it is ritualized at all, is celebrated through baptism. Also, ideally, everyone should go through a First Communion. Pictures from this event are among a family's most treasured possessions. For economic reasons, most Haitians enter plasaj (common-law) partnerships rather than have legal marriages. However, where there is a wedding, it is understood that it should be a church wedding. The church also buries the dead, although Vodou rituals are woven in and out of the wake, the entombment (burial is aboveground in Haiti), and the memorial Mass that comes nine days following the death.

Vodou ritual pervades the life of the great majority of Haitian people. For example, candles are lighted and libations poured at countless family altars every day. There are also large ceremonies that have a more social and celebratory air. Among these are the sumptuous feasts for the spirits that occur with some frequency throughout the calendar year at large urban temples. These are a source of entertainment and celebration for curious onlookers and invited guests as well as for the members of that particular Vodou family. Even though all guests may not be offered drinks and plates of food, it is a tradition that the doors of the Vodou temple are closed to no one. Furthermore, the more people present at one of these events, the more chance it has of being a success. The spirits will not come until the crowd is *byen es-hofe*, "well heated up." When sweat is streaming down the bodies of the drummers and they have found that vast reserve of energy on the other side of fatigue, when their intricate polyrhythms drive the dancers to new heights of grace and spirit, when the voices of the leader of songs and the ounsi cho-rus challenge one another in an ascending spiral of statement and response, that is when the ceremony is byen eshofe, and that is when the lwa will mount their horses and ride.

Spirit Possession

Once the spirit is in charge of the horse, the crescendo of energy stops and people settle in to watch the possession performance. The term "possession performance" is not used here to indicate that there is anything false or con-trived about these visits from the spirits. Vodou priest and priestess alike condemn the occasional person in their midst who may *pran poz,* act disin-genuously as if possessed. The term is used rather to indicate what has often been noticed about possession in the Vodou temple: it has a theatrical qual-ity. The characters of the major Vodou spirits are well known. Even an out-sider such as myself can identify the possessing spirit within moments of its arrival because of certain stereotypical behavior as well as the ritual garb and implements that the spirit requests. However, the Vodou priests and priest-esses, the ones usually possessed at these large feasts, improvise freely within the character range of the spirit. Thus a lwa not only goes through standard ritual salutations and exhibits certain forms of behavior that are seen virtu-ally every time this spirit possesses someone, but the spirit also addresses particular persons and gives advice about specific problems. The spirits hug, hold, and dance with the devotees. They give ritual blessings and some-times ritual chastisement, both appropriate to the situation. They sing. They eat. They cry. At these large public events, the Vodou spirits process the problems of the community, fine-tuning human relationships. Some-times an intimate problem can be whispered into the ear of a sympathetic lwa, and the spirit will take the devotee aside for a discreet and private au-dience. More frequently, these interactions with the spirits become the oc-casion for an individual's problems to be aired (and healed) in the larger community context.

One specific example of this process will serve to make several points. There was an oungan in Carrefour (a town on the coast road south and west of Port-au-Prince) who had a reputation for being a strict and dour discipli-narian in his Vodou family. Because she had angered him, he sent away a woman named Simone, the song leader in his temple, and told her never to return. At a ceremony not long after, this oungan, whose name was Cesaire, was possessed by the warrior spirit, Ogou. Ogou arrived in a rage and im-mediately began to berate Cesaire (the very horse he was riding). Who did Cesaire think he was, Ogou asked, that he could send Simone out of the temple? Simone was one of Ogou's favorites, and besides, it was he, Ogou, who was in charge of the temple, not Cesaire. The gathered faithful were instructed to convey this message to the ill-mannered oungan without fail, and then the spirit departed, leaving the body of Cesaire in a crumpled heap on the temple floor. When he had barely regained his senses, the reluctant Cesaire was carried along in a procession of all the temple dignitaries, complete with the brightly colored, sequined banners of the temple, right to the home of Simone. They stood outside and sang Vodou songs of invitation and reconciliation. After much coaxing, Simone agreed to come back to the temple, and, accompanied by the full parade, she was ritually reintegrated into the Vodou family.

This example shows something of the complexity of the possession process, in which a lwa can chastise, even humiliate, his own horse. Yet, perhaps more significantly, it also shows the key role of the community in the interpretation and application of the wisdom of the spirits. Thus, the public airing of community problems and issues within the Vodou temple is a means of enforcing social sanctions, mobilizing the assistance of the community, and mending broken relationships. It is, in short, a way of healing.

Yet there are vast areas of Vodou ritual that are concerned with healing in a more direct way. These vary from the individual client-practitioner interactions (practices that will be discussed below in a section on the types of caring used in Vodou healing) to the expensive and elaborate cycles of initiation rituals.

Initiation

Vodou initiation ceremonies are never undertaken lightly or routinely. Almost always it is trouble with the spirits, manifesting in problems in the individual's life, that leads a person to undergo initiation. In the temples of the Port-au-Prince area, there are four levels of initiation possible. Each level involves a period of seclusion that may vary from three to twenty-one days, and most temples have a small interior room set aside for such purposes. Persons tend to be initiated in small groups. The men and women in these groups become "brothers" and "sisters" in a special way. Above all, they are committed to helping each other with ritual duties. This is the case even when the groups contain individuals who are seeking different grades of initiation. All grades of initiation have public rituals that occur intermittently in the exterior temple dancing area as well as rituals reserved for the already initiated members of the house that occur within the inner chamber.

The first level of initiation is called the *lave tèt* (head washing) and involves cooling and soothing as well as feeding of the spirits in a person's head. The second level is *kanzo,* a word that refers to a rite in which initiates are briefly removed from the initiation chamber in order to undergo a ritual trial. In the semipublic part of the kanzo ritual, small, hard dumplings are snatched from boiling pots and pressed into the palm of the left hand and the sole of the left foot of the initiate. When this ceremony is completed, the initiates are told: "Now you are *kwit* [cooked]; no one can eat you," that is to say, no one can do harm to you. They are also admonished: "Never say hot again, say strong!"

The third level is called *sou pwen,* on the point. *Pwen* is a complex, multivocal concept in Haitian Vodou, as it is in Haitian culture in general. Within the general culture, "singing the point" or "sending the point" refers to a socially appropriate means of indirect communication that is especially useful for conveying difficult messages. For example, one young man in Haiti told me this story: He was courting a young woman who came from a family as impoverished as his own. The girl's mother decided that the match offered neither one any chance of advancement, and yet she was loathe to insult her daughter's suitor. So when he visited, she went about her household tasks singing a popular song, the refrain of which was "Dè mèg pa fri" (Two lean [pieces of meat] do not fry). The young man got "the point" and broke off his relationship. In and out of the temples, it is often Vodou songs that are used for the purpose of singing the point. These songs have a sparse, even cryptic quality to them that lends itself to communicating several different, sometimes contradictory, meanings at once. The person who "sends a song" in the Vodou temple, that is, the one who suggests the next song to be sung by the group, is not only following a closely prescribed ritual order in which each important lwa is saluted in the proper order with his or her own songs and rhythms, but quite frequently is also sending the point, *pwen,* to a person or group of persons present at the ceremony. Such an observation both reveals the extent to which Vodou ritual intertwines with and comments on the life of the community and suggests a preliminary definition for the troublesome word *pwen.* At a level of abstraction uncharacteristic of the way people who serve the spirits speak, *pwen* may be said to mean the condensation or pith of something. At a concrete, ritual level, *pwen* are charms or medicines composed of words, objects, gestures, or some combination of the three. They may be drawn on the earth, spoken, sung over a person, placed under the skin, or ingested; they may be buried at the crossroads, in a cemetery, or in the courtyard of a house. When one is initiated "on the point," the reference is to the condensation of the power of a particular spirit who has been diagnosed as the mèt tèt.

The fourth and final level of initiation is the one that gives a person license to begin practicing as a healer. It is called *assògwe,* literally, "with the asson," the beaded rattle that gives priests and priestesses some measure of leverage in the spirit realm.

In Haitian Creole, the verb *kouche* (to lie down, to sleep, to make love, to give birth—less commonly, to die) is the general word used to describe initiation. Entering the initiation chamber is like dying. Friends and family members cry as they line up to kiss the initiates goodbye. Shortly after this genuinely emotional leave-taking, the initiates are blindfolded and led through a dizzying dance of spirals and turns before being taken into the small room where they will kouche. As in many other sorts of initiation around the world, to kouche is to be forced by ritual means to regress, to become a child again, to be fed and cared for as a child would be, only to be brought rapidly back to adulthood, a new kind of adulthood, again by ritual means. When the initiates leave the inner chamber after days of seclusion and ritualizing, they have their heads covered. Initiates must keep their heads covered for forty days. Like newborn babies with vulnerable soft spots, new initiates must protect the tops of their heads. The spirits within have been fed and are still changing and strengthening day by day. On an altar inside, the initiates have left their pò tèt (head pots), residues of the internal externalized, the self objectified, the spirits concretized. These pò tèt generally remain on the altar of the priest or priestess who performed the initiation and who will be ever after the initiates' spiritual mother or father. Thus, through initiation rites, bonds among the living—as well as between the living and the spirits—are reinforced.

The Vodou Spirits

In the preceding discussion, I have been using the term "spirit" in a generic sense, as the Haitians often do, to refer to what are in fact three distinguishable groups: the mò (the dead); the *màwasa* (the divine twins); and the *mistè* (the mysteries), more often referred to as the lwa, or, using the term in a more specific sense, the *espri* (the spirits). Generally speaking, the dead and the divine twins are more central to rural than to urban Vodou. As the structure of the large extended families unravels, the sources from which people seek wisdom and assistance change. In the cities, possessions by specific powerful ancestors decline, while more energy is focused on possessions by the major Vodou lwa, most of whom are known and venerated throughout Haiti. In similar fashion, as children lose some importance for the work of the family, the divine children, the màwasa, also lose some ritual significance. However, neither the mò nor the màwasa disappear completely in the urban context.

The dead are still venerated in the cities. As was mentioned above, the lwa are inherited in urban families, where they will be remembered for some time as the lwa of a particular ancestor, for example, Marie's Ogou. Also, in the urban context family graves continue to be important, as do the annual celebrations for the dead that occur on and near All Souls' Day.

The màwasa also continue to have a role in urban Vodou. In addition to being routinely saluted in most large dancing and drumming ceremonies, the divine twins are given special attention in two contexts, both of which have to do with enhancing the luck of a particular group or a particular enterprise. The first instance has to do with making a *promès* (promise). This is done when resources do not permit the immediate fulfillment of an obligation to the spirits. In such a case a small *manje màwasa,* a meal for the divine twins, can be prepared. The dishes, favorites of children, will be fed to the actual children in the group. When they take obvious pleasure in the food, this is taken as a sign that the spirits have agreed to accept the promise.

The second ritual in which the màwasa play a central role is the *manje pov* (feeding of the poor). This ritual is performed by families, both biological ones and those created around the urban Vodou temples. Ideally it is performed annually to ensure the good fortune of the group. Large quantities of all sorts of food are prepared. A small portion of this—a pot of soup, perhaps—along with coffee, soap, tobacco, and small change, is then sent to a gathering place for the poor. The steps of a church or the cemetery are likely places. These things are passed out to the poor along with an invitation to come to the temple or the home later in the day for a feast. Before any of those later assembled can eat from the overflowing pots prepared for the ceremonial meal, the children of the poor (a group doubly identified as the socially vulnerable) must first consume a separate manje màwasa.

Within the realm of the spirits, the màwasa play a role parallel to that of children in the social realm. They require more in terms of care and material goods than they can give back in the same media of exchange. However, because children are closely associated with the good fortune of a family as well as with its vulnerability (youngsters are said to be the most likely to "catch" destructive spirits sent against a family by its enemies), the exchange can be kept more or less balanced by the luck or blessing that children can uniquely bestow.

The manje pov reveals the connection that is made within Haitian Vodou between children and the poor. Both are socially vulnerable groups in need of care. Furthermore, the poor, like children, are understood to be sources of blessing. Almsgiving, particularly when on pilgrimage, is highly recommended in Vodou circles. The identical rituals that end both the promès and the manje pov reinforce the reading that helping children and the destitute brings good fortune. When the respective meals are finished, the guests—in one case the family children, in the other the poor, both children and adults—wash their hands in a basin containing water and basil leaves. The donor of the meal then stands in the center, and all guests wipe their hands on his or her clothing, face, arms, and legs.

By far the largest proportion of resources, time, and energy in the urban Vodou context is expended on service to the lwa. These lwa are both related to and different from their West African progenitors. The religious systems of the Fon and the Yoruba, both of which made central contributions to Haitian Vodou, have complex pantheons of spirits. These spirits have hegemony over a wide variety of life domains, including natural phenomena such as thunder, wind, rain, and smallpox, as well as cultural activities such as farming and hunting. When these rich spiritual systems were transported to the Caribbean, their considerable power to make sense of the world came to focus almost exclusively on the most problematic arena of life there, the social arena. For example, Shopona, the powerful Yoruba figure associated with smallpox, was completely forgotten. Others similarly associated with the powers of nature were lost unless their skills and proclivities translated readily into the social realm. In related fashion, many spirits were redefined in the New World setting. The Yoruba Ogun (the Fon Gu), a patron of metalsmithing, hunting, and warfare, came to be understood exclusively as a warrior in Haiti. This pervasive socialization of the divine occurred when West Africans were brought to the New World, and it happened again in new ways when their descendants were forced from rural homelands into the cities. Among the Gède (generalized spirits of the dead) recognized in Port-au-Prince are an automobile mechanic, a dentist, and a Protestant missionary. And Azaka, a lwa who is a peasant farmer, functions in his urban incarnations mainly as a voice reminding the dispersed of the importance of maintaining contacts with the extended family.

In the Haitian countryside (probably to a greater extent in former times than now) the various lwa are organized into several *nanchò* (nations). The names of these—for example, Kongo, Ibo, Wangol, Nago, Rada, Petro—almost all point to specific areas or groups in the African homeland. In the cities this complex of spirit nations has been synthesized into two major groupings, the Rada and the Petro. Within Vodou lore and practice these two groups are understood as fundamentally different, even oppositional. For example, mixing of the altars of the two pantheons is prohibited. Furthermore, even though both may be saluted in the course of a single evening, clearly articulated ritual transitions create buffer zones between the two groups.

The opposition between Rada and Petro can be best understood as a contrast between the quite different modes of relationship that each group represents. The Rada lwa are the "sweet" spirits. They are served with sweet foods and drink. The ambiance of their possession performances is intimate and warm. Even those Rada lwa who are awesome in their wisdom and power are treated with a respect that is transparent to the affection that underlies it. Rada spirits are *rasin* ("root") lwa. They are also said to be *frangine*

(African). They are, in short, family, and the mode in which one serves them reflects this. While fidelity and caution are required in the service of the Rada lwa, these spirits are not overly strict in their dealings with the living. If a promised feast cannot be offered to them one year, they can be persuaded to wait until the next. The Petro lwa by contrast are characterized as "hot" spirits. Their possession performances often play at the border of violence and destructiveness. In like fashion, the unfaithful or careless devotee does not escape punishment. Why then would anyone serve the Petro lwa? Because they have access to realms of life that the Rada spirits do not. The power of the Rada lwa derives from their wisdom, including herbal knowledge. The power of the Petro lwa by contrast extends over, but is not limited to, the arenas of money and commerce. The Petro lwa, whose iconographic repertoire includes intricate and intense drum rhythms as well as police whistles, whips, and knives are the spiritual incarnation of the plantation owners and their neocolonial equivalents—the mulatto elite who control the wealth of the country, and the American and European businesspeople who profit from the labor of the poor. The opposition between Rada and Petro is thus aptly described as that between family members and foreigners, or insiders and outsiders. Not incidentally, the Petro lwa also chart a course for the person who would assert his or her individual needs over and against the demands of family. The two pantheons, Rada and Petro, thus offer different rewards and are in turn characterized by different modes of sociality. Relationships with spirits in both realms require reciprocity. However, exchanges with the Rada spirits take place in a warm, familial atmosphere characterized by compassion, while those with the Petro lwa operate according to impersonal and inflexible rules and are thus pervaded with caution and anxiety.

The difficulty ethnographers have experienced in attempting to create a definitive list of the Vodou lwa is well known. The reason for this difficulty is rather simple: no such list is possible because the lwa are inherently mercurial. They are more accurately described as ways of being in the world, subject to endless transmutation through experience, than as beings per se. For example, the Haitians will say that there is one Ogou; they will also say that there are seven or twenty-one. In fact, there are probably many more than twenty-one that could be identified in the Port-au-Prince region alone. Each is an extension and elaboration of the central character of the warrior spirit Ogou. In his various manifestations Ogou plays across the full range of the constructive and destructive uses of power and aggression. For example, there is the politician Ogou Panama. There is the drunkard Ogou Yamson. There is Ogou Fèray the general, and Ogou Badagri the heroic soldier. Moreover, the individual personalities of the lwa are not exactly mercurial but similarly multifaceted. A particular lwa can exhibit power, dispense wisdom, and give solace and practical advice. But the same spirit can also—the particulars of his or her personality permitting—whine, pout, needle, harass, and become wantonly destructive. It is impossible, therefore, to group the Vodou spirits according to the moral categories of good and evil. Each spirit, Petro as well as Rada, has both constructive and destructive dimensions, and these change as the character of a lwa is applied to a particular life situation through the medium of possession performance. The lwa thus do not so much set examples for the living as they hold up mirrors that clarify certain aspects of the lives of those who serve them.

Treatment in the Vodou System

Vodou priests and priestesses treat a wide variety of *pwoblèm,* "problems." Clients come to them for help with love, work, and family problems as well as with sickness. The first determination that a Vodou healer must make is whether the problem "comes from God." If a problem is determined to have been sent by God, it is then seen as "natural" in the sense of that which is meant to be, that which is unavoidable.

When Catholicism was blended with African religious traditions to create Vodou, the great West African sky gods, progenitors of human and divine beings alike, were absorbed into *Bondyè* (God). Bondyè (literally, the "good god") is the one and only god and is clearly distinguishable from the lwa, who are sometimes said to be his "angels." A popular Haitian proverb emphasizes the message that is contained in the name of god itself: "Bondyè bon" (God is good). As a result, if a problem, usually a physical illness, is understood as coming from Bondyè, then it works to the greater good, even though this fact is unlikely to be apparent to the sufferer. No priest or priestess will interfere in such a case.

However, if a problem is determined to come from what some Haitians call "supernatural" causes, it is then thought to be appropriate for treatment within the Vodou system. It is important to remember that Haitians do not live in a two-story universe. God and the spirits are an intersecting dimension of life; they are not denizens of a separate realm. When they call a problem "supernatural," it means two things: the problem is not part of the natural order, meaning part of what is fated to be; and it is likely to have been caused by the spirits. Health problems that have a history of being resistant to scientific medical treatment often end up in the Vodou temple, where that very resistance is taken as a sign of the spirit-connected nature of the ailment. In fact, most problems are diagnosed as supernatural in origin or, if not specifically caused by the spirits, then at least falling within the province of their curative powers.

Once the preliminary determination is made that a particular problem is suitable for treatment, the manbo or oungan sets out to discover more about its nature and origins. Clients do not present themselves to Vodou healers with a detailed list of their symptoms. According to tradition, nothing more is required than a statement such as: "M'pa bon. M'pa genyen chans" ("I'm not well. I don't have any luck"). From this point, it is up to the priest or priestess to determine the nature of the problem, as well as its cause and cure. This is usually accomplished through divination.

The most popular form of divination used in Port-au-Prince is card reading. However, gazing into a candle flame may be used, as may other, more exotic techniques, such as pouring a small amount of alcohol into the top of a human skull and then reading the patterns made by the liquid moving along the cranial grooves—a very graphic appeal to the wisdom of the ancestors! For card divination, an ordinary deck is used, with all cards below the seven removed. After lighting a candle and praying, the manbo or oungan offers the cards to the client for cutting. These are then laid out in four rows of eight in front of the healer. The whole process is repeated twice, once to determine the best description of the problem and once to track down its supernatural connections. After the first spread, the healer begins tapping the cards in patterns dictated by his or her own inner perceptions. Occasionally a question will be raised or a statement made. For example: "There is trouble in your house. I see fighting." The client is free to say yes or no without prejudice. Gradually, through a series of such statements and responses, the contours of the problem reveal themselves. It should be emphasized that while this is clearly not a miraculous procedure or even one requiring extrasensory perception, it nevertheless calls on the intuitive skills of the practitioner and represents an important step in the curing. When the problem is articulated through this gradual dialectical process, its definition may well surprise even the client. I once witnessed a session in which a mother brought her young daughter for help because the child would not eat, was losing her hair, and had run away from home. In the course of settling on the appropriate description of the problem, the manbo uncovered something that was unknown to the mother and unspoken before by the daughter: the girl's stepfather was sexually abusing her.

Once a full picture of the problem emerges, the healer then lays out the cards once more to determine its cause or origin: "I see the spirits love you a lot. Ezili especially. Did you promise you were going to do something for her and then not do it?" By this means a complete diagnosis is made.

Diagnoses point to disruptions in relationships. Often the relationship in question is with the spirits themselves. Broken promises, lax or insufficient offerings, or refusal of the spiritual vocation the lwa have chosen for a person can all be reasons for trouble. Many manbo and oungan have stories to tell about their own efforts to resist the desire of the dramatic lwa that they take the asson, that is, undergo initiation into the priesthood. One woman was hospitalized three times and given last rites on two occasions for an intestinal disorder, the cause of which medical doctors could never determine. Eventually she obeyed the lwa, and thereafter she reported that she experienced no further health problems. Obligations incurred or promises broken by family members generations back can emerge as the cause of the present individual's troubles.

However, as was seen in the case of the sexually abused child, it is not always the spirits who cause a problem. For example, the cards often reveal that someone is suffering because of the "jealousy" of other persons. Jealousy is understood to be such a strong emotion that the lives of its targets can be seriously disrupted. Within the Vodou system the object of jealousy rarely escapes at least part of the burden of blame. Such an attitude reflects a society in which it is expected that anyone who has much should give much. Thus, a wealthy person is almost by definition thought to be stingy, and a very lucky person is suspected of having done "work with the left hand." A less serious but related diagnosis is that someone is suffering from "eyes." This mildly unsettling condition comes from the fact that too many people are paying attention to that individual. It may be that there is gossip circulating. With both jealousy and eyes, as with several other diagnostic categories, the troubled relationships are among the living. In such situations the spirits are called on for help, but there is no sense in which they are seen as causing the problem.

Sorcery and Ethics

Disruptions in relations with the spirits cause serious problems, yet in many ways it is an even more serious situation if, in the course of a "treatment," it is discovered that a person's problems arise from the fact that another human being has done "work" against them. The range of magical actions that fall under the category of "work" is considerable. It may only be that a rejected lover has gone to the manbo or oungan for a love charm, or it may be something more serious, such as an act of sorcery performed by a vengeful neighbor.

For example, sorcery is frequently implicated when a diagnosis is made that a woman has "fallen into perdition." "Perdition" is a condition that befalls a pregnant woman in which the child in her womb is "held" or "tied" to prevent it from growing. When a woman who has missed one or more menstrual periods and assumes herself to be pregnant experiences a discharge of blood, she suspects that she may have "fallen into perdition." In all pregnancies it is believed that the menstrual blood that would ordinarily exit from the body each month is held in the womb, where it serves as nourishment for the child. In a state of perdition the nourishing blood bypasses the fetus. The fetus, however, is not expelled but held inside the mother. Fetuses are believed to be able to stay in a state of arrested growth for years until something is done to "cut off" the perdition or "untie" the child. When that is accomplished the monthly blood flow stops, and the child begins to do its "work" within the womb. The infant born nine months later is the one who was conceived before the state of perdition began. Falling into perdition can be caused by several things. It can be caused if "cold" is allowed to enter the womb. It can be caused by restive lwa or ancestral spirits. However, work of the left hand, specifically sorcery, is the most frequent diagnosis. All children, but especially the unborn, are said to be susceptible to being "caught" by a work of sorcery directed against a family.[7]

There is an underlying belief in what might be called an economy of energy in Haitian attitudes toward sorcery or the work of the left hand. A rather flat-footed way of articulating the content of this belief would be to say: nothing comes for free. For example, there is a significant distinction made in the types of powers that a person can call on for help in this life. There are first of all *espri fami* (family spirits), and then there are *pwe achte* (literally, "points that have been purchased"). Most often residing in some tangible object such as a stone or bottle (the "point"), these spirits are either the souls of persons who died without family, ceremony, or burial, or they are the free-floating spirits of another, often malevolent, sort.

Serving family spirits entails obligations that may strain resources and energy; however, the demands of family spirits theoretically never escalate beyond reason. Within a given family the living and the spirits are interdependent in a way that makes both parties exercise restraint. Powers that have been purchased are another matter. While it is understood that they may be extremely effective, they have neither history nor loyalty to curb their rapacious appetites. Consequently, working with the left hand leads all too easily to an ascending spiral of obligations. Stories are frequently told of manbo and oungan who turned to sorcery in a desperate moment and then found it impossible to extricate themselves. First they lost members of their family; finally they lost their own lives. This belief that a person ultimately pays for what is gained through illegitimate means is one moral force within Vodou that curbs the wanton practice of sorcery.

Another moral force is the belief that only in extreme circumstances may one use sorcery to harm another, and only if one is absolutely just in doing so. For example, there was a manbo who lost her home through the deception of a woman friend who stole the title papers. The former friend actually went to court in an effort to claim the house for herself. The manbo performed a very simple act of magic (there is a widespread belief that the simplest ritual acts are the most powerful)[8] that involved dropping a "point" or charm into a latrine. As a result of this, three people either fell sick or died: the judge, the lawyer, and the erstwhile friend. When this incident was discussed within the family, someone invariably noted that the manbo could do this with no fear of reprisal from humans or spirits because she was so clearly in the right. The house was hers.

Yet another belief that acts to curb destructive uses of spiritual power centers on that part of Vodou associated with cemeteries. Although a version of this system operates within the cities, the pattern is clearest in the rural areas, where cemeteries are still family property. The first male to be buried in a cemetery is known as the Baron Simityè, Baron of the Cemetery. When a wrong has been done to an individual or family by someone from outside that group, a simple ritual performed in the cemetery calls on Baron to send a mò, one of the souls of the dead, to avenge that wrong. The Baron's power can never be used, by definition, by one family member against another.

What complicates this discussion of morality and the uses of power within Vodou is the fact that it is not always possible to keep the categories clear and distinct. What is sorcery from one person's perspective is no more than what was required for an effective treatment from another's point of view. For example, love magic may heal a broken heart or soothe wounded pride, but it also necessarily involves the manipulation of the will of another. Cemeteries in Haiti are littered with the evidence of this common sort of "work." Small male and female rag dolls bound face to face and stood on their heads (inversion creates change) in a jar or drinking glass are evidence of a work designed to bring about a reunion. The same dolls bound back to back indicate that the dissolution of a troublesome relationship was the desired result. One bound with its face to the back of the other is said to be in a position to "eat" the other, that is, to take revenge. Such routine magic is within the repertoire of most Vodou healers and does not involve trafficking with suspect or "purchased" spirits.

Understandably, most priests and priestesses claim to eschew the work of the left hand. Equally understandably, rumors circulate that this one or that one "serves with both hands." It is not unlikely that most sorcery rumors can be attributed to individuals or groups in conflict wherein each party, knowing its own spirituality to be rooted in family and tradition, can only assume that the practices of its enemies are not so rooted.

Knowledge and Power

In the course of treating a troubled person, Vodou priests and priestesses call on a variety of different types of knowledge and power. The word *konesans* (knowledge) is used to refer to learned skills such as herbalism and divination as well as to what might be called intuitive powers. The different degrees of initiation are seen as increasing konesans. At least part of what is meant by this is sensitivity to a sense of foreboding. The attuned person, the one with konesans, knows when to cancel a trip or a business appointment. At a higher level of development it may be the gift of "seeing" what is wrong with people just by looking at them. (Although called seeing, one manbo described its physical manifestation as a prickling in the scalp.) Many of the most sought-after Vodou healers are said to have this gift.

In addition to their own developed talents, priests and priestesses also call on a range of higher authorities in the healing process. Possession allows the healer access to the awesome wisdom and power of the lwa, and in fact it is often one of the lwa who prescribes the specifics of a cure. Quite detailed information about what should be done to treat a particular case can also come in dreams. One manbo said that it was usually her dead mother (a powerful manbo herself, appearing to her in dreams) who provided the solutions to her most difficult cases.

Dreams can also function in healing ways in the lives of ordinary devotees. Dreams can give warnings about bad things to come, thus providing the means of possibly avoiding sickness or anger, robbery or accident. Both the dead and the lwa routinely appear in dreams to give warnings and advice. The spirits sometimes appear in dreams in the same form as they are depicted on Vodou altars. Individual lwa have been conflated with particular Catholic saints, and the inexpensive and popular chromolithographs of the saints have thus become the most common images of the spirits. However, it seems that even more frequently the lwa appear in dreams in disguise. Each dreamer has his or her own code that must be applied to interpret the dream. Often it is a friend who has a name or personal qualities reminiscent of the lwa's who comes to stand for that spirit in the dream world. Thus one manbo said: "Last night I dreamed about Gerard. [Saint Gerard is the Catholic saint conflated with Gède, the spirit of death.] Gerard asked me how my daughter was doing, if she was out of the hospital yet. That is when I got scared for my daughter. I was afraid she might really get sick because I know every time I dream about Gerard, that's Papa Gède."

The care given by Vodou healers ranges from truly awesome displays of power to tender solace. I know of one manbo who brought her severely depressed female client into her home as part of the curing process. The woman had not spoken for nearly a year following the loss of a child. This mute condition, well known in Haiti and generally seen in young women, is considered especially difficult to treat. In the early stages of the treatment the manbo actually took the woman into her bed and held her until she slept. Yet treatments can also involve humiliation (e.g., being sent to the market to beg) and angry lectures from the spirits. In my experience, women healers routinely use the full range of care, from the solacing to the jarring, that is possible within the Vodou system. Male healers, by contrast, tend to remain authority figures throughout the healing process.

From a more general perspective, the jarring or confrontational aspects of Vodou healing are never separated from the overall context of familial care in which healing takes place. In fact, to make the distinction is to miss the coherence of the system. An image drawn from Haitian culture may make it easier to articulate this subtle point about the tone or ambience of caring within Vodou. Haiti is a child-centered culture. There are no events from which children are excluded. Yet the crying of infants and the misbehavior of older children are not tolerated. Crying babies are grabbed and rather roughly jostled into silence with unspoken messages that communicate at once the full attention of the caretaker and that person's unwillingness to tolerate the behavior. Older children can be given a harsh reproof at one moment and then a quick hug and kiss soon after. In a similar way traditional healers in Haiti can be possessed by an angry lwa without having that anger shape their personal relationship to the person seeking the cure.

The Creole verb *balanse* (to balance) has a special significance in Vodou and in healing within Vodou. When devotees take ritual objects off the altar they are instructed to "balanse," to swing the objects from side to side. This is thought to awaken or enliven the objects and the spirits associated with them. The word can, however, be used in less constructive contexts. For example, when death touches a family it is said to "balance their house." The sense that balance is a dynamic condition is revealing, as is the notion that it comes out of opposition, whether that be the back-and-forth motion of the ritual balanse or the harsher clash of death against life. Within the Vodou view of things, life is stirred up through opposition. This stirring and jarring, which can wound, is nevertheless healing when the clash of opposites is wisely orchestrated by the Vodou healer.

One example of a specific problem and cure will illustrate the confrontational dimension of Vodou healing. A young woman came to a manbo distraught, in fact nearly hysterical, because her husband had left her. In one moment the woman said she wanted her husband back; in the next she recounted a long history of his abuse. Finally, with a shrug of impatience, the manbo said harshly: "Pran tèt ou!" ("Get ahold of your head!") Three ritual baths were prescribed to be administered, one each week for the next three weeks. The first bath was made from warm milk in which cinnamon sticks had been steeped. About four cups of the liquid were placed in a small enamel basin and the woman was instructed to remove her clothes. Because this was a good luck bath, the liquid was applied to the body from bottom to top, starting at the feet and stroking upward. (The reverse would operate in a bath designed to remove bad luck, a more serious condition.) The second bath was composed of various liquors and perfumes. It was applied in a similar fashion, as was the third and final glorious combination of champagne, roses, and perfume.[9] After each treatment the woman was instructed to leave the infusion on her skin without washing for three days. The first bath, she reported, made her smell of sour milk "like a baby." After it she took to her bed and cried for most of a week. She said that the second bath, in which alcohol was the dominant ingredient, burned her eyes and genitals. The second ended the tears, but she was flooded with anger. She sought out her former husband and screamed and yelled at him until the neighbors intervened. She reported nothing remarkable from the third bath beyond the fact that she no longer felt so unhappy. This sequence of baths took a woman's ambivalence about the man in her life and concretized it. The first and second baths shook loose contradictory emotions; they jarred her into powerful and direct experiences of sadness and anger. From the resulting dynamic "balance" came the possibility of the third bath, which moved her beyond the extreme moods of the first two to a less precarious emotional state, one in which she gradually was able to let go of the destructive relationship. These baths, like so many of the Vodou treatments, can also be seen as a ritual regression, a regression to infancy and then a movement back, or even as a ritual rebirth not entirely unlike that which is accomplished through the initiation ceremonies.

Conclusion

"Moun fèt pou mouri," people are born to die—the saying reveals the Haitian's sense that life is both short and painful. This verdict cannot change; it can only be accepted. Yet in the midst of the struggle that is life it is possible to enhance one's chans (luck) and minimize the mizè (suffering). This is accomplished in two ways: first, by respectful attention to the web of sustaining human relationships that defines family, and second, through conscientious service to the spirits who are after all members of one's own extended family, even—from one perspective, at least—parts of oneself. The spirits are served by the parent (fictive or actual) in the name of the family. In order to serve the family well in this role, the priest or priestess must have konesans: knowledge, intuition, insight into human and spiritual affairs. Such knowledge is most often rooted in the oungan's or manbo's own experience of suffering. To kouche (lie down, sleep, give birth, die, and, specifically, to be initiated) is to take the risk necessary to be healed oneself and through that process to enhance and focus one's power and knowledge in order to heal others. Once gained, konesans carries with it a moral obligation that it be used justly and respectfully. Thus, the manbo or oungan is one who knows how to eshofe, to raise the life energy in individuals and groups, human and divine. Power thus mobilized can then be concentrated in pwe (points) that are the concrete embodiments of relationships, both human and divine. Problems properly articulated in the concrete can be healed. One can pick up the pwe and balanse—turn the point upside down and bring about change that heals.

Chapter 5 🖾

Santería as a Healing Practice in Diaspora Communities: My Cuban Jewish Journey with Oshún

Ester Rebeca Shapiro Rok

For quite some time now, I have realized that my professional commitments to culturally informed, community-based teaching and practice are intertwined with a personal quest: to understand my own Cuban–eastern-European–Jewish family and how our multiple diasporas redirected the flow of our family lives. Dissatisfied with the received knowledge of an individualistic, psychopathology-oriented mental health field, I have tried to understand my own life course, and that of others, as deeply intertwined with the many souls, among the living and the dead, with whom we share our evolving family lives. My life as a woman between cultures has not been easy, as I sought and failed to find personally acceptable choices among my family's and society's prescriptions for a good daughter, wife, mother, teacher, psychologist, healer. But the struggle to discover more inclusive life sources, to learn how to learn from life's inevitable losses, has been rich with cherished opportunities to discover, again and again, unexpected harmonies in apparent contradictions. I have found that sharing the lessons learned from my own profoundly human struggle is itself one of my most powerful resources as a teacher and healer.

🖾 🖾 🖾

Many of the world's communities commence an important new enterprise with a prayer to the fates, recognizing the potential dangers that accompany

any voyage into new territory. In this essay, I would like to tell you the story of a journey between worlds. Because the telling is itself a journey, I will begin by invoking Elegguá, the Orisha in the Afro-Cuban religion of Santería who guards the entries and crossroads of our lives' many paths. The stories tell us that at a young age, he cured Olofi—humankind's personal God, and an aspect of Oloddumare, the creative force of the universe—with herbs he had gathered from his forest wanderings. For his talent as a healer, Olofi awarded him the right to always enter first. As gluttonous for food as for adventure, he is always first at the table. But do not be deceived by Elegguá's youthful, playful appearance into taking him less than seriously. He has the body and energy of a mischievous child, but the face of a wise old man. Guardian of all the doors that open on this world and the next, he ushers us in at birth and walks us to the cemetery entrance as we approach death. He is intimately familiar with the many paths that lead us on our human adventures and misadventures. He is intensely ethical, and some say he is justice personified. He may appear as a trickster in his penchant for placing thorny moral dilemmas in our path, but he is an impatient and implacable judge of our will to do good in the world. In one set of New World Santería stories, responding to the powerful image of the devil in Catholicism, Elegguá is described as having himself made the ultimate commitment to goodness. Elegguá offered to take evil into his being so as to battle evil in the form of Olosi, the Santería equivalent of the devil. This later legend of Elegguá understands fully what the Orishas know so well, that to be purely and simply good presents us with no challenge. Our true, great tests in life come from the temptations placed in our path, which resonate to the dark side of our own soul's desires. Having invoked Elegguá's presence, I cannot stop there, without making the offering that requests his blessing for the difficult and risky road to come. It doesn't take much to help Elegguá feel recognized: a large fresh yuca root, or a handful of sweets, will persuade him that you are aware of the need to carefully consider your path.

❊　❊　❊

Life's most sumptuous banquet of learning unfolds before us at times of disruptive change. Yet learning feels like an inaccessible luxury at just those times, so desperate are we to rebuild, to reach the other shore and arrive at stable ground beneath our feet. Eventually, we become more sympathetic to the inevitably partial, provisional nature of our life's certainties. We become better able to shoulder our share of sorrow's burdens, and therefore are more capable of joy at the surprises that might unfold at the next crossroads in life's journey. When my first marriage to an assimilated North American Jew ended, I discovered that the life I had so carefully crafted to be my very own turned out to be a secret duplication of my self-sacrificing mother's. I went back to my psychoanalyst and asked him, how did we miss this, after all those years of careful sifting? We explored the missing longings and loyalties, the self-subversive strategies for continuity and connection, from which I had unconsciously and cleverly crafted life, career, and marriage. Armed with these insights, I also learned the limits of what my words and text-based therapeutic methods were prepared to see of life's eternal struggles. I began to study and transform my own life with my own tools, a model of human development over the course of the family life cycle, in which I understood our collective selves as a negotiated conversation with family, community, culture in sociopolitical space and historical time. I left a psychology practice to teach full-time at an urban university; I went back to Cuba and found much that I believed had been forever lost and that I could now refashion as my own legacy.

I thought I had changed everything. Then my second husband, a Cuban exile of my generation with whom I shared so much of my carefully reconstructed life, told me he was leaving me for another woman. I experienced once again the terrible sense of absolute loss I had dedicated my life to evading, and which I seemed to have once again built into the core of my marriage. I thought my husband and I had built the partnership of my dreams, in which our shared foundation of loving commitments would bless us during the best times and the worst. Instead, I found myself drowning in an ocean of grief. I resolved to search more deeply for the sources that would help me build a new life, that would help me understand how I once again in the name of love had turned a blind eye to the troubles before me. I understood my husband's affair with a Cuban exile of our generation as a chapter in our shared *telenovela* (soap opera), which I began to call, with all the ironic humor I could muster, "Love and Exile/*Amor y exilio.*" I had faith that our marriage was fundamentally sound, even if a romantic delusion had proved for the moment an irresistible lure. Yet once again, in this second unexpected collapse of my carefully constructed life, I was the last one to see it coming. The last thing I needed were more therapeutic certainties, offered by trained professionals without a clue as to the seismic forces of landscape and history that had shaped my intimate struggles with birth and death, love and hate, loss and rebuilding. I needed to listen more respectfully and attentively to the chorus of ancestral voices and spiritual guides who surrounded me.

I went to see Steve Quintana,[1] a local Cuban Santería priest, or babalao, whom I had met many times as part of my life and work in our Boston community. I had gotten to know Santería through a patchwork of sources in music and dance, through readings in cultural anthropology, and through my many Cuban friends for whom Santería was thoroughly woven into the texture of our transplanted island imagery. I had once heard Puntilla, a

Cuban santero and musician based in New York, at an intimate Boston club where he and his musicians offered a program closely based on sacred *batá* drumming, immediately followed by a program of more popular, accessible rumba. I was riveted by the realization that right beneath the surface of the Cuban rhythms that had formed me flowed Africa's lifeblood, its pulse punctuated by the drumbeat and chant of a sacred calling, in compelling synchrony with my own heart. Mostly, I had channeled my emerging energies into Yemayá, the Orisha that is the universal mother, as she offered images of the sea and embodied my maternal strivings. But I was still a dabbler on the surface of far deeper waters than I knew. Steve's divination suggested I had neglected Oshún, the Orisha of potable waters, and it was her he suggested I get to know. I began to travel on a road guarded by the mischievous yet ethically demanding Elegguá, accompanied by Oshún, the great seductress and patroness of marriages, and by Oya, the guardian of markets and cemeteries. Thanks to the Orishas, in all their splendid, quarrelsome complexity and practical divinity, I was able to bear my burden of loss enough to experience the pleasure of new learning even in the depths of my absolute grief.

❊   ❊   ❊

Our Judeo-Christian traditions, translated into scientific Cartesian reasoning, have taught us that the world's religions fill our landscapes with meaning. We have forgotten the most basic evolutionary lesson, that our lives, the struggle for survival that we share with all living things, and the uniquely human search for meaning, are rooted in a very particular landscape of earth and stone and tree. Exile only deepens the profound desire to re-create the promised land in ritual and memory. For one brief but intensely powerful and meaningful generation, our wandering Hebrew tribe became part of Cuba's thoroughly transcultural mix. From Byelorussia on my father's side and Polish Galitsia on my mother's side, my grandparents made the long transatlantic journey from rural Polish villages to rural Cuba, just a short step ahead of certain death in the Holocaust. Both my maternal grandmother Abuela Adela in Las Villas, the central province town of Cabaiguán, and my paternal grandmother Abuela Berta in the Matanzas province town of Bolondrón, told me separately how fully they appreciated their newfound freedoms: to stay alive, to earn a living, and to come out from under the tyranny of a daily life deeply constrained by the daily ritual obligations of Jewish law. They each rejoiced that their openhearted, curious new neighbors did not enforce their *shabbat* observance, their keeping the dietary laws of *kashrut*, or any of the other of the more than 600 sacred obligations. My uprooted relatives resonated to the deep familiarity in the rhythm of rural life, and already knew how to sell necessities to hardworking farmers. Our families reforged a Jewish identity based less on strict religious observance and more on family ties and financial security, which became the center of our New World religion.

I was eight years old when I too was uprooted, as our family fled from the Cuban revolution for Miami. Like many of my generation, I was asked to participate in the polarized politics of our exile community and reject all we had absorbed of a socialist quest for justice. My Cuban childhood images of La Víbora and El Vedado in Havana, of the coastal road on the way to Varadero's beaches, of the long bus trip through the mountains to my grandparents' home in Cabaiguán, filled with verdant landscape and vibrant people, became part of the psychologically and politically repressed. I came back to the Cuba I had deeply internalized through a personal search for these cherished, necessary, and forbidden images. In doing so, I resumed an interrupted personal and political education still in progress, whose aim it is to make one life out of these ruptured fragments of multiple diasporas. At the core of this personal exploration, I have discovered a tangle of images interweaving race and religion, landscape and longing. In order to make sense of these many strands and remain connected to my Jewish faith, I have reached way back in my ancestral memories. I traveled past the relatively brief accidents of fate which brought us into racist Poland, transported to the arid desert lands that bridge Africa and Asia. My tribe has wandered in the parched deserts of Asia and Africa, in the dense woods of Poland, across the Mediterranean coast, and to the cold white North. As Jews, we have survived through our extraordinary capacity to both make new homes and keep our sacred scrolls mobile. By joining fully the joyful Cuban *ajiaco,* the transculturated stew of cultures, each transforming the next, I have discovered what both Yoruba and Israelite slaves learned in their long wait for emancipation: within every stone and stream we can find divinity.

🕱   🕱   🕱

My own deep connection to Santería as a healing practice is especially surprising given that my own tribe regards the Orisha iconography and purification rituals as totally *treif* (unkosher, impure). Our Jewish community's great gifts to civilization began when Abraham destroyed the idols in his father's workshop, and we have become people of the text, bound by over 600 rules of ritual obligation. As Jews, we are reluctant to recognize that we have become a diverse people whose dispersal throughout the world has transformed us, whose homes among many nations have created our own religious and racial *mestizaje.* Each generation must discover anew how to reaffirm Judaic traditions in our new place and time. Given how history turned out, it is all too easy to forget that Jesus was first Joshua, a Jew in the Messianic tradition who wished to bypass the Hebrew priesthood of the Cohanim to restore a missing personal connection to God. The Hassidim, who have made sacred ritual out of a moment of our Polish diaspora frozen in time, have sacralized the broad beaver hats, dense wool coats, and xenophobic feudal relationships. They make it easy for us to forget the ardor that gave birth to the Hassidic sect, born out of a deeply recognizable desire to infuse distant, abstracted Jewish law with direct, passionate prayer sung and danced and above all felt. In Jewish law, mothers are the guardians of ritual observance, which is why in rabbinical law we are considered Jews only if our mothers are Jews. When my two grandmothers left rural Polish villages to arrive in rural Cuban towns, both expressed the joy at the permissiveness of these new spaces for reinventing a safe, loving Jewish family life. No one would stone you for not keeping kashrut, and no one would kill you for being a Jew. They added garlic to their braised flanken and chicken soup recipes, and made noodle kugel with guava. In my own life, I honor the energetic inventiveness that helped them flourish in the New World, and try to bring their wisdom, their talent for both ancestral continuity and creative improvisation, to my work as a teacher and healer. It is simply one of life's expectable ironies that my loyalty to the fundamental values shaping my grandmothers' lives between cultures has been defined as treasonous rebellion by family in my own generation. Were they to read this essay, their worst fears would be confirmed.

�֍   ✖   ✖

I am still absorbing the many lessons of Santería in my own life, which began when I was born on December 17, 1952, the day of St. Lazarus, who came back from the dead, syncretized in Santería with the great healer, Babalú Ayé, protector of the ill and the crippled, who stands guard at the cemetery gates between life and death. San Lázaro is the least playful of the Orishas, perhaps because of his own infirmities and suffering: he is depicted as totally covered in suppurating sores, limping painfully on crutches. He is the Orisha of smallpox, syphilis, leprosy, and now AIDS, who if approached with the proper attitude of self-flagellating reverence can cure and heal. Because of his own experiences of suffering, he is said to be the most empathic of the Orishas, and to appreciate that the love offered by sufferers is of far greater value than that unmarked by illness and the hardships of fate. My grandfather Eliezer (in Hebrew), Leizer (in Yiddish) and Lázaro (in Spanish), who suffered from violent epileptic seizures, understood immediately that with my sacred birth date and his namesake I would be doubly protected and perhaps infused with the healer's power. He fought hard to name me Lázara, but he was no match for my two formidable grandmothers, whose fight to honor the Jewish tradition and name me for their dead mothers ended in a draw. My name is Esterrifke, Ester Rebeca, after maternal great-grandmother Ester, who died in a Polish concentration camp, and paternal great-grandmother Rifkeh, who emigrated to Palestine in 1939 and was buried in Eretz Ysrael in 1952. I do not carry San Lázaro's name, yet my Hebrew naming made me an intermediary between the world of the dead and the world of the living.

✢ ✢ ✢

Santería is an Afro-Cuban religion with its roots in the Yoruba traditions, faithfully preserved and richly transformed by the slaves brought to Cuba. In the United States, the slave masters practiced the annihilation of African cultural and religious identities, knowing that to sever our ancestral ties is to break our human spirits. In Cuba, for whatever historical accidents of fate, the colonizers were less severe in policing the religious practice of their African slaves. Communities of slaves and free blacks created energetic transplantations of the Yoruba deities, mixing the African Orishas with a liberal dose of Catholic images, adding a generous serving of European Spiritism, and rooting the new mix in Cuba's distinctive landscape. The new, improved Orishas are improvisational wonders, richly textured icons that embody elements of the divine, the human, and the natural world. The resulting Santería mythology is as intricately woven, poetically crafted, and richly evocative of philosophical reflection as the celebrated Greek Pantheon. Santería thrives as a living tradition, in Cuba and in the new postrevolutionary Cuban diaspora, because of its exiles' willingness to embrace elements of the new even as it strives to preserve the essence of a soul-satisfying ancestral continuity.

Santería, the syncretic Afro-Cuban religion of the Yoruba slave diaspora, has shown me how much its rich pantheon, transplanted and transformed, connects the exile to enduring images of nature in her splendid generosity and terrifying power. Santería offers surprising succor to those of us who are forced to sing our sacred songs in a strange land and make them once again our own. For me, the landscape animated by Santería's Orishas, with their practical, earthbound divinity, has become unexpectedly intertwined with the spiritual world of my Jewish traditions in an altogether new diaspora. I have come to appreciate the way Santería speaks to a long-neglected impulse in my bookish people, whose reverence for the written law and its detailed observance has obscured our fundamental human need to relate to the natural world with immediacy and passion. My desert tribe knows fully that our nourishment depends on the sacrifice of life that must be ritually recognized and respected. We, too, sacrificed animals and let their blood flow as a reverential offering to potentially vengeful God whose protection we craved. I grew up selecting live chickens with my mother in the Havana market, as did my rural Polish grandparents before us. Our nourishment demands a moment of recognition that life and death hang in the balance.

❈   ❈   ❈

When I was in high school in Hollywood, Florida, and receiving alluring piles of college recruiting mail, my parents insisted that I attend the University of Miami, where they could keep a watchful eye on my dangerous rebelliousness and unpardonable streak of intellectual and sexual curiosity. If the University of Miami was already good enough for my cousins, it was certainly good enough for me. Anyway, didn't I know that too much education would make me unmarriageable? Enraged at being deprived of freedoms my friends could take for granted, I was at the same time profoundly excited by the extraordinary menu of interdisciplinary seminars our elite corps of honors students was offered (we even got to register first, along with the football players). In a freshman seminar on Culture and Mental Health offered by an anthropologist, we met a Cuban anthropologist who had studied Santería with the eminent authority Lydia Cabrera and who had recently emigrated to Miami. A youngish woman in her thirties, she looked much older to my early-seventies hippie-identified eyes because of her tall, lacquered, dyed-blonde hair and prim, conservative white blouse and skirt, exactly like those of so many other Cuban women of indeterminate middle age. She told us the story of her Santería studies, which became the story of her "going native" and becoming an initiate in the Santería faith, in the spirit of Yemayá. She described a scene I can still see in my mind's eye today, in which she walked the beaches of Miami at night and encountered Yemayá in her vibrant, generous divinity, a story of when she lost her objective scholar's hold on her subject and delivered herself into a rapturous romance with the Orishas. I did not know then to look for the blue and white necklaces underneath her tightly buttoned collar.

❈   ❈   ❈

My particular quest as a Cuban Jewish clinical psychologist–turned–public health educator has taught me to mistrust health and mental health industries that make their living from fragmenting and amplifying people's problems. Throughout my professional life, I have been working on a model of family development in historical and cultural context that can offer a foundation for healing practices rooted in cultural wisdom and community strengths. I seek to understand the mysteries of life's passage, its rhythms of seasons and years, of couplings and births and deaths, through the cultural images that connect us to ancestors and communities, soothe our soul's terrors, nourish us with music and meaning. My two communities, the Jewish and the deeply Africanized Cuban, share the wisdom forged in diaspora wanderings. Life in exile challenges us to find continuity in experiences of radical uprooting. Both the Jewish and the

Afro-Cuban traditions became, through cruel necessity, expert at refashioning severed connections into a unified, satisfying whole. We sit by unfamiliar rivers and sing sacred songs that connect us again deeply to each other, to our ancestral traditions, and to our new homes. We arrive in a new community and explore the earth's rhythms, with its cycle of seasons expressed distinctively in a new space and time. As we join the eternal cycles of our uprooted lives to our new home's cycle of seasons, we gratefully discover what the earth yields for our sustenance, we explore exactly how sun and moisture and hard work and prayer produce sustenance for body and soul, flesh and spirit. In a modern world, so distant from the daily acts of reverence that sustain the eternal cycles of life and death, we create those connections in ways that might surprise us.

❊ ❊ ❊

As a university professor of clinical psychology who worked with culturally diverse families in community health and mental health settings, I had known of Steve Quintana's Santería practice for quite some time. Tall and corpulent, with plump, cocoa-colored skin and mischievous, sparkling eyes, Steve is at the same time physically imposing yet uncharacteristically humble for a Cuban. He balances the intense dose of Cuban-style interpersonal electricity with a fundamental tranquillity. He always seemed to me both affectionate and accessible, dignified and serious about his position of responsibility, yet utterly approachable. I experienced Steve to be an immensely reassuring presence, and an articulate, credible voice for a much-maligned religion associated exclusively with animal sacrifice in the public eye. I had been working in ways inspired by the Cuban health system and my own work on family development, seeking with immigrant families the sources for nurturance and warmth in our cold New England city with its segregated ethnic enclaves and suspicion of strangers. I listened carefully to the tone and texture of their stories, seeking to build with them the new language and images that would weave a new destiny, that would preserve memory and create meaning, that would make hard lives in the present bearable by linking past and future in harmonious ways. Our new lives required creativity and flexibility rather than obedience and orthodoxy. Wherever in the world we came from, we now faced the demands of a life our ancestors could never have imagined. I was learning with the culturally diverse communities that make up the Boston immigration experience the importance of spiritual beliefs in the struggle to make one life out of wrenching displacements, whether chosen or imposed, by ship or plane, to save our lives or to make a better life. We Cubans in Boston were a small community, and cherished those connections we could make with other Cubanos. But when I consulted Steve

Quintana, I went for the same reasons that women from many Boston communities came to see him: my husband had left me for another woman.

※   ※   ※

When I finally visited Steve Quintana for myself, I entered an extraordinary space I had already entered twice before. Once, when the rumba group Los Muñequitos de Matanzas had traveled to Boston, the all-night party for the performers and their friends after one of the shows was held at the Quintanas' home. That night, I drove up to a white shingle Dorchester row house in a residential neighborhood and crossed the threshold into a space so filled with human energy it took a while for my uninitiated eye to notice the reverberations emanating from the other world that nourished it. The cubbyholes and closets so characteristic of our New England homes were unexpectedly filled with a jumble of objects, most of them quite ordinary in their individuality—a bowl of candy, a pumpkin, a pile of roots like yuca and malanga still smelling of earth, a porcelain doll in a yellow dress—that became transformed by some to me unknown yet identifiably intense energy pouring out from their assemblage. I wandered around the cozy house packed with people, I poked into the kitchen and sampled from the army-size pot of ajiaco, dimly aware that I had not yet crossed the threshold of the house's first parlor and receiving room. When a knowledgeable friend offered to serve as my escort and guide, I felt fortified and reassured. I stepped into the ritual heart of the house, lit by a scattering of candles. I found that the graceful bay windows of a New England parlor, offering three windows and two walls, each held an altar for an Orisha. The room was relatively silent compared to the party space, which made even more striking the palpably intense energy emanating from those multiple collections of objects and offerings. I had been ill with an immunological disorder some years before and, as part of my treatment, had studied Chinese medicine and learned to discern the flow of *chi,* or life energy, between my body and the people and spaces around me. In Santería, the flow of divine life energy is called *aché.* The intensity of aché in that modest space, overflowing with such ordinary objects—more baskets of root vegetables, bowls of both tropical and local fruit in every phase of ripeness and putrification, a riot of silk and plastic and natural flowers, sugarcane-cutting machetes and kitchen knives, dolls of varying sizes dressed in colorful costumes—made it hard to stand up, much less take in what I was seeing. I had just seen a program of music and dance devoted to Yemayá, Oshún, Changó, and Obatalá, each dancer dressed in the Orisha's colors, each dance with its chanting and drumming completely capturing their multifaceted personalities and playful, conflictive interrelationships. So I was prepared to make the most rudimentary identifications, and spotted the doll dressed in a full-skirted blue dress trimmed in white bands like ocean waves. Yemayá drew me like a magnet, and I approached her altar with pleasure and relief. Her, I could understand.

❈   ❈   ❈

From the exterior, the House of Obatalá, home to Steve Quintana's family and to the Orishas who dwell with him, is indistinguishable from the row of wood-framed houses on his residential street. As you walk up the wooden steps to an open porch and prepare to ring the doorbell, you first see a modest brass plaque, which you might easily overlook if you're not searching carefully for signs that this is indeed the space you have sought, in a desperate moment, seeking a reading of your future on behalf of a troubled present. Steve is available, preferably by appointment but if necessary on a walk-in basis, Tuesday through Saturday, from 9 A.M. to 8 P.M., and Sunday from 1 P.M. to 4 P.M. He distributes an occasional newsletter to a mailing list of subscribers, with a masthead that states on the top, "Santería in USA/Afro American Caribbean Cultural Magazine"; and on the bottom, "dedicated to the Afro-Cuban culture and education of the Lucumí religion." The back of the newsletter describes, in Spanish and English, what problems we might bring to a santero's door. The translations correspond only partially, and I found myself speculating about the aspects of the work in Spanish that were missing from the English. In English: "Do you have family problems? Health problems? Work problems? Business problems? No peace at home? 'Bad luck' instead of 'good luck'? I can help you overcome all of these problems." Then in smaller print: "I perform 'shell' and 'coconut' readings, and can come up with solutions to all of your problems." The description in Spanish approaches the reader from a slightly different angle. The list of questions adds, "Do you have enemies? Divination system can help you!" Then in smaller print: "Solutions, consultations, prayers for the head, the necklaces, Afro-spiritual cleansings, purification baths, cleansing of your home or business, and much more." In Spanish only: "It matters not if you are of another faith, our house will try to give you peace of mind about your problems." In Spanish and English, Steve Quintana III is described as an ordained Santero, Obatalá priest of the Yoruba religion. In Spanish only: "Son of Obatalá, extremely limited consultations of utmost necessity, through the mediums of cowrie shells or coconuts." I felt like Steve was speaking to us in culturally congruent ways, and for those of us who knew both English pragmatism and Spanish spiritualism, he spoke into both ears.

One sunny, cold Saturday on the cusp of spring, I accompanied a friend who wished to consult Steve. We joined an African American woman who smiled at us warmly from her seat by the window as we settled onto the living room couch. The muffled sounds of conversation behind the closed, curtained

French doors suggested that Steve was in consultation in the next room. Then the doors opened and a slightly built, dark-skinned young man walked out of the front parlor with Steve, who was busy with final instructions in Spanish concerning the purchase of necessary materials for an *ofrenda,* or offering, and a *despojo,* or purification bath. He greeted his next visitor in English, and they entered the consultation room. While we waited, we noted the remarkable diversity of souls, our Cuban Jewish selves included, who felt drawn to Santería by compelling forces we could not totally describe. When it was our turn to enter, the bright light of a spring day exposed the exquisite clutter of the *altares* that lined the circular bay as gracefully as if designed exclusively for that very purpose. I counted seven, and later learned they were altares for the major Orishas, "Las Siete Potencias (The Seven Powers)": Obatalá, Steve's own Orisha, had pride of place in the center, surrounded by the sisters Oshún and Yemayá, and the warriors Changó, Elegguá, Oggún, and Ochosi. Because I was not, at that moment, myself the afflicted seeker, I was able to observe the ritual and reflect on its intrinsic therapeutic properties. Steve asked a very few questions about my friend's dilemma, to start with, and moved very quickly to the *diloggún,* or divination ceremony. He began the diloggún by sprinkling water and invoking the Orishas and the deceased santeros who had preceded him. He placed 18 cowrie shells on the table, gathered them in his hand, and touched the hand clenching the shells to my friend's forehead, hands, and knees. He then repeatedly threw down the cowrie shells, and, depending on their array, identified one of 16 possible patterns, each associated with a number and therefore an Orisha and a special story. I did not find the divination as compelling as I did the discussion that came after. Steve did not relate the *patakis,* or stories, from the Orishas that were associated with the numbers that my friend's reading yielded. Rather, he went directly to the heart of my friend's dilemma, which he saw as requiring patience, commitment, and careful consideration of her blood ties—past, present, and future. Having practiced psychotherapy for two decades, I found Steve's approach to my friend's concerns as thoughtful, supportive, and substantive an intervention as anything I might have expected from a trained professional.

❈   ❈   ❈

When I went for my own consultation with Steve, I was no longer the discerning observer. In the weeks after my husband told me he had fallen in love with another woman, pulled as a writer toward a writer's inventive romance built exclusively of words, I turned toward my own work of rebuilding, although I did not yet know what it might require. I felt fortunate that I had a sabbatical year coming, which I had planned to dedicate to the development of my professional work. Instead, I prepared for a very different kind of learning. I cleared my desk of all my pending projects and planned a long, meandering trip that would balance companionship and solitude in any way I chose. Steve welcomed me into his front parlor, and when I tersely told him why I was there, he said, "You know, that's who mostly comes to see me, they are women and their husbands have left them." I was already feeling less alone as we began the diloggún. My numbers and patterns were very clear, as Steve told me in Spanish (my own translation): "Oshún, number 5, she is yours, she is the seductress that helps people change. She is the Blessed Virgin, Our Lady of Charity [*La Virgen de la Caridad del Cobre*], Cuba's patron saint. Here there are no malevolent forces from the outside, everything comes from between you and your husband. He will need to seek Elegguá's help with what's real. You have a lot of power, whoever tries to harm you will only harm herself. Keep the bat in your own hands." I loved that image, because the baseball metaphor captured the core of my own commitment to focus on my own deeply held values, to remain in control of my one and only life. I visualized myself, bat in hand, hitting the ball of selfish malevolence that had been pitched into my life, back to its rightful owner.

I told Steve I had been so focused on Yemayá, the great mother, Orisha of the sea and maternal fertility. I had needed her in my struggle to cope with the multiple miscarriages that had blighted my hopes of bearing my own child. I confessed to Steve that I knew nearly nothing about Oshún, Yemayá's sister. "Who is Oshún, you ask? She is 'la cabrona,' the great feminine power [literally, 'she-goat'] of this religion. She is the Orisha whose dominion is the rivers and potable water, she is also the messenger of the Orishas. She is a mulatta [racially mixed woman] who likes her sweets. You need to build a relationship with her, which you can do through your sweet offerings. And when she gives you what you ask for, you must give her what she asks for in return."

So far so good. But then I found Steve moving on to a far more disturbing aspect of the reading, reflected in the day's lengthening shadows and the suddenly darker atmosphere: "But first, you have to remove this dead spirit clinging to you, right away. The dead, they fall in love with you, and they place obstacles in your path so they can control you. They even bring your husband a lover, so they can keep you to themselves. You are at war with a dead spirit. But your own spirits, your achés, are stronger and protect you." I immediately thought of Abuela Berta, who had died at age 92 the previous year, Alzheimer's having decimated the mind and body of that iron-willed matriarch, her spirit freed by death. Her gravestone was placed over her grave in the Miami Beach cemetery, on the late spring day two months earlier that marked the one-year anniversary of her death on the lunar calendar, and I had not been able to attend the ritual. I fingered my Polish pink gold wedding band, which Abuelo Lázaro had given my grandmother in 1923 to consecrate their great love, the happiness they hoped to seize from the terror of World War I and the Russian Revolution's decimation of my grandfather's landowning family. Abuelo Lázaro had been dead for two years, and I was visiting Abuela Berta without having told her that my first husband and I were divorcing. She noticed my ringless hand and wordlessly took the simple band off her finger and handed it to me. I had worn the band on my right hand ever since.

Steve went on: "In another life you were a gypsy, and you must reclaim the gypsy again, in the company of Oya. You need to put on a skirt of many colors on the ninth of every month. Go dance in the streets, with your brilliantly colored skirt, and gather together the objects for Oya: a pack of tarot cards, a red handkerchief, castanets, a red flower, and a glass of water. Whatever else you do, do not forget the gypsy Oya, La Virgen de la Candelaria, because she lives with the dead in the cemetery, and she can help you out here." The gypsy was already one of my most cherished images for an aspect of myself. When I wrote my first personal narrative for Ruth Behar's *Bridges to Cuba* (1994), she asked all of us for a photograph, and I immediately offered my most precious one: my sisters and I at El Patronato, our neighborhood synagogue in El Vedado, in costume for our last Purim in Havana. Purim celebrates the Old Testament story of how Queen Esther the orphan married the Persian king Ahashuerus and with her brave, proud uncle Mordechai saved the Persian Jews from annihilation. A holiday of rare hilarity and revelry among my serious tribe, it allows children to come in costume to the synagogue. While the *Old Testament Book of Queen Esther* is read, the congregation boos every mention of the wicked, murderous Haman, who wished our people dead, and cheers Queen Esther and Mordechai for turning the tables on our people's certain genocide. Consistent with Old Testament bloodthirstiness, the story concludes with King Ahashuerus permitting the Jews of his kingdom to hang Haman, murder his many sons, and annihilate his followers, so that the enemy's blood flowed satisfyingly in the streets.

On Purim 1959, our childish excitement is fueled by the carnival atmosphere and the magic of donning costumes evoking another persona. In the picture, my younger sister, six-year-old Rachel, is dressed as Queen Esther, in a full-skirted gold satin dress and regal tiara; my baby sister, two-year-old Miriam, is wearing a blue sequined brocade dress that Rachel had worn in January 1959 as flower girl for Tio Nuñi and Tia Rosita's wedding. I am seven years old and dressed as a gypsy, in a costume I had assembled from Rachel's cast-off clothing, holding a child-size tambourine. I was entranced by the profound sensation of embodying my favorite fantasy, my private distillation of our European diaspora stories, and my profound sense of being a passionate, problematic outsider to my rigidly conventional family. I would later learn much more about Oya, the Orisha of winds and storms, a woman warrior who stole the power of lightning from Changó when he betrayed her with Oshún. Elegguá taught her to temper her violent rage with her loving passion so she could lure Changó back. Dressed as a gypsy, she receives the dead who have been walked to the cemetery gate by Babalú Ayé, and who now enter her dominion. I would not forget Oya.

We then turned to the practical matter of the remaining ofrendas. "Since all paths begin with Elegguá, you must make a modest offering for him. For Elegguá, you will need a sweet potato and a dried whole coconut. For Oshún, you will need to prepare yourself to make the offering with a ritual bath. For the ofrenda, you need to go get eight or ten sweet Italian cakes drenched in sugar syrup, and hold them in your home for five days. At the end of five days, you must deliver them to the river." I had to begin immediately to collect the objects I would need for the ofrendas, as well as for a ritual purification bath dedicated to Oshún, each step carefully timed.

At another time in my life, I might have found the observing North American Jewish psychologist keeping a skeptical eye on these prescribed rituals. Instead, my anguish and need had prepared me to enter the ritual from an altogether different vantage point. I explored each delightful element for its spiritual poetics, the most ordinary objects transformed by being brought together purposefully, their relationships creating an aesthetics of the sacred. I found filaments of meaning extending their reach beyond the here and now of space and time, adhering backward to memories and forward to hopeful anticipations, creating synchronicities as pleasing to the senses as to the soul. The immensely concrete symbols of my ritual, part archetype, part poem, part chant, part dream reverie, part dance, penetrated the darkness before me with a warm golden light. I did not really know Oshún, yet already I felt the excitement of an anticipated tryst, an enticing balm for my rejected soul. As instructed, I prepared my clothing, a bright yellow cotton tank and loose white pants, Oshún's colors, which could stand up to a full day in which I'd be drenched in Oshún's special bath. Early on Sunday morning, I would light a yellow candle for Oshún and prepare the sweet fragrant bath that would please us both: a gallon of orange juice, two tablespoons of sugar, one jar of honey, flower essences. I selected fragrant flower waters of rose, orange, and jasmine, and included fragrant yellow lilies from our garden, scattering their petals over the viscous, aromatic bath. After bathing myself clean in fresh water, I then bathed in the purification bath, following the strict instructions to drench my hair and body completely, pat myself dry only enough that I wouldn't drip, and then make sure I waited five hours before I bathed again. During that time, I was to bring to Steve's house the offering to Elegguá and a basket of Italian sweets for Oshún. I would also keep a basket of my own sweets, to hold for five days, at which time I would bring them to the river and offer them to Oshún directly.

The ofrenda was the easiest part: I knew the Italian North End of Boston well, and in the absence of Miami-style Cuban bakeries, I frequented the Italian bakeries regularly. I had selected my favorite for my second wedding cake (the first one, destined for the Miami Cuban Hebrew Congregation, was made by a kosher caterer), a voluptuous rum-soaked whipped cream cake. I had stored a piece in my freezer for a future anniversary celebration. I decided the cake, as saturated with love and hope as syrup and rum, would make a good addition to my ofrenda. I was certain the Oshún I was getting to know would approve.

⌧   ⌧   ⌧

My first surprise came the very first afternoon of my ritual bath and ofrenda. I had two hours yet to elapse before I could wash, the sticky, fragrant bath growing progressively more lacquered on my skin over the course of a sunny, humidly hot late July day. Feeling both languidly peaceful and restlessly energetic, I went to the Charles River, where a local rhythm and blues band was playing at the Hatch Shell. I had with me the folder of journal entries and notes for my journey that I was already calling "Love and Exile/*Amor y exilio.*" Although I had not planned it, I quickly and almost explosively wrote my husband a vivid, poetic, feverishly exuberant letter of love and seduction, letting him know I saw this volcanic explosion, this violent rupture between us, as an opportunity to renew our passion and our shared learning. More surprising, I wrote the letter in fluent, expressive Spanish, a language that I speak quite well but would never ever choose for writing if I could help it, as my Spanish schooling stopped at the beginning of third grade. In it, I lay out my hopes for my own journey's work: the renewal of my capacity to love outside of my desire for children; the renewal of my capacity to work and write first for myself and then for others; the alchemical transformation of my suffering into the accumulated wealth of wisdom, rose-golden bracelets that will musically clink together as I dance, whose sight and sound will be pleasing to Oshún. Then I got up and, moved by the music and the spirits within it, its rhythms resonating with heart's percussion, the dance moving through me as naturally as my blood's flow, I began to dance more gracefully and passionately than I knew how. When the concert was over, I walked west on the river's banks. The lengthening shadows softened the day's heat, the setting sun's angle lit each blade of grass, the river flowed gently like a sheet of blue sky, becoming dappled with soft coral turning deep reddish orange as it absorbed the sun's fireball. I stepped on the still warm rocks and bathed in the cool river waters, refreshed and reassured that I would be well accompanied on my new soul's journey.

⊠ ⊠ ⊠

Oshún did not once let me down. She was with me when I bathed in the conjunction of three rivers of the southern Sierras, when I swam across deep canyon pools in Baja California, all the time gathering my strengths for the battle before me, to more fully claim my own soul, my own life as a woman between cultures. I found my grief had drowned and my rage had incinerated the self-sacrificing wife I had secretly and once again well preserved, so much did I apparently feel I could not be a woman without her. Yet I had worked so hard in my life, to live by the light of the most loving woman I could be. I did not know how to keep her, that side of myself, alive in the presence of my deep resentment. I found a path toward an answer during the High Holy Days, the period between Rosh Hashanah, or New Year's, and Yom Kippur, the most sacred time in our calendar. During those ten days, the gates open between the world of the dead and the world of the living as God decides who will be inscribed in the Book of Life for the coming year. We are instructed to ask forgiveness of all we might have harmed, knowingly or inadvertently, that we might earn the gift of life. One Jewish ritual suggests that we take an offering of bread and cast it in the river, symbolizing our commitment to repent our sins and live by our best qualities. I went back to the Charles River, with the remains of a sweet challah from our Sabbath meal. Crumbling the slightly sticky crust and golden loaf, I knelt by the muddy shore and prayed to all the assembled spirits. I asked to be purified of the rage and resentment that had entered my life, to be guided toward rebuilding the bridges of love that I had always known to be the path between this world and the next. My prayers loosened the tightly clenched muscles of my heart, which opened with a torrential weeping. I remembered with renewed immediacy that I cannot dam up rage without harming my capacity to love, my most cherished treasure.

I spent Yom Kippur in Miami, where I could most easily visit my still living Abuela Adela and my still present Abuela Berta, letting them both know how much I brought them with me, even in faraway Boston. Later that year, after my husband and I had reconciled, I visited Cuba during the pope's visit. I traveled to the rural town in Matanzas that had sheltered Abuela Berta and Abuelo Lázaro when they fled from the coming Holocaust and were sheltered in the province that, after Santiago de Cuba, is most associated with Santería. I went with a cousin to visit the Jewish cemetery in Guanabacoa, soothed by the sight of its imposing arched gate and its wide vista of tropical fields, the Escambray foothills beyond. After the obliteration of our Jewish cemeteries in Rubyshevish and Galitsia, our desecrated graves used for paving stones, this New World space had become another verdant resting place for our far-flung migrating souls. Although I could not find the grave of my great aunt, Abuelo Lázaro's younger sister, who had survived the Bolsheviks and the Nazis to die in childbirth, I remembered her in my prayers. Because I have guided so many families through the dark days of grief and death to a reclaiming of life, I recognized the gift life had handed me in this opportunity to once again let loss be my great teacher. I embraced both Oshún and Oya, Elegguá and San Lázaro, as companions in my voyage from darkest sorrow to a new life. Traveling and learning with the Orishas, more open to the spirit world they inhabited, I was reassured that I was not alone, that I could touch bottom and reach the other side of the riverbank, that I could rebuild the shattered pieces of my life.

※　※　※

I recently described cooking as my most profound spiritual practice, as it is in the kitchen that I enter a creative, reverential space lovingly dedicated to the soul's sustenance. Natalia Bolívar Aróstegui, the Cuban anthropologist and force of nature whom I had the pleasure of meeting in her Miramar home, published a book called *Mitos y leyendas de la comida afrocubana* (*Myths and Legends of Afro-Cuban Food*, 1993). In the chapter "Foods for the Orishas," she has a section called "Eggún: Special Orishas," in which she describes the Eggún as the spirits of the dead who still cling to their homes, to their loved ones, to their memories and material belongings, who have not succeeded in elevating themselves from the terrestrial plane. She notes that these spirits are also offered food, usually ajiaco, at a beautifully set table with flowers, candles, dessert, coffee, *aguardiente* alcohol, and tobacco. She offers a selection of regionally diverse ajiacos.

I offer my own recipe, in honor of Abuela Berta and her Polish Cuban kitchen. First, you must begin with a ritually slaughtered kosher chicken, preferably one you have looked in the eye and thanked for its life's sacrifice. Carefully feather, clean, and cut the chicken into nine parts including the neck and feet, trimming the rich gold fat underneath the thick yellow skin. Put the chicken neck, gizzards, wings, and breastbones in a pot of simmering water on the back of your stove. Fill the pot replete with a handful of aromatic bay leaves and plenty of sweet root vegetables: a whole head of gently peeled slightly crushed garlic, a large quartered onion, five peeled carrots, four stalks of celery, and a cut-up fennel bulb complete with its feathery fronds. I use Goya *adobo* with extra cumin instead of salt, and a handful of freshly ground black pepper for seasoning. In the front of the stove, I make a *sofrito* in a large pot: I begin with the chicken fat, sautéing it gently until it is rendered, and removing the cracklings or *gribeneh* for another use, as they are too delectable to lose in a big pot. My grandmother would have reserved them to make *gehakte lever,* chopped liver, offering a few morsels to her favorites who wandered into the kitchen dazzled by the smells and greedy for the silken pleasure of crisp-fried fat that we associate in the marrow of our bones with life-sustaining times of plenitude. I add enough olive oil to cover the bottom of the pot and sauté another large chopped onion, a large green pepper, and eight crushed heads of garlic. Once the sofrito vegetables are soft and golden, I add the cut-up chicken pieces and stir them with the sofrito, adding enough sprinkled adobo salt, pepper, oregano, and cumin to coat and flavor them. While the chicken browns slightly, I peel 4 large yuca (*casava*), 5 medium ripe plantains, and a small sweet pumpkin, cutting them into serving-size pieces. I add the yuca first, along with 5 ears of corn, each cut into four pieces. By that time the chicken broth bubbling in the back has acquired some depth, and I ladle a couple of quarts of it into the ajiaco pot, along with a bottle of light brown beer and half a cup of sweet sherry. The liquid should cover the chicken and yuca, maintained at a low simmer. The smells should be so powerful that everyone in the house will be drawn into the kitchen to look in the pot and swoon with anticipation. After the chicken and yuca have simmered for an hour, add the pumpkin and plantains and taste the broth for additional seasoning. Cook for another half hour, until all the roots and fruits of the earth are tender and the chicken melts off the bones. Serve hot in deep bowls, and rest assured that all who share this nourishment will feel satisfied with your fiery soul's love offering. Let us say Amen, *Aché to.*

Chapter 6 ▨

Dolls and Healing
in a Santería House

Anna Wexler

S teve Quintana was born in Havana, Cuba, where he was trained and worked as a graphic designer. He came to New York City in 1957 and continued to practice his profession. Since 1960 Quintana has been devoted to Santería and was ordained as a priest of Obatalá in 1982. He opened the House of Obatalá in 1988 in Dorchester and is well known as a ritual leader, diviner/healer, and spokesperson for his religion in the Boston area.

In addition to conducting initiations, cleansing rituals, and regular ceremonies to honor specific Oricha, Quintana serves a large multiethnic clientele through private consultations involving divination with cowrie shells or *dilogún,* and ensuing healing treatments with herbs, flowers, perfumes, ocean water, and other elements. Dominicans, Puerto Ricans, Cubans, Cape Verdeans, Haitians, African Americans, and clients from other communities throughout Massachusetts seek his help for a range of problems often related to immigration barriers, poverty, job discrimination, dispersed families, and other consequences of oppression and legal marginalization within American society. As a public educator and representative of his religion emphasizing its nonsectarian, healing aspects, Steve Quintana gives presentations on Santería in universities and hospitals and on television programs, and currently publishes the *Afro-Cultural Magazine,* which combines cultural and health-related news. He recently conducted the first Oricha ceremony—including an altar, drumming, dancing, and a feast for Changó—to be sponsored by Harvard University.

During my first meetings with Steve, he encouraged my interest in making spiritual dolls by showing me cloth dolls like those his grandmother and great grandmother had used in their work as spiritualist mediums in Havana. The following interview grew out of these conversations as well as readings/divinations in which Steve suggested that I make a doll for my deceased grandmother as part of my own healing. This doll, like most of those discussed at length in the interview, is associated with the tradition of spiritualism [also known as Espiritismo], which is often intertwined with Santería. European in origin, it became influential in Cuba beginning in the mid-nineteenth century and developed there as a healing system based on mediumistic contact with the dead during spiritualist masses. The dolls for deceased family members and other spirit guides are therefore to be distinguished from those that represent the major deities of Santería, the Afro-Cuban Orichas, although, as in the House of Obatalá, both kinds of dolls may be used if a given priest or santero/santera also incorporates spiritualism into his or her religious practice.

—*Anna Wexler*

※ ※ ※

S. I have to start with my family. My mother, Elizabeth Romero de Quintana, and my father, Félix Esteban Quintana II, have already passed away. My father was well known in Havana as a sports leader and teacher and representative for Cuba for the Olympics in the forties. He was an ex–ball player for the Cuban leagues and also did track and field sports. I came from a family of Catholics, with a wonderful grandmother who was the one who raised my father. She was not my father's original mother, but she was very important in everything that I pursue today. She was a spiritualist; my great grandmother, her mother, was a medium too. People with problems came to see her, and she solved some of their problems with spiritual consultation. She was also a dressmaker and cleaned houses. At that time there were rich houses—there were a lot of customers. A lot of people were able to send their children to university by working five or six days cleaning houses and washing and ironing clothing, the white clothing and linens of the period. I remember my great grandmother did that until she got arthritis and couldn't do it anymore. But she was a very very strong medium, and I remember that white people used to bring problems of their own to her and used to love her. We had a relationship between black and white then. The sons and daughters of the Spaniards got very attached to the black families working for them.

A. What period was this?

S. We're talking about the 1940s. I remember my mother working in one of the most expensive stores in Havana. She would leave me with my grandmother and my great grandmother, so I was raised by them as baby-sitters. . . . My grandmother used to have ten different sewing machines in the living room, I remember, and she used to have women coming in and doing sewing, dresses for weddings. When carnival time came, she made all the carnival dresses for the neighborhood groups. Musicians like Celia Cruz and Olga Guillot and people like that came to get their dresses made by my grandmother. These are the things I remember as a child. . . .

A. Would you talk a little about how your grandmother practiced as a spiritualist and what you experienced.

S. She was a medium, a person who has spirits that speak through her, spirits of those who passed away, ancestors, or maybe Madamas or Negras or Negros or Congolese,[1] those spirits the medium has the ability to work with, who speak through her during masses. My grandmother didn't use cards, nothing except a glass of water. She lost her sight because she had cataracts. When she lost her sight she was still working, and she was a stronger medium without the sight than with it.

A. Did you actually participate in the masses?

S. No, I was too young—maybe I sat down a few times, but my head was not into learning. I was just curious to see what was happening. It was an influence. There were heavy-duty mediums. I saw ladies mounted by some powerful spirits—there was nothing you could hide from them. If you had something you didn't want someone to know, you better not go to the table because it would come out. It would come out in such a way that they would be able to tell you how to repair the problem or change your habits and your ways. I've seen guys say, "I came in here because I have a problem with my marriage," but right away it came out he had a woman somewhere else, and then the guy would be ashamed and walk out. But there's nothing you can say or do—when you are at a medium's table, the truth will always come out.

A. Did your grandmother and great grandmother have dolls or use dolls?

S. Yes. There was a collection of dolls—the dolls were attended to on different days. They used to bring them down. There was an old china cabinet—the dolls were of different sizes, and they sat there with a glass of water right next to them. There were also some glasses very high on top of the cabinet. I wondered about this, so I asked my great grandmother—it was '49 or '50, I was already growing up and going to a Catholic school—I asked her what that meant, and she said those are our spirits, our ancestors. The dolls were different colors—there was a brown-skinned one, one was white-skinned, one was a *gitana,* a gypsy.

A. Were they made out of cloth or were they factory made?

S. Some of them were regular dolls, made out of clay with very nice faces made in Spain, but others were made out of rag. Their clothing was very different; one was in white, the other was in different colors, in gingham dresses, gingham dresses like those we use for the Orichas. I saw them in different colors, but I didn't see any Orichas. I saw Elegguá—it was not an Elegguá, it was an *Eshu,* that means a stone—and they had it right next to the door. Everybody would say, "Hi Elegguá," and they used to knock on the door or on the floor. Some people, for one reason or another, out of gratitude or something, brought in candies, fruits, peanuts. I saw those things and was fascinated. . . . I was aware of being raised in a house where there were spiritual powers in every corner—in a glass of water or a plate of food, in a cup of coffee and a cigar together with a glass of water. They talked to those glasses and they knew what it meant. I learned how to respect all this and to value the feeding and the taking care of the spirits of the house.

A. Did your grandmother and great grandmother actually make some of the rag dolls?

S. Yes, they were all made in the house except for those that were bought, the bodies of the dolls which they dressed up depending on which spirits those dolls were dedicated to. If it was a gitana, they used a doll with a very Spanish face, of brown complexion, and dressed in a lot of colors and a lot of jewelry on top of it. That was a doll maybe 16 inches high.

A. A lot of the mediums used a gitana. It was a typical doll?

S. The gitana is not only typical, but offers a connection to the Spaniards and Portuguese. There were in Cuba many people from Zaragoza and the south of France; therefore we had a lot of gitanos in Cuba, traditionally descendants of what we call gitanos, or gypsies. And as mediums, we feel the gitanos have a tremendous connection with the spirits. A lot of people don't take them seriously—they feel they are just after making money. Maybe that is true in some cases today because we live in a different age, but in those times, gypsies worked with cards, the tarot cards, and they read your palms. You would give them a donation, so it was a completely different story, and sometimes some of them were so dedicated to spiritual work that they would not charge any money. It's a totally different story today. People live off the psychic situation, the telephone consultations which cost you per hour or per half an hour or fifteen minutes . . . and then they're not that good spiritually, they just learn how to read the cards. That's one thing we have to explain—the cards work through your spirits. If you just read a book on how to use them, then you learn the symbolism of the cards but not the spiritualism of the cards.

A. As far as the dolls are concerned, did they bring them out during the meetings?

S. Yes, they were like the best friends of the house. . . . For example, there were times and days when each doll was put down on the floor close to the mass because the mass was dedicated to that particular spirit, so the doll was part of it. Remember, for you to be able to synchronize the doll with the spirit, you must bring it over to the table. This way the spirit could come over and embrace his doll and say this is me, I look very nice in it. The spirit will live in that doll for the rest of the time, and therefore you will respect that doll just as you respect that spirit.

A. Maybe this sounds like a silly question to you, but why is it that the spirits like the dolls, like to see themselves in dolls?

S. Because when we are alive, we have things we like, like music . . . the sound of castanets, the mandolins. People die and those things they like—for example the famous cigar and coffee for the Congo—if you don't give them those things it's like not giving them what they used to like when they were alive.

A. But in the case of the dolls, it doesn't seem to be quite the same thing . . .

S. It's the image. . . . It has to be explained. Sometimes we see movies where a doll takes on life as a monstrous or negative spirit and kills people. We're talking about real things though, spirits who would like to see themselves better treated, so they're expecting that we give them an image. . . . A lot of people don't understand that the spiritual part of religion is portrayed in a figure that takes the life of a spirit. My mother likes me to change the clothing on her doll, every month or so, and I change her hairdo and put different necklaces on her because she was a woman who used to make her own dresses. She made a new dress for every weekend, every time they used to go out to one of the clubs where black Cubans gathered back then.

A. Is she the doll here with the white dress?

S. No, even though that was made by my mother. . . . I gave her another, larger image, the doll we have here, and I dressed her and gave her everything, the image of how she used to like to look. And the food—the *café con leche* she liked to drink and toasted bread—when you want to make her happy, you give her café con leche with toast. These are the things we do with the dolls. Because when spirits take the image of the dolls, they expect to be treated as they were when they were alive.

A. So is it mostly like the spirits, the ancestors—in this case you're talking about your mother—she feels your love because you're treating the doll as you would her?

S. Oh yes, yes. And it's a great deal of help. I didn't see any *Ocha* [Santería] over there, what I saw was the spirits.

A. In Cuba?

S. Oh yes, and I saw a lot of plates placed with dolls. Frankly I don't see much of that today, but I saw plates of food with coffee and water or rum, and they put it with a candle. Then the following morning when I'd get up, funny thing the food was reduced—it was maybe hard to believe, but I saw all that. They would come in and say, "Oh she ate it all up you know," and they would say, "Oh you like it, I'm going to do it for you next month again, mama." And thus they communicated with that doll.

A. There were other dolls?

S. There was also a Congo doll made out of wood in the backyard, placed amid a lot of bushes. They used to call him a name—I don't remember it now—and I used to see my great grandmother, a cigar in her mouth, talking to him, knocking on the floor with a stick and calling him, asking him if he's happy and if he has everything he wants. They used to dig a hole in the ground and give him vegetables such as yams. They had a can with food or plain black sugarless coffee which they placed in the hole and left overnight, only at night. That was a spirit who lived out of the house in the backyard, and, believe me, when there were storms, big winds, I saw them running to the back and putting something over him to cover him, to make sure he was protected. This is something I was brought up with.

A. What did the Congo figure look like?

S. I don't remember in detail, but it was a man sitting down on a chair. The whole thing was done as what we call a *taburete,* a typical Cuban chair with a frame made out of wood and the seat and back made from the hide of a cow. And the figure was sitting down, one hand open, the other holding something; you could place the cigar, a fruit, a vegetable, a stick of *guayaba,* a stick of wood in there. He always had a cane leaning on the chair, and when they wanted to call him, they used the cane.

A. Was that figure the one who received the most regular attention?

S. Yes, yes—but all of the dolls had different months and years when they were taken care of and had a spiritual mass. Sometimes they used to take me to church and dedicate a spiritual mass to the spirits of those ancestors who had passed away. They didn't take the dolls, but they put a fresh glass of water on the floor and told them they were going to dedicate a mass to them. At that time the priests knew we were mediums, and they used to reserve that day for the mass. All the family used to sit down in the front row and offer a donation—one or two dollars. Today it is still done, but sometimes the priests ask for more money, or, if they know it's for mediums or santeros, they refuse to do it.

A. Going back to the dolls your grandmother and great grandmother had—you said they often made the dolls?

S. In most cases, yes, but sometimes the doll was a gift. . . . In the old times all women used to sew wonderfully. They made all the clothing for their children, they were poor people without money to go to a Filene's or other expensive shops. Those people used to make the dolls not only for themselves but sometimes as a gift. So the gift came in very appropriately and with a lot of love. . . . You should have seen the dresses, how completely finished they were, and so nice in miniature size, so gorgeous, dresses made in long years past. Then when people died, the doll would pass from the grandmother to the daughter or granddaughter or grandson, from one hand to another.

A. The doll that represented the spirit?

S. Oh yes, and that's the reason why the spirits held such a powerful hold on the dolls.

A. When they made the dolls, what did they stuff them with?

S. Some people think everything that is inside should be talked about, and, as a matter of fact, at one time there were people opening the dolls to find out exactly what was inside. And they came back and said, "But this doll doesn't have anything"—and we said that maybe the spirit, knowing you were going to open it, didn't want you to get anything. The secrecy is very powerful. . . .

A. I wasn't asking about the secrets inside, just how they were made.

S. They were made out of rags, but they don't use rags with names or numbers. They used plain color cloth, with no pattern or paper. Or they used burlap to fill in the doll.

A. Why wouldn't they want patterns on it, what difference would that make?

S. Because that will bring different patterns in the role of the spirits. Let's say you're putting lines and crossed lines, you're crossing up the spirits. It's like the Haitians will do flags with some specific signals, with specific drawings, but if they change it, they're changing the meaning of the flag, so the flag will not function the way it is supposed to. It's the same thing with the figures.

A. So with the figures, in other words, they didn't want to put any patterns inside the doll that would confuse the spirit or bring the wrong spirit?

S. Not only confuse them but wouldn't bring them down with all that kind of messed-up situation inside. We have a lot of things inside of our body, but they are well put together by the Creator who made us. If I'm going to be a creator of a doll, I'm going to consult that specific spirit; so when I fill in the doll, I have to question what I should be putting inside, what should be done inside.

A. So people who were making dolls for the spiritualists in Cuba were going through the same thing, they were thinking about what the spirit wanted?

S. Exactly. And for example if it was a black spirit, Congolese, the dolls inside and outside should be black or brown. If it was a white person, they should stuff it with orange or pink or white that was close to the colors of the person. Then you are close to the image of who that person was. Inside or outside. You use ingredients that have been used throughout the years—herbs and things that to us are secret and that are used to call the spirit or Oricha. So we use those things and we add them up in a specific place to give them life; it's like a battery in a little doll or something that's going to move it. You've got to give them something that's going to give them life. So this is just like a battery, it will give them that charge.

A. Your grandmother and great grandmother and others who made the dolls, would they also put organic materials, like herbs and things, inside them?

S. Yes, definitely. Sometimes they had to be included in a very small pouch that would go inside the doll. Also, people should know . . . it won't work unless you are a spiritualist. If you are a spiritualist you can make it happen, but if you're not, you have to go to someone who is a spiritualist, and they will make it happen. They will have to put the secrets inside, and they will have to find out what that doll should take.

A. They didn't use divination, they just used the mediums.

S. Mediums—questions and answers. A medium has a connection to bring down the spirit of that person. By having the name and day of the person, that medium will be able to find out exactly how that person was and what they have to put inside to make that person in that doll.

A. They put herbs . . .

S. Yes, that is part of the secret. . . . That's how I look at it. A lot of people are reading books now about what we're doing. If we tell them the secret, we're losing the essence. It's like when you're cooking. You're using a style or some sort of recipe, a special recipe that not everybody has, so when you talk about that secret, you've got a problem because you open a Pandora's box. If you keep that secret, you will keep something important. So that is how the doll comes alive, and the doll can become a very important part of the family. Sometimes you see a child with a doll, and she is in love with that doll. Later on that doll becomes so much a member of her own room and life, sometimes she even talks to that doll. I would suggest not to take the doll away from that child because sometimes without even a preparation or anything there is a spirit helping that child through that doll. I think that is a very reasonable way of thinking. Sometimes that doll will take over and help out that child, protect her.

The doll can even be inherited by somebody else. I mean you sometimes go to secondhand stores, and you find a doll hanging in there, and it looks very attractive to you. You take it with you. It may be a very good spirit in that doll, or it may be the reverse. It may be some kind of spirit who belonged to somebody who was grouchy or who suffered in their life, and that spirit will be inherited by you, and then you don't know why you have so many problems in your own house. Since you brought that doll you got problems, and then if you don't take care of that doll and pay attention to it, the doll can become either a good spirit or negative spirit, and then it must be questioned—whether you should get rid of it or take care of it or attend to it. If you attend to it, you may be able to solve a lot of problems that the doll had before.

In most cases only the person who is visually a spiritualist can see the spirits in a doll. They will not permit anyone else to see them, but when they are in a doll and are respected, they will see themselves and therefore have no longer a need for a medium to see them. They say, "Now I can be here sitting down on this shelf, and from time to time they're going to bring me water, they're going to bring me coffee or milk or tea, and I will be very happy here. I will be able to protect and help this family who is giving me attention." Now if you leave town and somebody walks in through that door and breaks the lock to come in and rob you—the doll can see him and make a neighbor or somebody passing by see that man coming in and call the police. The guy would be caught with the help of the doll spirit who didn't permit anyone to do something wrong in that house or any wrong to any members of the family.

A. Could you compare it to the spirits liking to come down in people, to possess people? Is that the same thing with the doll in the sense that they come down and possess the doll?

S. Yes, yes . . . now the possession of dolls with spirits can be very useful. . . . If it's not useful, they have to be given the proper attention or funeral. You take that doll to the place where it would like to rest, and then that's it, you've finished the whole story there. Now remember this, we're talking about good things, how to take care of the dolls and of those spirits that are good to us and all the family. But what happens if the doll is angry or remembers mistreatment or sickness? It can bring problems to the family if not taken care of properly. So it's not a game or anything that a person can buy and say, "I have what the book says." We have to explain that the doll can become a negative force which can be very powerful. So there's got to be someone who knows about what they're doing, who can give life to that doll for good and profitable spirits, someone we can take care of and they can take care of us. . . .

But I would say the heritage of the dolls is important because I know my grandmother had one that belonged to her grandmother. . . . To me the dolls have a historical mystique in the family. . . . My grandmother's doll was an inheritance from her own grandmother when she died. She took it, and instead of throwing it away, it was brought up to the family. That doll was a very strong one, very big, already broken down in places. It was a rag doll—funny because they refused to repair it. There was something about the doll that they didn't want to repair it. [They wanted it] just the way it was. I don't know the story of those dolls now because we left Cuba in 1957, and I don't know what happened to the things in my grandmother's house. The revolution came in 1959, so eventually a lot of things changed. I wish I knew what happened with the dolls.

A. Would this doll your grandmother got from her grandmother, would this be a doll that your grandmother had for a spiritual doll?

S. Probably, because I saw her putting glasses by her and giving her food and fruits. They used to cook a lot for the dolls—the doll would be fed before anyone else. That means that you can be hungry, but I'm sorry, it may even be Noche Buena [Christmas Eve], they fed the dolls first. There won't be food for anybody until the dolls are fed. They used to go out to the patio over there and feed the man before everybody else was fed. That was a time when cooking was a big job because they used to cook with charcoal, with wood charcoal, and it takes a lot more time to prepare the food.

A. So having all these dolls required a big investment.

S. Yes, for example in that block were families that we all knew, and when masses were said, there were dolls sitting in the spiritual masses. They had their own chairs, their own space. I saw women coming in with their dolls in their hands. They used to sit down and put the dolls right by their side, and in some cases they were on the floor right near to them. They were the major spirits of their own houses. . . . Things you don't see anymore. These would be family spirits. And they used to dedicate the dolls, and sometimes the spirit of that person came out through those dolls, and speaking through the medium the spirit would say, "I'm glad I was invited here."

A. In other words, would the presence of the doll make it more likely that the spirit would come down?

S. Yes. Let me tell you, it was the good old times. By doing things that maybe today look funny, odd, I saw old people stay very healthy. They had rheumatism, they had arthritis, problems with bones, with heart attacks, cancer, intestines, but I didn't see too many operations. What I saw was people who were depending on the spirits they had around them, who were confident that these spirits would carry them on until their last days. There was no such thing as insurance and running around to the hospitals and getting pills for this and that. The majority of the time all the cures were done at home—those poor people were taking care of things with herbs and home remedies and the good old spirits helping. Remedies that were ordered by the spirits. Sometimes when the person was very sick, with a terminal sickness, they used to say a mass or two around the person's house and prepare the way for them to go. They knew doctors' operations would be a waste. They knew they were going to go, so they prepared the way for them to go. I saw a person die—the husband of my grandmother—and instead of being taken to the funeral parlor they did it in the living room, the same place where they used to say the masses. And I saw those old ladies, before they dressed and washed him and before they put him in a box on the table in the house, they did similar prayers that they did at the table. From that moment, they asked the spirit if it was in peace, and spiritually once they knew the person was in peace, they had a lot of talk about him and all the good things that he did. They used to put a table right next to him, and there always was one person taking notes. That person would record what the mediums were saying that would need to be done later on, maybe months later, for that spirit—to be maybe in a figure or a photograph or maybe in a glass of water—and what kind of food he would like to have.

A. Let me ask you this, when a spirit asked for a figure or a doll, was this considered to be a heavier or more serious request?

S. All depends. Sometimes they waited one or two years before doing it. And sometimes there was a person who didn't want to die, so when he did, it came as a shock. It's not very easy to take care of that spirit, so it takes two or three years, maybe five, to see to it that he gets his maximum elevation. When that happens it might not be a good idea to have him around the house in the form of a doll because he will be angry that he's gone—somebody who got killed or had a heart attack when he was young—and that person will not be totally elevated in a few years. Dolls are only done for those spirits who want to be in the dolls and not because we want it.

A. So if a spirit requested a doll, you would usually do it a year or two later?

S. Always at least a year or a year and a half later. It's the same thing with the glasses of water. We don't include glasses of water until one year after that person was buried. If you attend to that spirit you will keep his elevation from happening. You want him to have peace and elevation and to dispose himself from his body and go out from his closeness to the family, and then we will take care of the rest of the elevation. But if we don't, if we hold them down, that spirit will be more damaging, he will not be in peace or content that he passed.

A. I just had a question in terms of the making of the dolls for ancestors that passed: Were they more likely to have dolls for the female ancestors than the male?

S. No, it would not matter. As a matter of fact, sometimes even children. Sometimes a very beloved dog died in the house, a ten- or fifteen-year-old dog in that house. Sometimes when they heard a dog barking in the middle of the night, people would say that it was Blackie or whoever. So they get a figure of the dog and put it in the place, and that dog will be in peace. It could be a clay figure on the patio—that way you knew the dog spirit would quiet down. The dolls and all the figures would represent the quietness and the peace of the spirits according to the treatment you gave them.

A. You were saying before that many women in Cuba sewed during that period and made beautiful dolls and dresses. Was it just women who made dolls—did men ever make them also?

S. Yes, sometimes it was men. When they were making the secret preparations for those dolls, they were connecting spiritually with the doll they were making. Remember how I told you when you were going to make the doll for your grandmother, I told you to remember how your grandmother was, and by doing that you will be connecting the body with her.

A. So, in other words, the actual making of the doll is a way of making more spiritual contact with the ancestors?

S. Exactly. You're starting from that moment when you start sewing, when you begin doing the body and the dress. . . .

A. Would you say if you're actually making the doll with your hands as opposed to buying one and preparing it, the actual making it with your hands makes the doll more of a spiritual vessel because you're making contact with the spirit?

S. It's like the woman who gives birth—she's giving birth to a child, and the child is not coming with beautiful Filene's store clothing. The child comes naked with his own body. It's a precious gift from God that woman gave birth to, and they clean him and give him to the mother to feed for the first time. . . . The connection with the doll is the same. When you're giving birth to a doll, it is a connection from you to your own ancestors through that doll. From the moment you start to do the body, eyes, mouth, you will be thinking about that person who is going to take over that doll, and it will take place and be a very useful connection. It doesn't matter if later you want to ask somebody to do a wonderful dress or whatever, even if you're not a fancy dressmaker or you have to learn how to make the doll; one way or another, if you actually do it, you learn how to contact your own spirits.

A. I think that's what I like the most about the work that I do because when I make things I feel I'm in contact with the spirits. You must feel that too in your own work?

S. When I do an Elegguá . . . it's not just what goes inside. It's also how Elegguá would like to be seen. Some Elegguás you saw in the old days were ugly and disfigured, sometimes the eye was crooked. It still functioned as an Elegguá, but I think he would like to see himself in a nice body. If he feels good in it, I think it will function as well as he looks; and as well as he has been charged. We always say there is no need to be fancy because it's going to work anyway—that's fine, but it is the artistic part of this religion. . . .

A. Could you talk a little bit more about how the dolls you saw in Cuba looked. When you said people sewed clothes for the rag dolls, did they usually make the clothes out of gingham?

S. No, no, it all depends. Sometimes they made them with silk, sometimes with lace, sometimes with burlap. If the people had the spirit of Babalú Ayé, when they passed away they made the dresses or pants for their dolls with burlap. Whatever the spirits asked. If he doesn't want to be bothered being anyplace, don't force him, because then you're bringing problems on yourself. The dolls the majority of the time do good, but if you're using a doll or figure to do wrong to somebody else, the spirit you're putting in that doll to do wrong to somebody else is going to feel hurt. What you do to that doll you do to that person, but you have to use a spirit . . . so you're hurting the doll's spirit. Therefore that doll is going to say later on, "I did what you want because you ordered me to do it, but now you've been doing me wrong and you're going to have a problem."

A. When they made spirits to represent ancestors, how did they deal with the face? Did they embroider the features on the face?

S. You don't have to—just something for the eyes, nose, and mouth, and sometimes they used to put hair or rags or they painted it. They would put earrings and bracelets and necklaces the women used when they were alive.

A. Did they ever actually use real cloth? Did they ever cut up clothing of the dead to use?

S. No, no, that is not permitted. Usually if the doll is big, they put bracelets and rings to represent the person, something they liked very much.

A. But not the cloth?

S. No, I don't believe that was done. It shouldn't be done; it will keep the spirit too close to this planet, and you don't want to do too much to keep them in or you will have a problem.

A. You don't want to trap the spirit.

S. Exactly. You want to have him free enough so that one day he can say I want to go, and then you will release that doll and you will take it where they want it to go, to the forest or to the ocean, a river or cemetery. That's it. The doll did the work it was supposed to do on the earth, and you get rid of it. Just like a human being. The Chinese, the Hindus, many other religions had the same thing except they used to do it in stone or wood. . . . In Europe they used puppets and they said a lot of those puppets had life. In the history of the world, people have always used images of what used to be alive to keep alive the image of those who passed away.

My father had a very good friend about four hours drive from Havana, in a place called Guínez. The lady's name was Esperanza; she was an iyalocha, a daughter of Ochún, and she lived by the river. She had dolls in her house just like my grandmother, made the same way out of rag but dressed according to the Orichas they represented. There was Ochún dressed up in gingham sitting up in her swinging chair in the living room, and everyone would say "Hi" to Ochún in that chair. When the river used to swell in the heavy rain and flood the whole house, the first things she placed up high were the dolls.

Those dolls were not brought into a mass, they were brought into a drumming, a ceremony of the Orichas. Sometimes they would have a sacrifice, and the doll would sit in a corner somewhere where it could see all that was happening. That's the reason why the energy of those dolls was very strong. . . . But I grew up in a house where they used to be closer to spiritualism and

Christianity than Santería. Coming from Havana or Cuba doesn't necessarily mean that you come from a family with a history in Santería. I am the first santero in my family from my mother or my father's side. I left Cuba in 1957 and I met Pancho Mora in the same year, the first babalao in the USA. He did some herbals and cleansings for me, and he ordered me to do some things because he predicted a lot of things I am doing now. He was living downstairs where I was living on the second floor on Columbus Avenue in New York City and he had one of the first botánicas. Now we have a tremendous amount of [Santería] objects available here, but we're talking about a time that when you were doing Ocha you had to order clothing from Cuba. There were no *soperas,* nothing that was needed to do Ocha. In many cases people had to go to Cuba to do Ocha and come back with their godmothers.

A. In terms of your spiritual development in New York, were there ways the dolls were used in New York, or ways you learned to use the dolls in New York after your experiences with your grandmother and great grandmother in Cuba, that you now continue?

S. Yes, those experiences were carried on through my godmother, the godmother who ordained me, Rosa Leyva, a godchild of the house of my godfather Bebo Azcui. I met her there. When my godmother Olga died she was the prominent person for me to do Ocha with and be ordained. At that time, I visited all her masses—she was also a very strong medium. She had a regular white table,[2] and every Friday we used to get together and do a mass. I learned the use of the dolls, they were all over the place, and they were used not only as Orichas, but also as spirits. All these spirits were very sensitive and close, powers that were present in the house.

A. What would be the difference between the Oricha dolls, the dolls that represent the Orichas, and those that represent the spirits in terms of how they're used? Do they have different functions?

S. Same way, except one is for the Orichas, one is for spiritualism. Sometimes they work together.

A. How would they work together?

S. Because the spirit is very close to the Oricha itself. Most peoples' spirits who are ancestors through black history one way or another had connections with iyalochas or santeros or babalaos or *paleros.* They were together with those mediums and with the Orichas; they had some sort of relationship. So let's say that now I'm a son of Obatalá and I'm doing a reading. The spirit of my mother will talk to me and tell me what to say to the person. Now it's a spiritualist medium coming into Ocha, functioning as an iyalocha. . . . The affiliation of spirits and the Orichas is very close. That's why we say in this religion you have to go to the spirits first and then pass over to Ocha. Because they work together. . . .

A. For example, in terms of working with me, you were doing a reading and you recommended that I make a doll for my grandmother. That doll then becomes part of my life—I do certain things for that doll, and that doll helps me with problems I have, and I can communicate with that doll. Now is that different than if let's say I made a doll for Yemayá. Would that have a different function?

S. I would say that you would have protection from the side of Yemayá, but the majority of the time what I recommend for people who do not have Ocha is to take a statue of the Virgin and worship it as an Oricha. That will give the most Catholic or Christian way to bring the person to this Ocha religion. When you go to Cuba, you see statues everywhere—they carry them, dress them up, they light them up when their birthday comes, they do traditional ceremonies with the statues until they do Ocha. Once they do Ocha they become the symbols they were before, and they are respected. That's why we respect all these saints, all these things they have in church. They saved this religion. We were practicing this religion behind those Catholic statues, and therefore I will continue today paying my respect to the church. I take Yemayá and Ochún, who belongs to Olga Dummont—she brought the statue of La Caridad de Cobre [Ochún] from Cuba—and I take mine of Virgen de Regla [Yemayá], and together we will do a procession the first week of September. We will take them to the ocean and do a big ceremony. To me it's very important—it's what I call *cabildo* representation.

A. During the reading you did for me, why did you decide that I needed to have a doll of my grandmother?

S. Because then your grandmother will be more honored, more remembered, and therefore that spirit will be closer to you in all these trips, in all these conferences, all these religious services, and you will be participating with the authorization that your grandmother will be not only a participant but a guardian—that is the most important thing, the guardian. For example I'm working today to give her [a client in the waiting room] a statue of Ochún, and she will see the statue of Ochún in her house to open everything Ochún is supposed to give. Ochún gives love, Ochún gives money, Ochún protects the woman; the woman's womb and all the sex parts belong to

Ochún. It is Ochún who brings the man and woman together, and if there is some sort of obstacle, it is Ochún who is the one who makes sure that things will work. There is always some sort of a reason for your participation in this religion. The Oricha will come to be represented by an image, maybe not a doll for her but a statue.

A. Why would you recommend a statue for her instead of a doll?

S. It's just that I see the doll coming to her probably when she gets a little more deeply involved, but I don't want to give her something now that would have more responsibility than a statue. For the statue, lighting a candle will be enough, but with a doll you will have a full responsibility.

A. So what you're saying is that compared to a statue, the doll is a more powerful medium of connection and therefore requires more attention.

S. The statue is more conventional—even in Cuba you can find those without having Ocha, without being a medium or anything, who dedicate to the statue, make promises to the statue, and do a lot of things for the statue as a promise, and it works. A statue is more conventional, being more Christian than anything else. For us, the statue is like a photo, an image of the Oricha; but if you have a doll for an Oricha, it is more like an actual representation; it has more life.

A. Maybe now would be a good time to go over some of these dolls you have here from your personal ancestry, how they came to be in the house with you and how they are important for your own health and healing. There's one sitting right next to me that I know is fairly new, the one representing your mother.

S. That right, that's for my mother because I thought she needed to have a figure, because she was so intensively alert as a spirit.

A. Do you feel comfortable talking about this?

S. Yes, I feel very good because I'm sure she's passing some things on to me right now. . . . I considered that my mother would not like to be only in a photograph, that my father would not like to be only in a photograph, so we put their photographs on the spiritual table with the glasses, and we put coffee and food there when they are hungry, and flowers. There is a lot to do here for them, to keep them happy and content with me. Why? Because they are my instrumental way of communicating with my ancestors. My godfather who passed away was like a second father to me, Bebo Azcui, and when I lost him, my godmother, my father, my mother, everybody—it's like my family has been reduced to the minimum. I still have an uncle and an aunt, one in Cuba and one in Florida. I consider myself lucky to have them as family, but almost everybody else is gone. So it leaves me with the memories and leaves me with the spirits, so there we go with the dolls. The dolls will be affiliated to each of them, they will give me strength, they will protect me from people who like to either talk badly about me or just try to destroy us or stop us, or people who come in with a bad feeling or bad frame of mind; but also they give me strength for the healing, to continue doing the extensive work that I do. This is not a job that is from 9 to 5, and it's not a money track. When everyone else is sleeping or watching TV, I'm working trying to help people out, and if I didn't have the help that I receive from the dolls representing my mother, my father, my godmother, my grandmother, I would be in trouble because something is missing.

A. How did you decide on the form of the doll?

S. In the case of my mother I already had these two male and female dolls. One was designated for Sarabanda downstairs, and the other one was designated for my mother. I started to get things together—I fed the doll and prepared the doll in such a way that the doll can have the identity of my mother. So I asked the doll what she wanted. Right now I'm doing what she wants because originally I thought I knew what was the right thing to do, but now I know a little better, and I know that she wants a better dress, better shoes, she wants a hairpiece. . . . I'm trying to see if I can get her glasses. I'm going to paint her lighter because her skin was lighter [than the doll's], and I'm going to dress her with better things, and I have jewelry that belonged to her and she wants to wear. These are the things we are going to do, and that's what you do with dolls.

A. I think it's really interesting how much of a process it really is—didn't you have this dress made specifically for her?

S. Yes, but she didn't like it, it's too loud, she said it was too much color. . . .

A. I think that's interesting how you have to go through a process figuring out if they're contented with the form that they have. So in other words, this is not the style she had in real life, this is not the type of clothing she would wear that she's wearing now.

S. No, she doesn't like those types of clothes. That doll was in the attic for several years after I moved from the botánica. The arm was broken, and I kept looking at it when I was upstairs and kept on thinking I should give it to my mother. Eventually, I started to question [the mediums] and decided to fix her up. I found out that my mother was very attracted to that doll. We ordered the dress, and we got her slippers, panties, socks, everything she needed, even a bra. But the main concern now is that she doesn't like that dress—in the beginning, yes, but not now. Now we know we have to give it a more appropriate dress.

A. You found that out through a medium?

S. Exactly. The medium, that's where the power comes in. . . . For me my mother is self-protection, so I keep her in memory, and every time I pass by here I say, "Goodnight Mom" before I go to sleep, or early in the morning, "How you doing." I'm not the kind of guy who gives them something to eat every day, but I do believe that at least once a week I should take care of her and give her coffee and cookies or bread the way she used to like it. She doesn't smoke, so I don't have to put a cigar in her hand. She likes water, she likes soda, she likes milk and juice. I could put coffee one time and the other time juice. She likes apple juice because she had problems with her stomach. Like the old-fashioned people, instead of eating pills for high blood pressure, she used to take garlic and cut it round like pills and put it in her mouth and drink it with her breakfast and that would control her blood pressure. There are things that I feel—when I have people coming here with problems, it is my mother telling them or telling through me to that person, telling them that they should do this, they should do that.

A. Now this doll for your mother, since you got the doll and prepared it to take on your mother's spirit, have you felt that the doll has been helping you?

S. Oh yes. It's been a very funny year. It was predicted by the Orichas; it was a year where for the first time in my life since I was born I went to the hospital. It was told to me that I was going to be sick, and I was sick. I had a touch of pneumonia.

A. I remember that.

S. I remember in the hospital it was getting close to the time I was supposed to do Elegguá's birthday and feed them like I do every year. It was already the same week, and I was flat on the bed. And the doctor didn't know how or when I was going to get out. So I remember Monday morning I opened up the window at 5 o'clock and talked to my spirits, calling my spirits and calling Olofi. And telling them, give me a sign that you are there. I want to get out of here and do what I have to do for Elegguá, and I don't care if I'm sick or weak, it's going to be done. . . . That same day the doctor came in, and he said you're going to go, if not today then early in the morning. I think the communication we have with either the spirits or the ancestors or with the Orichas, it's always been heard if we have directed our feelings and our whole heart and our words to them. And this is to me proof that what we're doing, we are on the right track.

A. So it's like the doll in a way helps you to have more direct communication with your mother, and it gives it more reality. Is that right?

S. Yes. Three days later we were feeding Elegguá and preparing the festivities for Elegguá. It was five days after I got out of the hospital I was doing all these things. So this experience told me three things. You have to be careful because you're working too hard. If you want to avoid going down in your health, you're going to have to take it easy a little bit. Second, don't do everything on your own. You're going to have to start looking for people to help you out. And third, take care of your own spirits, take care of your own Orichas. Sometimes this is a very busy house. I'm working on everybody, but I'm not working on myself, so I have to take care of my business, designate days when I'm going to go into a room and take care of my own things.

A. Why don't we talk about that doll a little then, that's the one that's sitting in the back on the shelf on the chair in the white dress and headwrap. Could you tell me a little bit about that doll?

S. It belonged to my mother. My mother was the one who made it for her own ancestors. When I asked where she wanted to be, I thought my mother would want to be in that one she made herself, but she didn't. So now she is represented by this larger figure, and the doll that my mother made is representing Olga.

Then later on after I represented my mother in this larger doll, I asked the question who wants to be in that doll [with the white dress] because I thought it was my mother, and they [the mediums] said no, my mother is pleased to be in the big one. So I worked hard and right now I'm getting her set with hair and all that, and for Christmas I'm going to see to it that her granddaughter—whom she's always loved so much—is going to dress her and get all the things that she needs. We're going to do a ceremony on Christmas for my ancestors. We're going to sit down and have dinner for Noche Buena, Christmas Eve; we will prepare food for all our ancestors and feed them.

A. So her granddaughter, your daughter, is going to be the one to dress the doll.

S. She's going to help me out. It will be very nice, and she will get in touch with the doll. My daughter needs to have a doll in the house representing her grandmother. She dreams a lot of her, so I think she has my mother very close to her, helping her.

A. That's very moving.

S. It's a very emotional thing. If you go to many countries, those little things are symbolic in the family traditions. I feel that that is why my daughter has a head of her own and she's not into drugs, she's not into drinking or running around with boyfriends here or there, pregnant. She finished school, she's now going to nursing school, she has a head of her own. She works during the day and studies at night. She may be stubborn at times, but she's a young girl of nineteen. She calls me sometimes to say I dreamed of grandfather or I dreamed of grandmother, and I think that is the support she has from my ancestors. And that's the reason why we have to maintain our ancestors, because they are the great supporters of us here in life. I'm very happy that my mother and father are close to her because that tells me that we may be doing something right here, and what I'm requesting is happening—to be protected. . . . So the tradition continues. . . . We're still doing the same thing. . . .

And I would say that 70 to 80 percent of people in the world have problems because they are not taking care of their spirits. If they take care of their spirits the way we are discussing now, it becomes an aid in their life; the solution will come easier, the problem will be eased. If the person has a problem with healing, that doll can be the best companion they can have. . . . The doll will cooperate with this person to see to it that this person feels better; he will not be alone, he will not be treated badly, he will not feel like giving up on his own life. In this religion you do not give up until the last hour, and in this religion you don't think it's better to die and live in another world—yes, you will be living in another world, but you would like to live in this world that God gave you, if it could be five or ten more years, you will do anything.

A lot of medical people ask when they interview us in the hospital, "What do you do to save peoples' lives?" Well, number one is make the person's will strong. . . . I see the doctors today do everything they read in the medical books, from their classes and universities. With us, it is the spirits of life and death, and if it is the spirit who is weighing down on that human being, we have the connection to find that particular human being's spirits or ancestors to help them, to give them aid. A lot of people ask me how do I come up with all these answers. When I'm sitting doing my readings, my spirits will indicate to me what to say and what to do with that particular person in front of me, and before I start with my diloggún I already see so much, before I even throw the shells. I am not a medium, I am a visualist. A visualist in this religion has a lot of support from the Orichas and the spirits. I don't mount: that is the difference between the medium and the visualist.[3] The medium will get mounted, and the spirit will take over.

A. So when you say visualist, you mean you are receiving images?

S. Images from the spirits . . .

A. Of what is going on with this person?

S. Exactly. And sometimes they tell me things that I don't say. For example, the person has a death threat. When I see something like that I go deeper into my investigation with the diloggún, and I don't say anything until we can identify how we can save them from that danger.

A. Sure, you don't want to just say something that's going to scare somebody without some way to deal with it.

S. Exactly. That's the power that we do have. We have the power to identify the person near death; it could be an accident, or someone who wants to kill you . . . this will come out in the reading. I don't know any other religion that can tell you to be careful with something that's going to happen to you. . . . If you have communication with your spirits and the dolls are sitting there, the dolls are going to work in many forms. You may have a dream in which your mother or grandmother tells you be careful you are near death. . . . If you have a doll for that person, then you will go to her and say let's find out exactly what she's trying to say to me. Maybe we have to feed your grandmother. You can go to the doll before that danger happens, and you can receive a response of salvation, taking that danger away, and because of that advice, that alert, it is possible that the accident will not happen.

A. What about the dolls being used to take away a negative spirit, how does that work?

S. Well, in many forms. You have a spirit you want to get rid of. The reading says it's a horrible spirit, we have to get rid of it, and I will ask Elegguá in what form. I will have to do an *ebbó,* a cleansing, taking something away from a person . . . to use a specific Oricha to remove danger from that person. It may be that the ebbó includes having a doll to clean up the person and take the spirit away.

A. But how would that work, would that doll represent . . . ?

S. It doesn't have to represent anything. We bring in the doll to the ceremony, and we use it to take the spirit away. Instead of staying in the person, it will go into the doll, and we get rid of the doll. We bury it or take it to the ceremony. The doll will be gone with that spirit.

A. So it could be any kind of doll.

S. Yes. . . . [It's not like] the doll who stays in the house and becomes a family representation of those spirits and lives with you, with your children, everybody. But when we use something like this—a ceremony that is not even done in the house, it has to be done in the priest's or medium's house— the doll becomes a powerful object to take away the evil spirit. Sometimes if the person is sick, we use the doll to take that; it's what we call "changing heads," using the doll to take the sickness away from that person.

A. Is it within Ocha?

S. It could be spiritualism, it could be Ocha, in Palo Mayombe they do it a lot too. It is also very useful in Vodou.

A. What type of ceremony is involved?

S. It could be secret; it could be calling upon spirits to get that doll confirmed with the bad spirit the person has. Therefore we take the doll, and it will go with the ebbó, with the cleansing, and it could be a doll three or four inches, or three feet tall.

A. It doesn't really matter.

S. Exactly, unless there are details given in the reading. For example if the person is sick, you put the doll in the person's room to be used as a ceremonial healing point. The doll will have the strength of a doctor or a healer and it will drain out the sickness of that person.

A. But the doll would already have had to be through the ceremony to have that kind of power?

S. Exactly, it has to have the power, but later on after the job is done we have to go back to another ceremony and find out exactly what to do with that doll—if we should get rid of it some place, a cemetery, garbage dump somewhere, the forest. Sometimes people see things like that in the forest and have a tendency to pick it up. I think we should say when someone is walking by and sees something, they should be very careful what they pick up; they could be picking up the problem that someone else had got rid of. In the old times people used to go to *maniguas,* what we call the deep forest, that way nobody would find it in the deep forest, but today it's not easy to find that in the cities. When we do a job now people have to go to Franklin Park . . . could be in the garbage. . . . We have to very careful.

A. But these ceremonies in which the dolls are equipped to take away sickness or a negative spirit, you're saying they could be in a mass or . . .

S. Either. For me I would probably go first to the diloggún and Elegguá, and then Elegguá will tell me what to do. I've had people with problems, they can't cope with their lives—they can't find happiness or jobs, they find themselves very unlucky or negative, nothing is bright. In most cases these people are held up because of their own spirits. I invite them to a spiritual mass after the reading and the spirits will mount. They come in and say you have to take care of your own spirits, there are spirits keeping you like that because you're not doing your duty, you're not doing your work of maintaining them, and they want you to do so. . . . Just yesterday morning I spoke to my mother and my father here [the dolls] and said, "What's going on here, there's no money coming in, it's been two or three days and no one calling me?" By noon yesterday two or three people called for appointments, just like that; I was working until 11 at night. Sometimes they [the dolls] will say, "Why don't you talk to me?" They expect me to talk to them, feed them, give them sweets, some food. When we had Thanksgiving dinner, I put out a plate for them.

A. By the dolls?

S. Yes, I put a plate, a glass of wine and lit a candle and gave them some of the sweets we had that day. I did it before I ate myself.

A. So in that way you're continuing exactly what your grandmother and great grandmother did.

S. Exactly. That's what I used to see in my own country.

A. We've come around to the beginning; that's what you grew up with, and that's what you've brought into your house here, your work as a priest, and your personal life. Thank you for all you have given and taught me.

Chapter 7 ▨

Community Healing Among Puerto Ricans: *Espiritismo* as a Therapy for the Soul

Mario A. Núñez Molina

In the last three decades, Caribbean indigenous healing systems have been studied extensively by Western researchers in an attempt to increase our understanding of healing as a generic process.[1] Their studies suggest the need to consider the substantial role of culture in the nature of healing and disease. An appreciation of indigenous healing systems can be an important step in improving the delivery of health care, in particular of mental health services, to all populations.

Espiritismo (Spiritism) is one such indigenous healing system. Utilized by a significant number of Puerto Ricans as an alternative to professional health-care systems (an epidemiological study carried out in Puerto Rico in 1990 found that 18 percent of the Puerto Rican population consulted Espiritista healers to resolve emotional problems),[2] Espiritismo and Espiritista healers have been found by several studies to indeed be effective in the treatment of a variety of mental health-related issues.[3]

The central principle of Espiritismo is the belief in the communication with the spirit world through intermediaries who are called mediums. Espiritistas consider that good and bad spirits are involved in the material affairs of this life. It is a belief system practiced by Puerto Ricans living on the island as well as those living in the United States, by lower-class as well as upper-class individuals, by the undereducated as well as those with a college education.[4] Espiritismo functions as a religion for some Puerto Ricans, as a healing system in moments of crisis for others, and as a "philosophy" and "science" for the academically oriented.

Espiritismo in Puerto Rico

Historians agree that the practice of Espiritismo was introduced into Puerto Rico during the second half of the nineteenth century, when the island was still a colony of Spain and Catholicism the official religion.[5] Despite a repressive political environment and an almost total lack of civil rights, a good number of middle-class families on the island managed to send their sons abroad for a European education. Many of the Puerto Rican students in Europe became deeply influenced by a French educator and philosopher who wrote under the pseudonym of Allan Kardec (1804–69). Their return to the island from Europe introduced Espiritista philosophy. A significant number of these Puerto Rican intellectuals were also interested in reforming the Puerto Rican economic and political system. They discovered in Espiritismo a philosophy that addressed both the transformation of the individual as well as that of the community. Espiritismo became for Puerto Rican liberals an ideal doctrine that would liberate the oppressed community from Spanish colonialism. Kardec's most significant works, *The Book of the Spirits* (1857), *The Gospel According to Spiritism* (1864), and *The Book of the Mediums* (1859), gained great popularity within the Puerto Rican intellectual community.[6] At first they were brought to Puerto Rico clandestinely due to the Spanish government's opposition to Espiritista philosophy.[7] Despite this restriction, by 1873 Puerto Rican bookstores were selling Kardec's books and the new movement was gaining widespread acceptance among Puerto Ricans.

At first Espiritista groups, facing arrest and prosecution by the government, had to be organized secretly, as they were believed to be affiliated with revolutionary factions.[8] Cruz Moclova in *Historia de Puerto Rico* writes of the arrest of Mario Braschi Rodríguez, an Espiritista incarcerated for six months for the publication of an article offensive to the Catholic Church. Articles published in magazines and newspapers described Espiritismo as an "abominable social cancer" and the cause of mental illness.[9] In 1875, the *Boletín Mercantil*, a government newspaper, reported that Espiritismo was "invading the Island."[10] Similarly, the Catholic Church, in addition to publishing numerous articles condemning the practice of Espiritismo, denied known Espiritistas such sacraments as baptism, marriage, and last rites.

Despite this repression, the Espiritista movement grew rapidly, organizing centers in different parts of the island, the earliest one being *Luz del Progreso* (Light of Progress), founded in Mayagüez in 1888. During the last two decades of the nineteenth century, these centers promoted changes in the areas of education, health care, and social reform. Espiritista groups organized libraries and published at least eleven magazines (among them *El Heraldo,* 1880; *El Peregrino,* 1884; *El Nivel,* 1889; *El Estudio,* 1892; and *El Neófito,* 1893). Espiritista leaders considered the study of Espiritismo as essential to the intellectual and moral growth of the Puerto Rican community. In 1873, an Espiritista leader, Manuel Corchado y Juarbe, presented a project to the Spanish courts recommending the study of Espiritismo in Puerto Rican secondary schools. Espiritista groups contributed to improving health care for the people by creating several hospitals throughout the island and were also involved in the task of working for social and political reforms. In 1888, Espiritista groups from Mayagüez sent delegates to the First International Congress of Spiritists in Barcelona with the purpose of using it as a forum for the condemnation of the abuses and repression of the Spanish government. Such Espiritista leaders as Rosendo Matienzo Cintrón and Emeterio Bacon were prominent politicians committed to achieving freedom and justice in Puerto Rico.

The 1898 invasion of Puerto Rico by the United States, an event that took place a mere six months after liberal politicians in Puerto Rico had succeeded in wrenching the concession of autonomous governance from Spain, reinforced the perception among liberal politicians and Espiritista leaders that Puerto Rico had reverted to its previous status as an oppressed colony. The American takeover, however, eased some of the government interdictions against the Espiritista movement. In 1903, a group of Espiritistas founded the Spiritist Federation of Puerto Rico, an organization dedicated to the promulgation of Espiritismo and the coordination and cohesion of Espiritista centers and societies. The Federation began to hold annual conventions in which Espiritistas from many regions of Puerto Rico would meet to discuss the development of Espiritismo on the island. In 1913, Francisco Ponte, a dentist considered to be the first Puerto Rican parapsychologist because of his empirical approach to psychical research,[11] became president of the federation. He was best known for the many experiments he performed with a medium who produced materializations.

Espiritismo, as we have seen, began in Puerto Rico as a middle-class movement led by intellectuals and academically oriented Puerto Ricans who were primarily interested in Espiritismo as a philosophical system providing a framework for social and moral development. Some among them were attracted to Espiritismo because of its "scientific" orientation and emphasis on psychical research. There was, however, another group of Puerto Ricans, generally from the lower class, who were interested in Kardec's *Spiritismé* not because of its "scientific" and philosophical orientation but because this system offered a framework for understanding healing and treating illness. They syncretized Espiritismo with popular Catholicism, *curanderismo,* herbal medicine, and other healing practices derived from Arawak and African heritages. In the process, they adapted Kardec's Spiritismé to their own reality and needs, creating a unique healing system that I refer to here as "indigenous Espiritismo," using the term "indigenous" to describe a primarily sociocultural creation that integrates different healing systems and religious traditions that had evolved in Puerto Rico for hundreds of years.

At the time of the introduction of Kardec's Espiritismo, there was already a rich folk-healing tradition in Puerto Rico derived from the Indian, Afro-Caribbean, and Spanish cultural heritages.[12] Folk healing practices such as *santiguos* and herbal medicine were used by poor people to resolve their everyday problems. (*Santiguos* are the hand massages given for settling dislocated bones and curing various forms of intestinal diseases.) The origin of these healing practices can be traced primarily to the healing traditions of the Taíno (Arawak) Indians, who inhabited the island at the time of the Columbian encounter, and to the curative practices of African slaves.

▨   ▨   ▨

The foundation of the Espiritista belief system is the acknowledgment of a spirit world constantly interacting with the "material world" (*mundo material*). It is a world believed to be inhabited by spirits who are classified according to a hierarchy of moral development.[13] Those at the lowest level are identified as "ignorant," because they are too attached to the material world and interested in harming human beings. At the highest level, the evolved spirits, or "spirits of light" (*espíritus de luz*), have achieved a great degree of spiritual perfection and are able to protect people from the negative influence of ignorant spirits. Human beings, according to Espiritista belief, are composed of two major dimensions: a material body and a spirit. When a person's material body dies, his or her spirit leaves the body but continues living at another level of existence, where it maintains its identity as well as its moral and spiritual development. The essence of the person is his or her spirit; the body is merely an instrument.

In the Espiritista body of beliefs, one's spirit exists before one is born and survives after death. As one life is not enough to purify the spirit of its moral weaknesses, spirits must reincarnate several times in order to achieve moral perfection. Consequently, problems and conflicts in a present life are strongly determined by one's actions in past lives. Conflictive relationships from past lives, for example, may affect one's present relationships. A spirit wife or husband from a past life can cause problems in current intimate relationships if the spirit is ignorant and does not recognize that one is living another life. Related to the belief in reincarnation is the concept of *pruebas* (trials or tests). According to Espiritistas, pruebas are problems, sufferings, or illnesses that have been chosen by a person before birth in order to pay a spiritual debt from a past life. If a person suffers the pruebas with resignation, he or she will purify the spirit of moral imperfections.

Communication between the spirits and human beings is an essential element of Espiritismo. Individuals capable of contacting the spirit world are called mediums; they serve as intermediaries between the spirit world and the material world. Theoretically, every person is an actual or a potential medium because mediumnity is considered a natural capacity. Yet, in order to become a medium, an individual must undergo a process called *desarrollo de facultades* (development of faculties), the *facultades* being the different capacities a medium requires in order to communicate with the spirits and obtain their help.

Espiritistas believe that ignorant spirits can be the cause of physical as well as mental illness. These spirits can control the thoughts and actions of an individual, producing in him or her an *obsesión*. The individual who is experiencing an obsesión is under the influence of an ignorant spirit, subject to that spirit's will. The influence of these ignorant spirits can also produce physical disturbances, ranging from headaches to major illness. Every person is born with a guiding spirit who protects him or her from the influence of ignorant spirits. The guiding spirit is expected to provide assistance, guidance, and spiritual support when one encounters problems.

The most important event in the practice of Espiritismo is the Espiritista meeting. Espiritista centers have a similar physical setup. A long cloth-covered table is usually occupied by the group leader (*presidente*) and the various mediums. On the table there may be a goblet of water, flowers, cigars, statues of different Catholic saints, incense, and other paraphernalia. Generally, the room is adorned with pictures of Christ and the Virgin Mary along with other religious personalities. The session traditionally begins with a reading from Allan Kardec's *El Evangelio según el "Espiritismo"* (*The Gospel According to Spiritism*) and with the prayers contained in the *Collection of Selected Prayers* requesting the presence of guiding spirits, the education of ignorant spirits, and support for the health of the sick.

After this first stage, the mediums prepare for the "working" of the *causas* affecting the visitors, that is, the actions and influences of the ignorant spirits upon an individual. The "working of causas" is a process that involves several tasks. First, a medium identifies the individual's particular problem, classifying it according to two major categories, material or spiritual. When the causa is found to be material, if the individual's problem is not caused or influenced by the spirits, the mediums will refer the person to a modern health professional. They may, however, also offer a treatment based on their knowledge of herbal medicine.

If the causa is identified as spiritual, on the other hand, the healing process is oriented toward educating or "giving light" to the spirit who is totally or partially responsible for the problem. In cases of a spiritual causa, the role of the medium is to divine which of the symptoms the person is experiencing is produced by the ignorant spirit. After this has been done, the medium is prepared to be possessed by the spirit in order to create the opportunity for a dialogue among the spirit, the other mediums, and the affected individual.

This healing dialogue has two major functions. First, as the spirit expresses its feelings against an individual, those present become aware of the spirit's reasons for harming the person affected. Usually, ignorant spirits affect an individual seeking revenge for an act committed in this life or in a past one. The second and more important function of the dialogue is to educate or give light to the ignorant spirit so that it will cease doing harm. If the ignorant spirit decides to follow the medium's advice, then the causa has been lifted. The healing process is not complete, however, until the ignorant spirit repents for the evil it has caused.

Mediums also involve the afflicted person in the working of the causa by asking him or her to perform a number of tasks and rituals believed to be effective in giving light to the spirit. For example, a medium can prescribe such rituals as the lighting of candles and the reading of prayers. At the same time, the afflicted individual is asked to transform his/her own character; ignorant spirits, it is believed, affect those who lack the strength to resist their influence. When the presidente determines it is time to finish the working of causas, the meeting is closed with a prayer from the *Collection of Selected Prayers* called "At the End of the Meeting."

Towards an Experiential Model for Researching Traditional Healing Systems

An experiential approach to research is fundamental for an understanding of traditional healing systems; it allows for the possibility of capturing their complexity without degrading, reducing, or devaluating them. A significant number of person-centered ethnographers recognize the role of subjectivity and the research-participant relationship as sources of increased knowledge and understanding.[14] Their studies suggest the need to consider researchers as "positioned subjects" who have particular life experiences that both enable and inhibit particular kinds of insight. In support of the use of researchers' experiential data in the research process, Reinharz writes:

> If the experience of the research is omitted, then the discipline is limited to the study of the observable behavior and responses to instruments and contrived

situations such as questionnaires. Studies built on such a foundation lack . . . the experience of the researcher and of the subject since the information concerning the subject is experiential but an artifact of research procedures.[15]

The Roots of My Approach: A Personal Story

Research accounts in the social sciences emphasize the analysis of results without sufficiently reflecting the ways in which the researcher's cultural and personal background influence the selection of the research topic, the methodological approach, the relationship with participants, and the research process in general.[16] The general orientation among social science researchers is to describe their research as if they themselves were not present or involved in the act of interviewing, observing, participating, and interacting with the people studied. Research publications are dedicated to examining the Other (the subjects) without including a description of the Self (the researcher) and the process by which the research findings are influenced by the interaction of the Self and the Other. The researcher's personal experiences and reflections on the research process are most likely to be found in peripheral sections of a study—prefaces, postscripts, footnotes, acknowledgments, and appendices. Thus researchers disregard personal experiences and a reflective stance in order to secure an "objective" analysis of their findings.

Given my strong conviction that the researcher's personal narrative is essential for understanding the research process, I will risk telling mine. This personal story is composed of my preconceptions and assumptions, moments of vulnerability in which my worldview was challenged, and biographical data that influenced the research direction. My hope is that a description of the research process from a personal perspective will illuminate the methodological issues I confronted during this process.

Native researchers have been defined as those who conduct research on the ethnic group of which they are themselves members.[17] In studying Puerto Rican Espiritismo, I became a native researcher not only because I am a Puerto Rican, but also because, having participated in the activities of Espiritista centers in my community since my youth, I have experienced this healing system from the inside.

I was born in Lares, a small town in the mountains of Puerto Rico, into an extended family and a community of strong Espiritista believers; my worldview and concept of reality have been heavily influenced by my being a Puerto Rican socialized within the Espiritista subculture. My interest in the study of Espiritismo can be traced to my first contact with an Espiritista healer when I was seven years old. At the time, I was suffering from a disabling condition.

The doctors informed my parents that the basis for my condition was physiological and advised an operation as soon as possible.

Desperate and not knowing where to turn, my parents resorted to Espiritismo upon the advice of a friend who recommended a good Espiritista
healer near my town. They decided to take me to him. The healer, I remember well, was a fifty-five-year-old man named Gumersindo. The first
thing he did was to put a cup of water on a table. Then he laid his hand on
my head and stomach, performing several *pases* (spiritual cleansings). After
this, he took the cup of water and said to me: "Drink it, thinking you will
be cured." I drank the water as he told me, believing it to be the medicine I
needed to be healed. The last thing I remember from this experience was my
parents asking Gumersindo, "How much do we owe you?" He responded:
"It is free. The healing power has come from God and the good spirits. I am
not responsible for it. Your child has been cured." He was right: from that
moment my health problems completely disappeared. This pivotal healing
experience motivated me to study the therapeutic dimensions of Espiritismo. It also contributed significantly to the development of my experiential approach to the study of this healing system.

In describing the experiential approach, I am proposing a different paradigm for doing fieldwork, which stresses the vulnerability of researchers and
in turn facilitates their understanding of the participant's reality.[18] Experiences of vulnerability are intrinsic to field research, and perhaps to the research enterprise in general. I experienced my own vulnerability doing
research on Espiritismo at an Espiritista meeting:

Doña Gela, a Puerto Rican Espiritista healer, is known in her community
for her "spiritual injections." I spoke with several of Doña Gela's clients and
discovered they felt as if they had been injected with a needle when she had
touched a part of their bodies with just her finger. My initial reaction was to
interpret the "spiritual injections" as produced by suggestion or by the use
of some object. I decided to observe Doña Gela very carefully when she
worked with clients in order to see if she was carrying something in her
hands. She "injected" several people in front of me; I saw nothing in her
hands or fingers.

One day while doing participant observation at Doña Gela's center, I had
an experience that changed my perception about the reality of the "spiritual
injections." After having worked with two clients, she looked at me and said:
"You are very tired. You are working too much." She asked me to stand up
in front of her, and began to massage my back and stomach. Suddenly I felt
as if I had been injected in my stomach with a small needle. At that moment
I tried to deny the experience, thinking that I was imagining it. However,
after a few seconds I felt another injection, but this time it was of stronger
intensity. My mind was telling me: "You are a researcher, keep your objec-

tivity." Then Doña Gela took one of my arms and pressed gently with one of her fingers in the middle. At that moment I had to move away as if I had been injected with a larger needle. It was somewhat painful. I told Doña Gela: "These injections are too strong." Everybody in the room began to laugh, and Doña Gela smiled at me, continuing her massage. When she finished, I looked at my stomach and arm and saw three red dots at the places in my body where I had been "injected."

This experience contributed directly to the development of a better relationship with Doña Gela and the other participants of my research. Through this episode I was able to experience and understand their reality. More importantly, I learned to respect and value their experiences by accepting my own vulnerability, and relinquishing the security of my own worldview. The degree of a researcher's connectedness with and subsequent understanding of a culture may depend to some extent on the acceptance of his or her own experiences of vulnerability, which can become an essential resource in decreasing the experiential and epistemological gap between a researcher and the people studied. A female Korean shaman, discussing the fact of being a healer and becoming possessed, describes this gap as follows:

> You, though you say you are trying to understand how I became a *mudang* [shaman] and what it's done to me, you will never understand me. . . . You see, there cannot be any real understanding between the possessed and the nonpossessed. . . . The possessed have had experiences that the nonpossessed cannot begin to comprehend no matter how they try. At best, they can only see what your possession is doing to you and to them [her family] socially. They cannot really understand your inner feelings or experiences.[19]

The experiential approach has several advantages. It may help researchers achieve insights that have been overlooked by others as well as alternatives for collecting, analyzing, and understanding data in a way that is more consonant with the culture being studied. And another advantage of this approach is that it helps reduce the bias against religion that exists within the field of psychology. Given the widespread acceptance of Freud's conception of religious experiences as a sign of mental illness, psychologists have resisted acknowledging the therapeutic potential of religion.[20]

Generally, researchers who have studied Espiritismo implicitly or explicitly assume that spirits have no objective reality and proceed from there to analyze their data. An Espiritista healer in this study expressed the idea that no one can undertake serious research on Espiritismo assuming that spirits are products of the medium's mind. He argued that it is impossible to understand the process of becoming a healer if one begins with this preconception.

Being a native researcher and having a different epistemology than that of Western researchers, I find it more appropriate to examine Espiritismo from an emic (inside) perspective, remaining at the level of the medium's construction of reality, avoiding interpretations beyond the data collected. My goal was not to examine Espiritista healers' experiences using a framework borrowed from Western psychological theories but to examine them based on the healer's worldview. Since what interests me is precisely the way in which they experience reality, I do not find it helpful to analyze spirits as creations of their minds, nor to compare Espiritista concepts with Western psychological concepts. Thomas Csordas suggests the need to include sacred reality in the study of religious systems, asking "whether religious phenomena can legitimately be translated into psychiatric terms or whether in some cases they must be analyzed with respect to the structure of the sacred. . . ."[21] This dilemma is crucial for a better understanding of religious experiences, as the tendency is to translate these experiences into psychological terms without considering the spiritual dimension.

The research model that I am proposing is based on the paradigm of multiple or alternative realities.[22] This paradigm emphasizes that ordinary reality is just one of a number of possible realities and states of consciousness, as opposed to the concept that there is one reality with which everyone should be in contact in order to be considered "normal" and "mentally healthy." Mental health, within Espiritismo, is the capacity to live in a world of alternate realities and to control the possibility of connecting with each of them at will.

The reality of the spirits is not something that can be proved or denied; however, from a psychological perspective, the spirits can be conceived as psychic truths. The fact that people have experiences with spirits is enough to consider them as phenomenologically real. For spirit healers, of course, the reality of a transpersonal or spiritual realm becomes a lived experience, not just a simple belief. For them, spirits are not abstract concepts or symbols for explaining reality; they see the spirits, hear their voices, and experience their reality in the possession trance.

❊   ❊   ❊

My decision to study Espiritismo stemmed from my desire to know more about healing, illness, development, and the spiritual dimension. The healers that I met in the process shared their wisdom and helped me achieve an understanding of life as a meaningful journey. I discuss below, therefore, what I believe are the most important contributions of Espiritismo as a healing system.

Many Espiritista healers are very effective therapists. They use several techniques familiar to mental health professionals: reframing,[23] abreaction and catharsis,[24] therapeutic paradoxes,[25] role playing,[26] hypnotic techniques and suggestion,[27] and crisis intervention and rehabilitation theory.[28] They are acquainted with the placebo effect and its use in helping their clients.[29] But while comparisons between Espiritista healing and modern therapeutic approaches are important to some extent because they help us understand the therapeutic implications of Espiritismo, they may prevent us from a full understanding of Espiritismo as an indigenous healing system.[30] One might conclude that Espiritista healers are effective because they are very similar to modern psychotherapists. Comparing healing systems of different cultures at the psychological-conceptual level runs the risk of ignoring important differences at the cultural and social-dimensional level. There is a tendency to "psychologize" Espiritismo without considering the system's unique healing elements, many of which are very different from the techniques of mental health professionals:

1. Espiritista healing, unlike Western psychotherapy, is congruent with basic premises of Puerto Rican culture. Healers are actively engaged in bringing about therapeutic results, offering direct advice.[31] In this sense, healer and client share similar expectations because it has been found that advice and medication are the principal types of treatment expected by Puerto Rican patients.[32] Healers prescribe herbs and baths that represent a kind of medication for the clients. Most lower-class Puerto Ricans do not believe that they can resolve their problems through psychotherapy, therefore they do not expect to be questioned about or to discuss their psychic conflicts. Espiritista healing fulfills this expectation by involving the client in different activities, giving little emphasis to conversation as a way of achieving insight. Consequently, clients do not necessarily require verbal skills in order to be helped. Espiritista healing has been described as "exorcism by action as opposed to exorcism by thought and insight."[33]

2. In Espiritista healing, the client's problem is not a stigmatizing phenomenon. Rather than the manifestation of illness, it is the signal that the client is developing faculties. The healers interpret the symptoms as a gift. This is very important for Puerto Rican clients because of the fear of being labeled *locos* (mentally ill).

3. Espiritista healers attribute mental illness to external sources, relieving the client from feelings of guilt. The client is considered responsible for the recuperation but not for the illness.

4. The sociocultural differences between Espiritista healers and their clients are minimal. Healers live in the same community as their clients, "sharing the day-to-day frustrations of ghetto living: unemployment; lack of adequate sanitation, housing, and medical care; and

estrangement from the outside world."[34] Healers generally provide assistance any time of the day without the need for appointments. The services of healers are very inexpensive, and the payment for services is normally based on an optional voluntary offering. All of this provides the Espiritista healer with a better understanding of the client's problem.

Years of researching have led me to the conclusion that one of the most important therapeutic dimensions of Espiritismo is its function as a natural support system. Espiritista centers provide community members an alternative to professional mental health services, offering support, guidance, and specific information to individuals, referring them to professionals when deemed necessary. The Espiritista center functions as a voluntary organization and as a primary group outside the family. Before and after each meeting, Espiritistas have the opportunity to speak to each other, sharing concerns and problems. As one Espiritista participant commented: "Usually I don't go out, but every Sunday I need to come to the Espiritista meeting. I enjoy talking with other members and knowing what they have done in the week." The center provides a setting for the creation of intimate relationships within a safe environment.

Espiritista centers also offer recreational opportunities such as the celebration of special holidays, social gatherings, and birthday parties. The meeting itself can be considered "recreational" activity. Often Espiritista mediums tell jokes and interesting stories; they entertain people and make them laugh. Good spirits who communicate through the medium enjoy discussing humorous situations and singing happy songs. The sense of mystery and suspense, which is always part of the Espiritista meeting, contributes to its being a very special event.

In my experience, Espiritista centers may also prevent emotional problems. They offer support to those participants suffering grief due to the death of their relatives, for example. Participants have the opportunity to communicate with their dead relatives, to express feelings of guilt, to work out unresolved conflicts, or to deal with the process of grieving more effectively. An example from my work is illustrative:

A woman visited an Espiritista center because she was feeling depressed after the death of her young daughter in a car accident. She felt responsible for her daughter's death because she "shouldn't have given her permission to go out so late." In the meeting, the spirit of the daughter communicated through a medium, emphasizing the notion that she was happy and that the mother should not feel guilty because there was nothing anyone could have done to avoid her death. The mother cried intensely, telling her daughter how much she missed her. The experience was a very powerful one, and the group shared the mother's pain by crying with her.

At the end of the meeting I talked with the mother. She was very grateful for having the opportunity to talk with her daughter and knowing she was not suffering.

Empowerment or Alienation?

Do Espiritista practices truly empower people, or do they only promote dependency and an illusory sense of empowerment? Victor De La Cancela and Iris Zavala have argued that the belief system of Espiritismo and other folk healing systems may promote passivity, alienation from the sociopolitical sources of problems, and dependency on Espiritista healers. They state that the ideology of Espiritismo may help to maintain oppressive social conditions in the Puerto Rican community:

> Folk healing . . . may function to placate the action potential of angry and frustrated individuals by offering mystical and magical explanations and solutions to what are long-standing consequences of structural inequities within our society.[35]

The weakness of De La Cancela and Zavala's argument is that they do not present a case to support their claims; nor do they mention having done any formal research on Espiritismo. Although I agree that the ideology of traditional healing systems may contain oppressive elements, it is essential to investigate how this ideology actually guides people's actions in their daily lives. This kind of data may help one to appreciate the issue in all of its complexity.

To my knowledge the only research on Espiritismo as an ideology that promotes or discourages social change was carried out by Figueroa, whose goal was to determine the role that Espiritismo plays in enhancing or diminishing both national self-awareness and working-class consciousness.[36] Figueroa's data were based on participant observation in an Espiritista group, analysis of case studies, and a description of a collective action by an Espiritista group. Although Figueroa recognized that Espiritista participants see their problems as caused by spiritual rather than social forces, his analysis of four case studies shows Espiritista meetings contributing to resistance more than to accommodation. He argued that Espiritistas believe in a dialectical relationship between the material world and the spiritual world: the spiritual world can affect and shape the material world as much as the material world can affect and shape the spiritual world.

Figueroa described a group of tenants who used Espiritismo in order to act collectively against a landlord who refused to provide heat for their apartments and maintenance for the building. During one of their Espiritista meetings, they organized a rent strike and prepared for a demonstration in front of the landlord's home. Espiritista rituals were also used in order to ask for the help of good spirits. A "*limpieza*" (spiritual cleanup) was given to the building, and a "*trabajo*" (spell) was put on the landlord. The tenants' actions pressured the landlord to agree to their demands, and the following day their apartments were warm.

Other studies also belie the notion that Espiritista healers promote dependence on their clients.[37] Salgado describes the relationship between an Espiritista healer and her client as follows:

> The process was accomplished through a definite plan of action that [required] commitment and effort on the part of the client, with the support and encouragement of the Espiritista. In helping families, she taught them how to work with their problems rather than working out solutions for them.[38]

It has been argued that Espiritista healers encourage clients to dismiss responsibility for their own problems and to believe rather that they are caused by ignorant spirits.[39] This can be therapeutic, of course, as it relieves the clients from feelings of guilt. However, this treatment approach can reinforce the idea that an individual lacks control over his/her life or the power to change his/her behavior. Harwood, attempting to reconcile this apparent contradiction, distinguishes between responsibility for the problem and responsibility for the cure.[40] He observes that the Espiritista healer denies the client's responsibility for the problem but encourages responsibility for its resolution. Espiritista healers usually make an effort to involve the client in the healing process through activities such as rituals, baths, and prayers, transmitting the attitude that the client is responsible for the treatment outcomes. Clients are, however, held responsible for their problems in Espiritismo. The cause of a problem need not be perceived as internal in order for one to be responsible for it. The wish of an ignorant spirit to harm a client can be explained as being caused by the client's bad actions against this spirit in a past life. In this sense, the client is accountable for the problem because it is a consequence of his or her actions.

One can argue that a dependence on spirits to resolve problems works against the process of empowerment. But Espiritista mediums believe that besides asking for help from the spirits, a client must assume an active involvement in treatment. The help from the spirit world is seen as complementary to the efforts of clients themselves. Data from my work suggest that several Espiritista mediums emphasize the need for the clients' accountability; as one of the mediums said: "People cannot become dependent on you because then you are not really helping them." Espiritista mediums consider it their responsibility to educate community members so that they can achieve better control of their lives. One of the mediums declared: "The major purpose of Espiritismo is not to cure people or to communicate with the spirits but to teach people how to develop their own spiritual powers in order to become better human beings." Espiritista centers strongly emphasize developing the participants' strengths. Individuals who arrive asking for help are guided to develop their own healing power through mediumship development; those who are suffering have the opportunity to become healers. In this sense, therefore, Espiritista healing is based on the empowerment of clients; they can develop the power to heal themselves and then be involved in the process of healing others.

Espiritista healers do not explain their effectiveness in psychosocial dimensions; their success depends on the connection they maintain with the dimension of the spiritual world. It is from the spiritual world that they derive the resources to help others. Healing is produced by transpersonal factors such as faith, the disposition of good spirits, and God's will. Espiritista healers see themselves as channels of God's energy, reflecting the universal idea of an energy in nature that can be used to heal. The essential role of the spiritual dimension within Espiritismo can be seen as a source of empowerment for the community. Patients undergo transformations of consciousness; through spirit possession, community members experience a sense of transcendence in their lives, finding healing resources beyond their individual selves. Through these rituals of transformation, one's individuality is subordinate to the service of community goals, with the result that one's sense of community is enhanced.[41]

❊ ❊ ❊

Espiritismo is a healing system created by and for the community to deal with its problems, using its own resources and strengths. At Espiritista centers, the community heals itself without relying on professional "experts." Community members are in control of their own resources, increasing their sense of empowerment. The Espiritista meeting is a community-oriented ritual that enhances the individual's sense of community and belonging. As a preventive and therapeutic system, Espiritismo is based on the particular strengths and cultural realities of the Puerto Rican community. Instead of imposing therapeutic and preventive models that fail to consider the resources of a people, we should support and collaborate with those healing systems that are already functioning in the community. From indigenous healing systems such as Espiritismo, we may learn how to offer better preventive human services to culturally diverse communities.

Part II 🔲

Artistic Healing

Chapter 8 ▨

A Particular Blessing:
Storytelling as Healing
in the Novels of Julia Alvarez

Karen Castellucci Cox

A borderland is a vague and undetermined place created by the emotional residue of an unnatural boundary. It is in a constant state of transition. The prohibited and forbidden are its inhabitants.

—Gloria Anzaldúa, *Borderlands/La Frontera*

Illness is the night-side of life, a more onerous citizenship. Everyone who is born holds dual citizenship, in the kingdom of the well and in the kingdom of the sick. Although we all prefer to use only the good passport, sooner or later each of us is obliged, at least for a spell, to identify ourselves as citizens of that other place.

—Susan Sontag, *Illness as Metaphor*

I

While Susan Sontag refers in her classic essay, of course, to the experience of pathologically fatal disease,[1] her reflection could as easily hold for the experience of mental illness or breakdown, that more inscrutable world of psychological dysfunction that resides as much in the human spirit as it does in the physical body. As Western science reaches for new palliatives for the troubled mind, applying medications, therapies, and analytic treatments to the myriad forms of mental affliction, socioreligious communities in Western and non-Western cultures have looked historically to the spirit world for healing. The Caribbean, with its multicultural matrix of blended religions and beliefs, is a unique site of such mystical curatives. While a thorough description of the richly varied tradition of Caribbean religious rites and healing cures is beyond this essay's scope,[2] tracing the influence of Haitian vodou and its healing practices in the fiction of Dominican American writer Julia Alvarez is useful in elucidating the episodes of mental breakdown and recovery in her novels. Though occasional vodou elements appear without elaboration in the novels, as in the "magic waters" that grace her fictional alter ego's desk and windowsills, Alvarez makes neither the sacred practices of Afro-Caribbean spirituality, learned from Haitians in her household, nor the symbolic world of her family's Dominican Catholicism central to her fiction. Rather than treating these competing (and, in the Dominican Republic, often syncretic) traditions overtly, Alvarez addresses the absence of a spiritual realm in the lives of her characters, women who suffer from various maladies for which Western medicine has no adequate cure. It is finally only the memory of a single episode of mystical healing that offers psychological wholeness to these Dominican American women characters living between two cultures in the mental borderland of the exiled.

A writer of novels and poetry, Alvarez spent her early girlhood in the Dominican Republic, living a comfortable, upper-class life within the superficially safe confines of her mother's extended family. Alvarez's father, a medical doctor, was politically active and participated in the underground movement to overthrow dictator Rafael Trujillo. Fearing discovery and serious reprisal after an aborted assassination attempt by his organization, in 1960 Alvarez's father secured passage for his wife and four daughters to move to New York City on a "temporary basis." Four months after the family's escape, the famous Mirabal sisters were killed for their political activities.[3] Shortly thereafter, on May 30, 1961, the same underground group to which Alvarez's father belonged succeeded in assassinating "El Jefe," unwittingly setting in motion a series of unstable governments in the country. The political turmoil of these years encouraged Alvarez's parents to put down roots in the United States and enroll their children in reputable boarding schools to accelerate the transition to American life. Though Alvarez and her sisters would return to "the Island" many times as visiting relations, this original migration to the United States would mark the end of their citizenship in the Dominican Republic.

In much of her work, Alvarez interrogates this tenuous category of belonging fully to neither the homeland nor the adopted country. For participants in the Caribbean diaspora in the United States, whose migrations were precipitated in so many cases by dictatorial persecution or menacing poverty brought on by a (post)colonial culture, the break with the past results in an alienation common to both immigrants and political refugees, who find themselves immersed in a new society that does not recognize the values these newcomers wish to retain. Thus, living between two cultures creates its own kind of "dis-ease"—a discomforting consciousness of things missing, neither a language, nor a culture, nor an extended family within which to position oneself. For people like Alvarez's parents, whose hearts remained with the homeland but whose future dreams were firmly planted in the new country, such a position necessitates an ambiguous melding of divided loyalties and conflicting customs. Julia Alvarez, who characterizes herself as a "U.S.A. Latina"[4] writer, suggests that her identity and many themes in her fiction grow out of this hybridity of two languages and cultures, a potentially positive amalgamation. Yet, the mental affliction that often signals such a split identity, where one experiences authentic citizenship only in the shadowy borderland between juxtaposed worlds, haunts much of Alvarez's written work.

In her first and third novels, Alvarez leans heavily on personal experience to create a fictional Dominican family, the Garcías, whose lives are thrown into turmoil when they must leave all they know to learn to negotiate the 1960s world of New York City. Alvarez's first novel, *How the García Girls Lost Their Accents,*[5] and its sequel, *¡Yo!,*[6] follow the four sisters—Carla, Sandi, Yolanda, and Sofía—as they straddle the borderland between two cultures. Despite the abrupt removal to a foreign country in preadolescence, there are ways in which these young women's initiations into adulthood seem very "American." They sneak away to meet boys, experiment with drugs, elope, marry, divorce, struggle with anorexia, depression, anxiety, and mental breakdown; in short, their lives can be read as not atypical outgrowths of the sixties culture in the United States. Yet, behind these apparently conventional narratives lurks the specter of difference. With every act of American conformity, these Dominican daughters act against a cultural code of behavior that values feminine deference, sexual purity, and familial devotion. The García girls are reminded incessantly that their allegiance lies in another place, their conduct measured by another standard. Even their subtle accents mark them, as they are encouraged as children in the Dominican Republic to "use your English" and then reprimanded as adults visiting the island to "say it in Spanish," as if language were a bulwark against the dangerous influences of the opposing culture, a country all its own, claiming its denizens by voice. Perhaps due to this attention to language, the central character Yolanda experiences her dual (or internally dueling) citizenship as a linguistic balancing act, one in which the requisite split between two languages represents the break between cultures and even the split self that initiates

Yolanda's mental breakdown. The pressure of growing up walking a tightrope of conflicting identities is even more apparent in Alvarez's latest book, the collection of essays *Something to Declare*.[7] Episodes recalled here provide important background material and additional evidence for the cycle of hurt and healing present in the novels.

How the García Girls Lost Their Accents is a novel made up of interconnected stories grouped into three segments that move backward through time. Part 1 comprises the years 1989–72, when the girls are teenagers and adults; Part 2 recounts the decade of 1970–60, the first ten years in New York; and Part 3 returns to the years 1960–56, when the family is still in the Dominican Republic. Because the narrative recedes rather than proceeds, the reading experience becomes one of simultaneous loss and recovery. Even as the narrative unfolds in reverse to reveal what feels like the recouping of a relinquished culture, the stories record a past that is not actually recoverable but irretrievably abandoned. Julie Barak has compared this narrative structure usefully to a "widening gyre," which highlights in its "spiral movement the centripetal and centrifugal forces that pull [the García girls] toward and away from their island home, toward and away from the United States, toward and away from an integrated adulthood."[8] The recurring sense of an island community, to which one's belonging is forever altered, is magnified by its disparity to New York City, which offers freedom within anonymity but at the cost of familial identity. The narrative pattern balances this perception of loss with an equal feeling of extrication and salvation, however, in that forays into the past are not simply nostalgic remembrances but critical turning points juxtaposed with increasing frequency against the harsh realities of life under Trujillo's dictatorship. Given the recurrence of anxiety and mental breakdown in the book, the incremental revelation of the narrative, told from the perspective—and occasionally the first-person voice—of different sisters in turn, could be compared superficially to the recursive process of psychoanalysis, during which the patient is directed to peel back the layers of adult protection to discover the repressed childhood nightmares that have given rise to the illness. The crucial difference, however, is that in the case of these characters the methods of Western science fail to alleviate a mental anguish whose original injury and restorative antidote both emanate from a complex Dominican past. The first episode, an experience of violence and violation for the future writer, documents the injunction of silence that plagues her art.

The key scene to which I allude is an episode in the life of the third daughter, Yolanda. Like the author who created her, Yo (her nickname and the Spanish word for "I") is a writer, a teller of stories from childhood who "always lied like the truth is just something you make up."[9] Alvarez identifies both Yo's first muse and her own as a picture-book version of the heroic

Scheherazade, whose life is preserved rather than plagued by an inclination toward tall tales.[10] As Yo grows up, her mother seems especially concerned that the child learn the difference between fact and fiction, inflicting punishment on her child whenever Yo tells stories: "Often, I put Tabasco in that mouth hoping to burn away the lies that seemed to spring from her lips. For Yo, talking was like an exercise in what you could make up."[11] In ¡Yo!, Alvarez interrogates the full measure of what her fictional family's escape and survival has cost each of them, but especially the writer, whose inheritance from growing up in a police state has been a command to silence herself. Like the first novel, its sequel is a collection of stories, each narrated by a different character whose life has been altered by Yolanda's fictionalizing. Alvarez paints a picture of a family frustrated by the writing daughter who insists on turning all their lives into, as one sister puts it, "fictional fodder."[12] And yet, despite a childhood of punishments and a family infuriated by her revelatory fiction, Yo's adult struggles with mental breakdown and identity crisis are rooted more deeply in the political turmoil of her homeland, the fallout of that persecution in the private home, and the scars it inflicts on Yo's authorial voice.

The dark episode at the core of Yo's artistic troubles takes place prior to the family's exile. As a member of the underground resistance, Papi knows he is being watched at all times. In addition to having a secret closet where he can hide in times of extreme danger, he has also concealed an illegal gun in the floorboards of his study. Though no one in the household may enter the father's study, Yo has been allowed to play there unsupervised because she has shown such an interest in his medical books. When her father asks what she whispers to the photographs of diseased and misshapen people in the books, she tells him, "I am telling the sick people stories to make them feel better."[13] Despite the girl's childish admiration of her father's medical skill, telling her friends, "My papi can do anything!," the future writer already seeks an alternative healing in words.[14] Through this innocent urge to tell stories, Yo lets slip the inadvertent betrayal that is rehearsed multiple times in the cyclic narrative, as if to repeat this singular event is to unlock the mystery of the writer's artistic urge and anxiety at once.

Each time the third-person narrator or a García speaks the story of Yo's betrayal, its details change and its significance grows. In the first brief telling, Yo remembers that she "told their neighbor, the old general, a made-up story about Papi having a gun, a story which turned out to be true because Papi did really have a hidden gun for some reason . . . and her parents hit her very hard with a belt in the bathroom, with the shower on so no one could hear her screams."[15] Later in this version, the mother silently admits that the parents' reaction was inappropriately harsh but excuses it with the comment, "[Y]ou lose your head in this crazy hellhole, you do, and different rules apply."[16] Interestingly, in a return to the episode early on in the second book, the mother's version of the story has been purged of its unsavory center, and Yo is questioned but not punished. The scene ends with the weeping Mami explaining how she "hated being at the mercy of my own child, but in that house we were all at the mercy of her silence from that day on."[17] From this cleaned-up version in which both the betrayal and the violation have been erased, the narrative gradually moves to the close of the novel *¡Yo!*, where Carlos García, "el Doctor" and patriarch of his family, finally tells what he promises is the "undoctored truth"[18] of that terrible day:

> We took her into the bathroom and turned on the shower to drown out her cries. "Ay, Papi, Mami, no, por favor," she wailed. As my wife held her, I brought down that belt over and over, not with all my strength or I could have killed her, but with enough force to leave marks on her backside and legs. It was as if I had forgotten that she was a child, my child, and all I could think was that I had to silence our betrayer. "This should teach you a lesson," I kept saying. "You must never ever tell stories!"[19]

Through the words and the beating, the child learns that her destiny to become a writer is forbidden; the "lesson" burned into her conscious is one of the danger lurking in words. Moments before the punishment, the father describes her shocked face as the lie gradually comes to light: "It was as if she were finally realizing that a story could kill as well as cure someone."[20]

The violent conclusion to Yo's childish storytelling sheds light on the close of *How the García Girls Lost Their Accents*, in which the adult artist laments the "violation that lies at the center of [her] art."[21] As a girl, she had violated the code of silence, and in turn her artistic nature has been permanently marred. The injury done to the artist's sensibility is not simply one of a father's beating, however. That private act of abuse is the outgrowth of a public political climate in which silence is the mandate. Mami notices that her other small girls seem already to have internalized the lesson beaten into Yo: "[S]he sees with a twinge of pain that they are quickly picking up the national language of a police state: every word, every gesture, a possible mine field, watch what you say, look where you go."[22] Alvarez explains that in her actual family, even removal to the United States did little to calm her parents' fears. If the children asked any questions about the state of the Dominican Republic, her mother answered, "'En boca cerrada no entran moscas.' No flies fly into a closed mouth." Alvarez discovered only later that "this very saying had been scratched on the lintel of the entrance of the SIM's torture center at La Cuarenta."[23] For Alvarez's characters, then, silence becomes the partner of dictatorship and death. The trauma of living in an environment of unquestioned obedience, suppression of personal desire, and absolute secrecy, coupled with the father's mandate that the artist must tell no stories[24] together make up Yolanda's violation—and the specter of mental illness that figures in the first novel.

II

Hysterics suffer mainly from reminiscences.

—Breuer and Freud, *Studies on Hysteria*

How the García Girls Lost Their Accents documents two episodes of mental breakdown and hospitalization, the first in the older sister Sandi and the second in the artist, Yolanda.[25] The narratives share important characteristics in their emphasis on speech and silence and on the dangers of the written word. Thus, the fragility of these women in adulthood seems easily attributable to the traumatizing vigilance with which their words and intellects were monitored as children, and to the emotional strain inherent in learning to adapt to a foreign culture and language. At the same time, the sense of a misplaced self that plagues each sister's breakdown could be traced as readily to the types of identity crises characterizing many women's awakenings as the feminist movement gained momentum in the American 1970s. Allowing the complex factors that coalesce in the periods of illness in the novel, I wish to focus principally on the role of the "doctor" in these episodes, both the psychiatrists who treat the women and the father who stands idly by throughout. Though as a child Yo believed her Papi could "cure anything," what comes through in these narratives of mental illness is the ineffectuality of Western medicine to make whole the brokenness of the García sisters. While their cases may in many ways bear the marks of classic depression, anxiety, and psychoneurosis, the real "illness" from which these sisters suffer resists clinical diagnosis and scientific treatment.

It is nearly impossible to read the narrative of Sandi's mental breakdown and not think of the case history of "Fräulein Anna O.," Josef Breuer's famous account of his therapy sessions with Bertha Pappenheim that mark the beginnings of the psychoanalytic movement.[26] Like Anna O., Sandi refuses to eat anything prepared for her, literally starving herself. In this, she displays classic symptoms of anorexia nervosa, a contemporary diagnosis for a historically female illness. Also markedly similar to the first case, Sandi has begun to read obsessively, as if words have replaced physical nourishment. She tells her mother that "[s]he had to read all the great works of man because soon . . . she wouldn't be human."[27] Trapped in a patriarchal canon, Sandi heads her compulsory reading list not surprisingly with the father of psychoanalysis, Freud. Nietzsche and Erikson also figure in the string of great male authors whose books her mother claims are "driving her crazy."[28]

Alvarez recalls as a child hearing the same words from an aunt about a poetry-writing cousin and feeling unsettled: "I had never in the world considered that books had that kind of power. They could make a person sick."[29] It is not the books alone that afflict Sandi, however. She is also haunted by a sense that her intellect is deteriorating. Asserting that "[e]volution had reached its peak and was going backward," Sandi worries that she is "becoming a monkey," and eventually loses her ability to speak.[30] Her clinical aphasia mimics that of Anna O., whose devolving communication skills Breuer documents:

> It first became noticeable that she was at a loss to find words, and this difficulty gradually increased. . . . In the process of time she became almost completely deprived of words. She put them together laboriously out of four or five languages and became almost unintelligible.[31]

Sandi's parents choose hospitalization only when she too reaches a state of complete incoherence, "making these awful sounds like she's a zoo." [32]

In the episode of Sandi's hospital admission, her role is subordinated to the presence of the two doctors, her treating psychiatrist Dr. Tandlemann and her father, "el Doctor" García. The effect of the scene is one of miscommunications, evasions, and half-truths. While Dr. Tandlemann asks mundane, stock questions (How many siblings? Did they get along?, etc.) and even has to glance at the folder to remember the patient's name, the mother offers a subjective case history while anxiously folding and refolding a Kleenex tissue until it disintegrates into bits. The father stands passively to the side, pressing his face tighter against the window, at one point "timing the gardener's treks across the rolling lawns" as if to fix himself in the everyday.[33] Reduced from medical colleague to detached listener, Dr. García makes no effort to help with the case history or diagnosis, breaking in only twice to categorize the breakdown as "small." At the close of this scene, Sandi, outside walking the grounds with a nurse, encounters the gardener's lawn mower, experiencing it as a ferocious animal. Watched by her father, Sandi capitulates to a horror he is powerless to assuage: "The girl screamed and broke into a panicked run towards the building where her father, whom she could not see, stood at the window, waving."[34] A relentless silence closes this section, as the incoherent daughter's screams are muffled behind glass and the father's efforts at contact are equally muted. The failure of these two to speak their terrors only magnifies the disastrous effect of the childhood mandate of silence, distorting words and books—any unchecked speech at all—into a dangerous illness that isolates and dehumanizes.

What is most painfully evident in Sandi's narrative of breakdown is the ineffectual presence of the doctors, whose mundane exchange going on literally above and beyond her cannot begin to offer authentic healing. When the reader encounters Sandi in the text postdischarge, it seems that the only objects shoring up her sanity are the Kleenex tissues and antidepressants she carries in her purse, the first reminiscent of the mother's obsessive attentions, the second of the father's medical correctives. No account is given of her treatment, and she seems to have been left, much like Breuer's abruptly dismissed Anna O., to fend for herself. She reveals sadly to her sisters, "I just want to forget the past, you know?"[35] But in this statement, relinquishing not just her immediate past but the whole bittersweet past to which she might lay claim, Sandi misses the one possibility for healing that could free her from the sickness of words and make her shattered identity whole.

Like Sandi's breakdown, which begins with her "crazy diet," Yo's depression and mental instability are precipitated by a concrete event, the dissolution of her marriage. The episode is less about relationships, however, than it is about Yo's attempts to reconcile the dual languages that threaten her identity. She complains of the permutations of her very name since she has moved to the United States: "Yolanda, nicknamed *Yo* in Spanish, misunderstood *Joe* in English, doubled and pronounced like the toy, *Yoyo*—or when forced to select from a rack of personalized key chains, *Joey*."[36] Her sense of self is likewise divided into "*head*-slash-*heart*-slash-*soul*," as if to match the multiplying names. When Yo fights with her husband, he pries open her mouth with a kiss, "pushing her words back in her throat" and overpowering her with the old injunction of silence.[37] As if in response, Yo discovers that the English language of her husband has become indecipherable: "[S]he could not make out his words. They were clean, bright sounds, but they meant nothing to her."[38] Contrary to Sandi, who devolves into wordlessness, Yo develops a condition of perseveration, in which she cannot stop talking for months and months, but during which time she invents no ideas of her own. Instead, her voice becomes a stream of others' words, as she quotes and misquotes all the great writers, "drowning in the flooded streams of her consciousness."[39]

Admitted to a private facility, where her doctor can "keep an eye on her," Yo briefly places her faith in the claims of the medical world, though a visit from her parents suggests such reliance will prove futile. In a repetition of the earlier scene with Sandi, the mother talks anxiously and the father averts his eyes out a window—both powerless to restore their daughter's health. When Mami tells Yo that they love her, Papi cannot even say the words, simply adding, "There's no question at all."[40] Recalling life with her medical father, Alvarez describes a similar detachment:

> To take hold of a hand, to graze a cheek and whisper an endearment were beyond him. Tenderness had to be mothered by necessity: he was a good doctor.

Under the cover of Hippocrates' oath, with the stethoscope around his neck and the bright examination light flushing out the personal and making any interchange completely professional, he was amazingly delicate: tapping a bone as if it were the fontanelle of a baby, easing a patient back on a pillow like a lover, his sleeping beloved, stroking hair away from a feverish forehead.[41]

Despite the signs her father has given her that medicine offers only impersonal intimacy and no magical cures, Yo continues to trust in Western science. Calling her psychiatrist "Doc" "secretly for luck," Yo believes he will "save her body-slash-mind-slash-soul by taking all the slashes out, making her one whole Yolanda."[42] Like Anna O., Yo engages in a modern-day "talking cure," daily sharing all manner of personal thoughts with her doctor and even effecting a classic act of transference by falling in love with him.[43] Nevertheless, psychotherapy fails Yo. While the definitive goal in the process of psychoanalysis is to achieve a picture of "the Truth," to uncover the past exactly as it happened and transform those memories into language,[44] this is not the path to healing for the storytelling Yo, who seeks freedom to stray from truth into art.

When Yo loses faith in the power of psychotherapy to repair her "slashed" self, events in the narrative shift toward an alternative to Western medicine, a dependence on the mystical rather than medical to heal the soul. In a small step back toward her roots in a Dominican culture that embraces the corporeal/spiritual duality of life, the writer recognizes the power of words, the spells they cast, and the authority they wield over the artist. At this point, psychotherapy fails to meet Yo's quest for meaning, even as she develops a symbolic allergy to the most important words in both her tongues. Speaking "love" and "amor" aloud, Yo discovers that "[e]ven in Spanish, the word makes a rash erupt on the backs of her hands."[45] Yet she determines to build up an "immunity" to the threatening words and learn how to speak the stories that have been silenced in her.

In his essay "The Healing Word: Its Past, Present, and Future," Thomas Szasz criticizes the usefulness of any "talking cure" that dispels the mystery of words in and of themselves to hurt or heal:

Since ancient times, people have recognized that words powerfully affect the listener and that, like double-edged swords, they cut both ways. Indeed, our vocabulary possesses numerous adjectives for characterizing both types of speech acts, such as blasphemous, impious, obscene, perjurious, pornographic, profane, and sacrilegious for words deemed to be harmful; and calming, cheering, comforting, consoling, encouraging, heartening, inspiring, motivating, and reassuring for words deemed to be helpful.[46]

In her empowering "speech act," Yo conjures up a hallucinatory vision that enacts a spiritual return to wholeness as an artist, "the real Yolanda resurrecting" in the figure of a "huge, black bird" who emerges from her mouth.[47] Like Poe's black raven perched on Pallas' bust, Yo's personal muse and secret phoenix rises up, seeking out a representative of the force that has silenced its fancy. Finding the doctor sunning outside on the lawn, the bird plummets: "Beak first, a dark and secret complex, a personality disorder let loose on the world, it plunges!"[48] After the murder of Western science, Yo is set free to begin her mental healing. The episode ends far more triumphantly than Sandi's narrative, with the poet mouthing "offending" words, exulting that "[t]here is no end to what can be said about the world."[49]

III

El papel lo aguanta todo.
(Paper holds everything.)
Mami

—Alvarez, "Ten of My Writing Commandments"[50]

When Yo unleashes her dark, flying muse and embraces both her languages—Spanish and English—she repudiates the law of the father and frees herself to take up the writing profession. That she achieves such a goal is evidenced by the legions of angry friends and relatives in *¡Yo!,* who complain that the first book exposed their lives. Echoing the father's injunction to "never tell stories," they condemn Yo's lifework and her *destino*. Alvarez describes the actual difficulty she encountered in lifting the silence:

> "My mother told me never ever to repeat this story," Maxine Hong Kingston begins her memoir, *The Woman Warrior.* And those same words could have been spoken to me by any number of women and men in my family. I had transgressed an unspoken rule of la familia. By opening my mouth, I had disobeyed. By opening my mouth on paper, I had done even worse. I had broadcast my disobedience."[51]

For Alvarez's fictional manifestation Yo, personal doubts about her indecorous profession haunt her into middle age, the "violation" at the core of her artistic self. In the final section of *¡Yo!,* the daughter, again anxious and depressed about her life immersed in words, worries that she should have become a mother, followed another path. When her father suggests that it is a blessing to get to fulfill one's destiny, she asks him, "But how can I be sure this is my destino?"[52] Splitting again into halves or "should haves," the artist—Yo or Alvarez in her place—must enact a final ritual of healing that returns to the scene of injury and invents a new story.

While the painful genesis of the artist's anxiety can be traced back to the silence demanded in a police state, the curative for what ails her is likewise located outside Yo's adopted *norteamericana* culture, in the hands of a Haitian maid back in the Dominican Republic. A deceptively minor character in *How the García Girls Lost Their Accents,* Chucha has lived with the de la Torre family for over fifty years, having sought asylum at their compound on the terrible night in 1937 when Trujillo authorized the slaughter of thousands of Haitian canecutters in the Dominican Republic. Chucha's unique religious fervor replicates that of much Haitian spiritual belief in that it is a syncretism of African vodou and the conquistador Catholicism of the family she serves.[53] Unmarried and forever grateful to her guardians, she spends her free days praying in her room for "any de la Torre souls stuck up in purgatory" and insists on sleeping in a coffin to "prepare herself for dying," as in certain monastic orders.[54] Side by side with this eccentric Catholicism, Chucha "always had a voodoo job going, some spell she was casting or spirit she was courting or enemy she was punishing."[55] The other Dominican maids fear and shun the Haitian, gossiping that she "got mounted by spirits" and that "she cast spells on them." Such rumors attest to Chucha's direct connection to her gods, her role as a *hounsi,* a spirit-wife or "horse," as described by Joan Dayan:

> The language of possession, or the *crise de loa*—that moment when the god inhabits the head of his or her servitor—articulates the reciprocal abiding of human and god. The "horse" is said to be mounted and ridden by the god. The event is not a matter of domination, but a kind of double movement of attenuation and expansion. For make no mistake about it, the loa cannot appear in epiphany, cannot be made manifest on earth without the person who becomes the temporary receptacle or mount. And the possessed gives herself up to become an instrument in a social and collective drama.[56]

Despite the García family's skepticism of their maid's strange practices, Chucha's connection to the gods is directly instrumental in their protection and safe escape. When a menacing pair of *guardias* visit the house, only little Yo exhibits confidence in the maid's vodou. Dropping a fine powder as she leaves the room, Chucha mumbles under her breath, and "Yoyo knows she is casting a spell that will leave the men powerless, becalmed."[57] Not only is the Haitian spell effective in delivering the family from these thugs, it is finally Chucha's "farewell voodoo," performed hours before the García family flees the Dominican Republic, which casts the right spell to release Yo's artistic muse forever.

The youngest sister, Fifi, narrates the episode of vodou, her only memory of her previous life. Chucha speaks:

> "When I was a girl, I left my country too and never went back. Never saw fa-
> ther or mother or sisters or brothers. I brought only this along." She held the
> bundle up and finished unwrapping it from its white sheet. It was a statue
> carved out of wood. . . .
>   Chucha stood this brown figure up on Carla's vanity. He had a grimacing
> expression on his face, deep grooves by his eyes and his nose and lips, as if he
> were trying to go but was real constipated. On top of his head was a little plat-
> form, and on it, Chucha placed a small cup of water. Soon, on account of the
> heat, I guess, that water started evaporating and drops ran down the grooves
> carved in that wooden face so that the statue looked as if it were crying.
> Chucha held each of our heads in her hands and wailed a prayer over us. We
> were used to some of this strange stuff from daily contact with her, but maybe
> it was because today we could feel an ending in the air, anyhow, we all started
> to cry as if Chucha had finally released her own tears in each of us.[58]

Barak rightly notes that Chucha's "voodoo good-bye" sits at the very center of the gyre that pulls the sisters away from and back to the Island.[59] The protective ritual the old Haitian maid enacts ties the sisters forever to their Dominican roots, and the final spell she casts after them offers the antidote for whatever still haunts their memories.

When the family has gone, Chucha consults the voices of her *santos* and hears her *loa* whispering stories to her of the future. Swinging her can of "cleaning smoke" in the bedroom of the García sisters, Chucha has a vision of their new American life:

> In the girls' room I remember each one as a certain heaviness, now in my
> heart, now in my shoulders, now in my head or feet; I feel their losses pile up
> like dirt thrown on a box after it has been lowered into the earth. I see their
> future, the troublesome life ahead. They will be haunted by what they do and
> don't remember. But they have spirit in them. *They will invent what they need
> to survive.*[60]

Like her role as "horse" to her *loa*, Chucha becomes a temporary receptacle of the daughters' pain. She gives a deathlike quality to the García girls' loss, as if the exile from their homeland is a kind of spiritual burial. She prophesies the coming anxieties, breakdowns, and identity crises that will mar their journeys into adulthood. In all this, Chucha does not deny the long-term repercussions of dictatorial oppression, forced migration to a foreign country, and a life spent negotiating between the haunted past and unpredictable future. The spell that Chucha sends after the children is not a promise of protection from the inevitable but an incantation of healing to equal it. Knowing that the family spirits have already gone (she saw Carlos' *loa* leave out the back door), Chucha invokes the García girls' special voodoo god-spirits to travel with them, to give them *invention,* voices to tell stories with which these silenced daughters can re-create a livable past from words.

This mystical call to invention—originating from the same Dominican past as the edict of silence—is finally what frees the third daughter, the artist, from her anguished self-doubts and mental exhaustion. In the final episode of *¡Yo!,* the father admits his wrong and resolves to return one final time to the scene of the violation in order to reinvent the past: "I beat her. I told her that she must never ever tell stories again. And so maybe that is why she has never believed in her destiny, why I have to go back to that past and let go the belt and put my hands on her head instead. I have to tell her I was wrong. I have to lift the old injunction."[61] Calling it a "magical solution," Papi promises, like a Biblical patriarch, to give his "particular" blessing to the writing daughter. In this part, he plays as well the Afro-Caribbean role of Orúmila or the "witness of destiny, he who knows the whole of our lives."[62] In giving his particular blessing, the father, in effect, heals them both:

> I have promised her a blessing to take the doubt away. A story whose true facts cannot be changed. But I can add my own invention—that much I have learned from Yo. A new ending can be made out of what I now know.
>
> So let us go back to that moment. Let us enter that small, green-tiled bathroom. . . . I lift the belt, but then as I said, forty years pass, and my hand comes down gently on my child's graying head.
>
> And I say, "My daughter, the future has come and we were in such a rush to get here! We left everything behind and forgot so much. Ours is now an orphan family. My grandchildren and great grandchildren will not know the way back unless they have a story. Tell them our journey. Tell them the secret heart of your father and undo the old wrong. My Yo, embrace your destino. You have my blessing, pass it on."[63]

This new story of an old horror should not be read as a classic psychoanalytic catharsis.[64] Nor should the Judeo-Christian overtones of the patriarchal blessing prompt a misconstrual of the episode as a Catholic confession.[65] In prompting her father's return to the bathroom episode—the revision that ends with a blessing rather than a beating, a call to speak rather than to suppress the family's stories, the artist has summoned Chucha's decades-old invocation to invent the words that can cure the "dis-ease" of the past. The protective spell Chucha casts echoes the healing cures of the Afro-Caribbean Ifá tradition, a religious system that invests the speech act with medicinal properties. In speaking of Ifá's sacred oracles, Eugenio Matibag explains that in the Afro-Caribbean belief system, "'literature' is medicine, therapy, counsel, soothsaying, and value clarification: it gives equipment, strategies, and instructions for living."[66] This notion exactly parallels the purpose of Chucha's call to the spirits to inspire the García daughters with healing fictions rather than self-limiting truths.

The ending of *¡Yo!*, in fact, has curative powers even beyond its reparation of old wounds between the father and daughter characters. Alvarez has written of the personal value for her in receiving the rare blessing from a relative, at one time her grandfather and at another an aunt.[67] As for the father's blessing that closes her novel, she reveals in an interview:

> The father's blessing at the end is something I could give myself. We all grow beyond it, but there's a way which we all want the blessing of our *antepasados*. Especially from a Latino culture, you are a bead on a string. You don't think of yourself separately, of me and my feelings and who I really am. I'm also Alvarez and my *abuelito* and my *abuelita*. To feel that blessing coming down from the past, even though I broke the rules of what I should have been as a woman in my culture, it made me feel good—at least on paper.[68]

The ending of *¡Yo!*, then, offers a triple healing in that it first resolves the anxiety of the character Yo, naming her destino and saving her from further depression and crisis. In an equally important capacity, however, the episode allows the father, the original perpetrator of the violent silencing, a fictional forum in which to repent and return his daughter's voice to her.[69] Finally, as the revelation above suggests, these fictional blessings result in a very genuine healing for their creator, Alvarez. The daughter who "broke the rules," she literally invents her own medicine by writing down what she needs to survive.[70]

❈   ❈   ❈

The epigraph to this essay, a quote by Gloria Anzaldúa, describes the indeterminacy experienced by those who live on the nameless borderland between two cultures. Anzaldúa's words suggest that the inhabitants of that shadowy country never reconcile themselves to its duality. The novels of Julia Alvarez, on the other hand, assert that a life lived between these binary worlds—in spite of the alienation and pain it engenders—can be embraced and celebrated with words. In fact, Alvarez calls books her "portable homeland,"[71] the country to which she claims a most comfortable citizenship. She also suggests in a recent essay that blazing a trail into the borderland can be the writer's finest role:

> Sometimes I hear Spanish in English (and of course, vice versa). That's why I describe myself as a Dominican American writer. That's not just a term. I'm

mapping a country that's not on a map, and that's why I'm trying to put it down on paper.

It's a world formed of contradictions, clashes, comminglings—the gringa and the Dominican, and it is precisely that tension and richness that interests me. Being in and out of both worlds, looking at one side from the other side. . . . These unusual perspectives are often what I write about. A duality that I hope in the writing transcends itself and becomes a new consciousness, a new place on the map, a synthesizing way of looking at the world.[72]

Alvarez's fearless melding in her novels of all the dualities of her life experience—of doubled religions, languages, cultures, and consciousness—suggests that such a "new place on the map" can be traced in the world of books. If writing on the borderland creates such narratives, it assures that Alvarez's fictional double, Yo, had it right from the beginning: stories do in fact have the power to heal.

Chapter 9 ▨

The Film Cure:
Responses to Modernity
in the Cinemas of the Caribbean

Jerry W. Carlson

The Caribbean, in the memorable phrase of Martinican critic and
novelist Edouard Glissant, has experienced an *"irruption into modernity."*[1] Catapulted from colonial societies organized around plantation economies to nation-states with intricate ties to the developed world,
Caribbean countries have had to (and will continue to have to) adopt certain features of industrial and postindustrial reality. Even so, they have
sought to retain those features of their own Creole cultures that not merely
define what it means to be Caribbean but also provide ways of negotiating
with a modernity that has been as ferocious in its effects as it has been rapid
in its onslaught.[2] The arts, popular culture, and Afro-Atlantic religions play
key roles in this process of accommodation; cinema contributes by providing a potential medium (actually, multimedia) for combining the other elements while creating its own effects. Cinema links the Caribbean with
modernity both by its industrial mode of production and by its nature as a
baroque medium capable of gathering an archipelago of cultural materials.
Consider first how films are made as a product and then the variety of fiction films that offer stories of how modernity has been suffered, confronted,
absorbed, rejected, embraced, or transformed by Caribbean peoples.

To work in the film medium is to experience an industrial mode of production and its new postindustrial developments. Requiring significant in-
vestments of capital and labor, feature films are made by coordinated
teams of craft professionals working under the supervision of the director
and producer. Specialized kinds of equipment, no less than well-trained

employees, are essential. Thus, no matter how deeply dedicated to traditional culture a filmmaker may be in subject matter, she or he must have achieved a metropolitan modernity in order to tell the story in the audiovisual medium. One cannot choose, for instance, between full-scale 35 mm feature film production and highly mobile, economical digital video to tell a tale without access to and knowledge of contemporary technologies that are concentrated in metropolitan centers such as Miami, Paris, London, New York, and Mexico City.

This need to be cosmopolitan both precedes and follows the stage of production. Cuba is the sole country of the Caribbean to develop a distinguished tradition of audiovisual education. This means that most filmmakers have to go abroad for their education (of course, that can mean Cuba if you are, say, Venezuelan) and in many instances master a second or third language. The possibility of a Caribbean cinema is thus impeded by all of the difficulties that imagining, seeking, and achieving an advanced education in another country impose. Moreover, the difficulties do not end once one has an education. As an industrial art form, film requires significant capital investment and thus forces those who come from societies without those resources to explore and secure international sources of finance, whether those contacts be based in motives of profit (banks or media corporations) or in cultural development (governments or foundations). In order to complete a budget, filmmakers must engage with these metropolitan, most commonly multinational circuits.

After production, finishing a film requires a hybrid of expensive visual and auditory technologies. Again, these are located in metropolitan centers because it is here that they may be rented to as many clients as possible and thus remain profitable in relation to the high investment necessary to purchase and maintain them. Fancifully put, the great Caribbean novel might be written with a cheap ballpoint pen and several pads of paper while the author sits on the beach or overlooks a valley from a mountain hut or shivers in exile in a cheap apartment—but the Caribbean films need a darkened room full of equipment and staffed with trained assistants. No beach or hut or shared apartment will provide that. Cuba and Venezuela have had these facilities, but their relative availability and reliability depend upon capricious economic circumstances. Elsewhere when facilities have been brought to the Caribbean, as they have been for certain aspects of the recording industry, their presence is more an injection of the metropolitan than a development of the local. Given these conditions, one must recognize that the ambition to chronicle Caribbean life on film is a struggle *within* modernity to portray a struggle *with* modernity.

Why, then, make a film? The extraordinary social, economic, and technological difficulties would certainly seem to argue against it. After all, the novels of Alejo Carpentier, the canvases of Wilfredo Lam, or the recordings of Celia Cruz render a rich Caribbean without the material burden demanded by the audiovisual medium. The answer lies within their works (and those of countless other artists). One characteristic of Caribbean artists is their reach for multimedia expression within a single medium. Hence, we *read* Carpentier, among other things, to *hear* his references to music; we *look* at a scene by Lam to *imagine* the movement between the human and spirit worlds; and we *listen* to Celia Cruz to *feel* the movement of Caribbean dance as it inhabits the body for secular or religious celebration. Film promises to provide an experience that can embody and braid together these multiple forms of expressive culture. This is significant not only to portray Caribbean culture to its own public but also to suggest its intricacies of experience to audiences that know it, if they think about it at all, from the packaged reductions offered by streamlined tourist culture.

The Caribbean shares this need for self-representation with other cultures that exist at the margin of our audiovisual imagination. What makes the issue especially charged for the Caribbean is the fact that as a cultural zone it has contributed most profoundly to world culture by its cultural mixture and its ongoing capacity to mix and remix. In this sense, Caribbeanness is an example of process without end, process with fruitful production but without a terminating product. At its best, film offers the chance to construct this process, the discourse worlds, the experienced cultures of the Caribbean, through the specific qualities of light, color, texture, movement, rhythm, dialect, sound, music, place, character, and story. The well-known preference of Caribbean artists for baroque styles finds its greatest promise for fulfillment (if perhaps not its greatest accomplishments thus far) in the multiple codes of cinema.[3] The extent to which there is already a significant body of films that deal with the Caribbean experience of modernity in a probing, accomplished way remains largely unrecognized.[4] The remainder of this essay outlines the main concerns of those films and the variety of stylistic and narrative strategies that they engage.

There are four general groupings of films based upon the aspects of modernity that they portray and how they address the narrative of healing the cultural fissures created by history in the Caribbean. In the first, the task is recovering the past, showing histories that have been forgotten, neglected, or suppressed. Dedicated to resisting cultural amnesia or obfuscation, these are histories that challenge a unified official history passed down by colonial or neocolonial mandate and reclaim the narrative agency for the formerly colonized. How, after all, can one understand the present if there is no accurate view of the past? In the second grouping, the issue is chronicling the passage from isolated communities to modern urban societies without losing the human values associated with community life. How was the change experienced? What does it mean? How does one tally a before and an after when neither nostalgia for the past nor uncritical acceptance of the present can be embraced? In the third grouping, the conditions of the present are the object of investigation. What are the special qualities of Caribbean modernity? What makes up—and can help us heal from—a tropical season of discontent? How can one live today? The final grouping pushes those questions into the diaspora. What happens to Caribbean identity as it experiences modernity in Paris, Miami, London, or New York? How can one find a balance between absorption of the other and assertion of the self? Taken together, these issues and questions animate a body of diverse works that share investigative aims and, equally important, reject the common protocols of commercial cinema as inappropriate—indeed, inapplicable—to their task.

This textual diversity can be studied adequately only if the questions about it are themselves multiple. What specific aspects of the Caribbean modernity do individual films address? What stories do they choose to tell? How do they select and arrange characters and events as plots? Who tells them and in what mode? And what resources of cinematic style are most important to the aims of the films? How do sound, editing, cinematography, and mise en scène (acting, costume, and setting) contribute to a construction of the Caribbean?

Among the films that reconstruct the Caribbean past, *Oriana* (France/Venezuela, 1985), directed by Fina Torres, holds a special place not only because it was honored with the Camera d'Or award at the Cannes Film Festival and therefore received wide distribution in Latin America and Europe, but also because it tells a story of Caribbean women from the point of view of a Caribbean woman.[5] Inspired by a short story by the Colombian writer Marvel Moreno, the film takes as its premise the idea that the past of the Plantation—the founding social structure of Caribbean society once Europeans arrived—has been lost as a cultural memory to many who live in cities. This is not a nostalgic view, especially when it comes from a society such as Venezuela, which has experienced the most rapid and profound displacement of peoples from the countryside to the city (Caracas) of any country in the Caribbean. It is a quest to link past and present, an act that is the necessary first step in understanding what the present truly is.

Oriana actually begins at a further distance. Marie, a woman roughly forty years old living in France, receives a telephone call informing her that she has inherited a country home from her aunt Oriana, who remained unwed at the hacienda of the family's plantation while her other siblings moved to the city. Upon arriving with her French husband at the house by the Caribbean, Marie begins an initially involuntary journey into the past. In a Proustian manner, images, objects, and sounds trigger memories of her initial trip there during her first summer of adolescence. The film moves by slow disclosure of the past. While the narration remains focalized through Marie, it shifts in its mode of focalization. At times, the memories are involuntary; at others, voluntary; and at still others, conditional. These last are hypotheses about what could have happened in the past but cannot be proved by evidential argumentation. Marie's reconstruction of the past has two objects: remembering what happened to her that summer and linking that story to what she discovered about the early life of Oriana. Each influences the other. It was an important summer for Marie because it marked her sexual awakening. Bored by the pace of country life but animated by her body's changes, she begins to look for a story about Oriana that will feed her new erotic curiosity. Her aunt has counted on this because she has a tale that she wants passed down and preserved but kept—at least for the moment—outside the official family record.

What Marie discovers is a story that outlines the conditions of women in the era of plantations. Oriana is raised under patriarchal control in genteel isolation at the hacienda, where her best companion is Sergio, a boy brought home by her father after a tour of his property. As Oriana matures, so does her love for Sergio. Although everyone knows that Sergio is her half brother—the product of her father's liaison with a woman of color—Oriana refuses to obey the incest taboo because she knows that Sergio cannot be included officially in her family history. To her, the hypocrisy of the system permits Sergio to stand apart from the family and frees her to love him. Her father, needless to say, does not share this interpretation. The father kills Sergio; Oriana poisons the father; and the family covers up the crimes by keeping Oriana at the hacienda where she can raise her son by Sergio. Oriana's double strategy is, first, to let the adolescent Marie discover the true family history, and, second, to draw the adult Marie back to the hacienda where she can rediscover the truth and distribute the family property in an equitable manner. She succeeds. Marie relinquishes the plantation to Sergio's son, who may have been her own first lover. As a film, *Oriana* is as important for the way it suggests the psychological struggles of recovering suppressed history as it is for revealing truths about how Venezuela became a nation of "café con leche" people. This "recovery"—a term associated just as closely with repossession (property) and recovery (health)—leads to personal fulfillment and social justice.

While *Oriana* takes a family chronicle as an emblem of Caribbean history, *Barroco* (Mexico/Cuba/Spain, 1990), directed by Paul Leduc, intends to do no less than tell five hundred years of Latin American and Caribbean history in two hours and do so without the benefit of dialogue. Derived from the novel *Concierto Barroco* by Alejo Carpentier and partaking of multiple, overlapping organizing principles, the film begins in all its complexity from the simple question posed by one of the songs repeated in multiple variations and styles throughout the film. It is Miguel Matamoros' "De dónde son los cantantes?" ("Where Do the Singers Come From?"). From everywhere, the film answers in many styles and voices. What Roberto González Echevarría observes about the novel is no less true about the film. The title is a "contradictio in adjecto, for the idea of harmony implied by 'concert' is undermined by that disorder and heterogeneity suggested by 'baroque.'" The film itself is presented as a baroque concert, "the indeterminate fusion of European, American, classical, and popular elements, as well as instruments of the most varied origins, to produce a new music, a new conglomerate in which there is no synthesis. The heterogeneous, the amalgam is also an abandonment of the notion of origins, to which none of the sundry elements need remain faithful; instead it is in itself an origin, a new beginning—it is already the future contained in the beginning."[6]

The concerto structure contains within it several other organizing principles. The broadest of them is the ambition to give a survey of key trends in the history of the Americas (especially the Caribbean) since the encounter of 1492. To be complete, the film must cover five hundred years. Also, the film traces a more modest journey in space. A Creole gentleman with strongly indigenous features sets out from Mexico and travels across the Caribbean and the Atlantic to Spain on a voyage of discovery about origins and relations. The journey and the film cannot be complete until he returns home again. The room in which the Creole is first seen contemplating his upcoming journey is a model of baroque space that will be duplicated in various forms throughout the film. Filled with mirrors and with a maze of objects of different colors and textures, materials and shapes, the room seems enclosed and infinite. Each major section of the film also sports a carnivalesque concert within the concert structure itself. Each of these illustrates the syncretic features of musical styles born of different cultures and mixed in the New World. Moreover, these parties, which take place over the span of five centuries, maintain the same guest list. Personages that are constant across the film appear as different characters in different fiestas.

To suggest that history is made by many forces, many of whose origins will remain unknown, the film denies unified psychology to its characters and imbues them instead with multiple historical functions. Thus the European is in one epoch an amazed explorer, in another an exploitative slave owner, and finally a happy tourist at the Tropicana nightclub. By the same principle, the film uses blocks of narrative to form tableaux that portray historically representative events. Sailors spy mermaids when they first sail the mangroves of the New World; slaves plot rebellion and maintain African traditions in the basement of a merchant's warehouse; a Creole sings of his desire for a nation; or a Latin American woman is killed fighting against Franco in the Spanish Civil War. History here is both profoundly discontinuous and overlapping. Generous in visual and musical detail, the film's narrational patterning refuses to draw lines linking the actions of individual characters. By constructing a compelling narrative world of multiplicity, irregularity, and flamboyance, the film suggests a baroque historiography that challenges univocal versions of Caribbean history; it is an antidote to the damage created by a narrative of history that dispossessed those marginal to the centers of power and different from the "norm" of colonial whiteness.

Oriana and *Barroco* may differ greatly in style, narrative, and historiographic assumptions, but they share the concern of finding new ways to understand the past of the Caribbean, a knowledge that can become the surest path to the healing from colonial wounds. A host of other films contributes to the quest. Although produced by Americans and directed by an Italian, *Burn!* (USA/Italy, 1969), directed by Gillo Pontecorvo, chronicles a fictitious slave revolt and offers a structural analysis of how colonial powers manipulated and controlled Creole rebels. The Cuban cinema is unusually rich in interpretations of the Caribbean past. The films of Sergio Giral, for example, explore issues of race in different historical epochs. In *The Other Francisco* (1975), two versions of slave history—liberal romantic and Marxist—are applied to the same story. In *Maria Antonia* (1991) the fate of a working-class woman who refuses to compromise with the standards of her community is seen from the perspective of Santería, the Afro-Cuban religion. How women have contributed to Cuban history is the subject of *Lucia* (1969), directed by Humberto Solas; the stories of three women in different historical epochs are presented in three different styles. *La Bella del Alhambra* (1990), directed by Enrique Pineda Barnet, uses shifting styles in the popular arts to offer an allegory of Cuban political history in the 1920s and 1930s. In Venezuela, several important films have explored the relations between the land itself and the idea that it must be tamed to enter history. *Jerico* (1988), directed by Luis Alberto Lamata, chronicles the defection of a sixteenth-century Catholic priest to the life of the indigenous peoples. *Rio Negro* (1990), directed by Atahualpa Lichy, exposes the exploitation of natural resources in the name of historical progress. *Orinoco—Nuevo Mundo* (1986), directed by Diego Risquez, explores the issue of who determines what history is by staging sequences as envisioned differently by Europeans and indigenous peoples. From the French-speaking Caribbean, *West Indies* (France, 1979), directed by Med Hondo and based on a play by Daniel Boukman, tackles the issue of ongoing black resistance to slavery and oppression. *L'Homme sur les quais/ Man by the Shore* (France/Canada, 1993), directed by Raoul Peck, shows how the memories of a young girl are forever affected by visions of torture inflicted by Duvalier's secret police in Haiti. Felix de Rooy from Curaçao, has made two films that strive to offer the historical experience of Dutch Caribbean culture: *Almacita* (1986) draws from oral traditions of folktales, while *Ava & Gabriel* (1990) explores the effects a visiting black painter has on a small colonial society in the 1940s.

All of these films interrogate the relations between the past and the present, signaling the healing possibilities of the process of recovering the historical past. Others emphasize the transition from the earlier ways of life to modernity. Perhaps the most famous of these works is *Rue cases negres/Sugar Cane Alley* (France, 1983), directed by Euzhan Palcy and adapted from the classic novel by Joseph Zobel. Both novel and film tell how the narrator, a boy from the *kreyol*-speaking laborers' compound of a sugarcane plantation, comes to be someone who can narrate his story in the form of a novel written in French. It is a specific variation upon the narrative pattern of coming-of-age stories. The protagonist must journey to new domains and gain expertise there. But he does not do so to conquer and remain in that world, as is typical of characters in Balzac or Flaubert. Instead, he wishes to use his new position as a means of returning to his own people and explaining their own conditions to them and to others who disparage or misunderstand them.

Rue cases negres is structured by the forces that impede the progress of José to gain an education. The most obvious of these is simply poverty. José is an orphan and depends upon the labor of his grandmother in the fields to support them both. The temptation is constant for him to join her there, but she insists that he remain apart. She knows that the step forward to agricultural work is a step backward to no future. Other characters provide false models or counsel. A woman who promises to provide José with lunch wishes to use him as free labor. The steward of the daily boat to Fort-de-France dresses in chic clothes, speaks of fashions in France, and dreams of being a movie star, but José is cautious, as his friend is illiterate and needs tutoring from the boy. The starkest contrast with José is a mulatto school friend, the child of a happy liaison between a Frenchman and a black Martinican woman. Once the father dies in an accident without legally recognizing his son, the boy loses his status in the closed colonial society. He descends to criminality as José ascends through the educational system. Even José's progress to higher academic achievements is marked in the film by signs of how few pupils will earn that privilege, how many will be left behind with few prospects. Yet all is not negative in the film. Apart from the shrewd analysis of the colonial system that José's grandmother makes, he benefits also from his association with an old man in the workers' compound, the last among them to have a memory of people who came from Africa. One of the most powerful scenes in the film returns the audience to the past through his reenactment of ritualized oral storytelling. Skillfully using torches and the fire-lit faces of the innocent children of the small community, the character Medouze marks the path of the return to Guinée and communion with the ancestral spirits. The lesson helps José reconcile himself with death and passing—both that of Medouze himself and of his own grandmother, whose dead body is prepared in the ancestral way for the soul's return to Guinée. On a more pragmatic level, Medouze's message of the possibilities of reconciling modernity with the ancestral ways motivates José to acquire the literate skills that will allow him to preserve at least partially the traditions that the man carries.

The impediments to José's development are made more credible by the film's attention to mise en scène. This is more than an accurate duplication of the material conditions of Martinique in the first half of the twentieth century. Settings and costumes must be read carefully. The workers' compound reveals poverty, but it can also be transformed by children into a magic kingdom. A beautiful colonial home is also a temptation to shallow fantasies of wealth and consumerism. And a deserted shack at the city's edge can be a home where education flourishes. *Rue cases negres* closes as José prepares to venture beyond Martinique to France. Without sentimentality, the film asserts that the greatest privilege of those from the margins who master modernity is to return anew to worlds and traditions that perhaps only they can save.

Destroying rather than saving is the subject of *Un Señor muy viejo con unas alas enormes/A Very Old Man with Enormous Wings* (Cuba, 1988), directed by Fernando Birri and based on a story by Gabriel García Márquez. Eschewing psychology for broad social satire, the film follows the life of a family as they care for a strange creature whom they find in the sea one night during a storm. The film's semantic game never confirms that the creature is an angel; rather the film develops around how different parties interpret and exploit what they think he is. The film follows both the fortunes of the family that finds him and the broader response of the community.

On the night that they find the creature, the family seems to have reached a low point. Desperately poor, they are threatened by a terrible storm and invading crabs. The arrival of the creature turns their fortunes. It pushes forward their material well-being, but inspires no sense of genuine awe. Their most profound discovery is that there are ways to make money using the creature. As their schemes grow, so do their desires for consumer goods. We see their world transformed from poverty to nouveau riche luxury. Their shack becomes a mansion equipped with the latest gadgetry. By the end of the narrative, they have even lost interest in the creature whose arrival marked the change of their lives. Only their small son seems to have inherited a measure of unworldly powers. Before the creature flies away, the boy hovers off the ground for him.

What the family suggests, the community proves. No one is capable of responding to the creature in a sincerely spiritual fashion. Many claim to have a religious interest but demonstrate only concerns for themselves. The local priest develops a grudge against the creature because he sees him as a rival. As an atmosphere of carnival develops around the area where the creature is displayed, a sleazy carnival act pulls into town. The film measures the depravity of rapid modernization by showing that the town's people can no longer distinguish between the genuine questions raised by the presence of the creature and the antics of the cheap carnival. They too lose interest in a visitor who has stayed too long.

The film not only portrays a carnival but is itself carnivalesque in style. Unconcerned with individualized psychology, the film sees its characters (apart from the creature) as objects of ridicule. An old woman is the Gossip. The priest is the Hypocrite. These character types, among others, are offered in quick scenes of dialogue or are pictured in long shots as part of the on-going festivities that surround the creature's presence. The creature retains his dignity and mystery by remaining silent. At the film's end, only he escapes from the banalities of modernity by flying away, and only the boy may follow someday.

A relatively small group of other films consider the difficulties of traveling from traditional societies into modernity. Winner of a major prize at the Cannes Film Festival in 1959, *Araya* (Venezuela), directed by Margot Benacerraf, documents the life of two families who work in the salt industry on the northeastern coast of Venezuela. Little has changed since the Spanish first began exploiting the region in the sixteenth century. Here, sadly, is an outpost not yet touched by modernity. *Cumbite* (Cuba, 1964), directed by Tomás Gutiérrez Alea, and adapted from the Haitian novel *Les Governeurs de la rosee/Masters of the Dew* by Jacques Romain, shows how peasants respond ferociously to the return to their village of a man who wishes to bring modern methods of agriculture. *The Harder They Come* (Jamaica, 1972), directed by Perry Henzell, blends a now-classic reggae score with a story of a young man from the country corrupted by the city. *La gran fiesta/The Big Party* (Puerto Rico, 1985), directed by Marcos Zurinaga, pictures a crucial moment in World War II in which Puerto Rico had to make clear its allegiance to the United States rather than to Spain, tilting an entire younger generation toward the mainland and North American modernity. Similarly, *Hello Hemingway* (Cuba, 1991), directed by Fernando Pérez, examines the trials of a young working-class girl in the 1950s who wishes to go to the United States to study.

It should come as no surprise that the dominance of Cuba in Caribbean filmmaking includes a claim to the best film about the dis-ease or contradictions of living in modernity: *Memorias del subdesarrollo/Memories of Underdevelopment* (Cuba, 1968), directed by Tomás Gutiérrez Alea and adapted from a novel by Edmundo Desnoes.[7] Sergio, the film's bourgeois intellectual protagonist, who is surveying postrevolutionary Cuba, suffers a collapse of faith in his life and class but finds no way to attach himself to the history being made in his midst. In fact, Sergio's agenda is vague: simply observing what new form of modernity the revolution will create. Sergio first appears in the film as he delivers his parents and wife to the airport so that they may fly to exile in Miami. Once settled again in his penthouse apartment, his one concrete goal is seducing a young woman who could replace his departed wife's sexual and social functions. The primary audience for his observation about his circumstances is himself, and as the film progresses he loses what other potential listeners he had. Yet, as this occurs, other narrators created by the historical transformations of the Cuban revolution multiply. History and its voices are everywhere: on the street among the people, in radio, television, and film, in newspapers, books, and magazines, and in the speeches of Presidents Kennedy and Castro. Here, as elsewhere in the film, a collage aesthetic expresses the collective nature of making and experiencing modernity, a nature that Sergio can never fully experience from the solipsistic isolation of his penthouse apartment. This isolation also alienates him from the strategies for adaptation that signal the resilience and esprit of the Cuban national character.

Sergio is an unusual protagonist for a revolutionary film precisely because he embodies no revolutionary values. But he is a fine protagonist for a film that wishes to dramatize the difficulties of living within a minefield of conflicting claims as to what constitutes a proper modernity for the Caribbean. A son of the bourgeoisie and the former owner of a department store, he is an outsider looking in, not a participant, much less a paragon, in revolutionary Cuba. Still, much of the film privileges him as the center of interest, a person who embodies negative traits but who can never be treated as only an example, as evidence merely illustrating a thesis. The film creates this interest in Sergio by means of narration, style, and narrative structure. His voice narrates much of the film, thus positioning him by sheer proportion of presence. In addition, his narration demonstrates that he is witty, knowledgeable, intelligent, self-reflective, and trenchant in his analysis of the past, if perplexed by the present. The camera frequently allies itself with his experience, giving us optical shots from his point of view or following him as he wanders the streets or engages with women. The spectator spends much time in Sergio's experiential field. Most important, however, is the fact that the plot is structured by a series of encounters between Sergio and friends or lovers, meetings that paint a broad portrait of Caribbean modernity and a damning portrait of Sergio. The principle of selection that rules the episodes is subtraction. Sergio's chances to engage in his society, to find a place for himself in modernity, to recover the vital ties to his nation and culture, are subtracted from possibility, character by character, aspect by aspect. As Cuba prepares to defend itself against a possible American invasion in October 1962, Sergio sits in his apartment alone, paralyzed by conflicting demands. Neither revolutionary nor counterrevolutionary, unable to find connections between past and present, incapable of reconciling the stresses between modern and ancestral ways, he experiences the nothingness that he fears is at the heart of modernity.

Even more skeptical about the possibilities of Caribbean modernity is *El Camino de las hormigas/ The Track of the Ants* (Venezuela, 1993), directed by Rafael Marziano Tinoco. Taking the city of Caracas itself rather than an individual as its protagonist, the film fits in the genre of city symphonies made popular in the 1920s by Walter Rutmann's *Berlin: Symphony of a Great City* and Dziga Vertov's *Man with a Movie Camera.* However, those films were products of the Machine Age, not merely positive but positivist in outlook. The new film envisions Caracas not as a machine but as a kaleidoscope of experiences for which no mode of representation is adequate. It is not one story; it is too many stories, too many experiences. What holds the film together is the structure of observing one day, following the circadian cycle. To explain as much as possible about the city within that framework, the film adopts multiple styles. Entering the minds of multiple drivers who are stuck in Caracas' traffic jams, the spectator hears their internal monologues. Shifting to the visual, the spectator sees signboards and vendors pass in slow motion like canvases seen through a car window. Later, a camera records all of the social and criminal activities in a plaza over a single night. At other moments, the experience of the city is suggested by rhythmic cutting or by visual analogy. A lone tractor moves in to clear a path in the jungle. Over Caracas, a single corporate jet cuts through a landscape of skyscrapers. Questions become more and more prominent: Where is the Caribbean in this? Has it been obliterated by modernity? Are only the faces different from Shanghai or São Paulo? Finally, in bits of sound, in snatches of speech, in textures of light, and in the faces that can be found, the Caribbean peeks through the concrete and mirrored glass, emerging—as it does in *Memories of Underdevelopment*—as a space of adaptability and possibility, a space where ancestral ways can coexist with the drives of modernity.

If *El Camino* is an urgent cry from the end of the millennium, it is encouraging to know that Caribbean filmmakers have been chronicling the processes of urban modernity for forty years. From the neorealism of *Caín Adolescente* (1959) to the outrageous expressionism of *Pandemonium* (1997), the cinema of Venezuelan director Roman Chalbaud has always interrogated the seismic changes in Caracas. Perhaps his most famous film is *El Pez que fuma/ The Fish That Smokes* (1977), in which a brothel on the outskirts of the city becomes a rich metaphor for the entire process of modernization. Two later Venezuelan works deal with the changes in social and ethical culture wrought by rapid urbanization that fails to meet its promises. *Macu, la mujer de la policía/Macu, the Policeman's Wife* (1987), directed by Solveig Hoogesteijn, uses a murder investigation to show the texture of an urban neighborhood. *Disparen a matar/Shoot to Kill* (1990), directed by Carlos Azpurua, takes on the touchy issue of police corruption and shows its relations to various levels of political and economic power. In *Latino Bar* (Venezuela, 1991), Paul Leduc applies his narrative method of visual tableaux, music, and sound without dialogue to show how migrant urban workers live in the bars and brothels of the waterfront. Several films by the Puerto Rican director Jacobo Morales take a gentler, more comic, though no less tough-minded look at what has been lost and gained as San Juan comes to be more and more like the mainland. *Lo que le pasó a Santiago/What Happened to Santiago* (1989) chronicles the discontents of a retired white-collar worker who seeks comfort in the fantasy world of a mysterious younger woman; *Linda Sara* (1994) explores how a selfish aristocratic family finds itself bankrupt and without a place in contemporary Puerto Rico. Two films by the Cuban Fernando Pérez might be called updates of *Memorias del subdesarrollo*. *Madagascar* (1994) examines generational tensions during the severe economic crisis in Cuba in the 1990s between those who came of age during the revolution and their children who were born into it; *La Vida es silbar/Life Is Whistling* (1998) asks how anyone could find satisfaction in today's Cuba. Responses from Cubans outside the island to the collapse of Cuban utopian dreams are unequivocal in their criticism of the form of modernity claimed by the revolution. *Azúcar amarga/Bitter Sugar* (USA, 1996), directed by León Ichaso, catalogues schematically but truthfully the conditions of Cuban austerity today; *8-A* (USA, 1993), directed by Leal Jiménez Orlando, investigates the trial of Cuban general Arnaldo Ochoa Sánchez, a high-ranking military officer who was executed in 1989 for betraying his office. In the French-speaking Caribbean, Christina Lara has created a trilogy of films about local political history: *Coco, la fleur candidat/Coco, the Flower Candidate* (1978), *Mamito* (1980), and *Vivre libre ou mourir/Live Free or Die* (1980).

One specific feature of modern Caribbean life—emigration—has created a separate grouping of films, made by Caribbean peoples to represent their experiences of diaspora. A pioneering work in this tradition is *El Super* (USA, 1979), jointly directed by León Ichaso and Orlando Jiménez Leal, and based on a play by Ivan Acosta. The story unfolds as a forty-two-year-old Cuban immigrant, who has spent his last ten years as the superintendent of a building in a Spanish-speaking neighborhood of upper Broadway in Manhattan, decides that he must move his family to Miami. Caught in a blizzard, he believes that he is trapped in hell, an image underlined for him by the furnace that he must stoke. Primed to make the decision, he suffers several intense days of conflict with family, friends, tenants, city officials, and the weather itself. While the conflicts force him to make a decision, they inform the spectators about the complex of pressures that distinguish the experiences of an involuntary exile from those of a citizen.

His first barrier, of course, is language. The film maps tensions that arise because "el super" never intended to learn English. He feels surrounded by walls of linguistic difference. The first threat of the morning is radio or television in English, which he and his wife Aurelia consider an invasion of their domesticity. It is not an opinion held by their daughter, who will soon graduate from an English-speaking high school. There is then the daily possibility that he must negotiate with officials in English, a prospect only more frightening than it is unpleasant. Finally, there is the fact that not all Spanish speakers in the city speak Cuban Spanish. He remains uncomfortable without his mother tongue, the ground of his identity.

Space represents another barrier. At times, he claims to dislike his family's living arrangements, but he still prefers staying at home far more than suffering the cold or exploring the city. At home he can try to re-create and control a Cuba that has been lost. The film's visual scheme emphasizes that he tries to burrow himself into an artificial Cuba to avoid being assaulted by the tenants' demands and by his daughter's Americanization. The film alternates these interior scenes with shots of him on the snow-packed streets. The color design of the cinematography paints the city in blues and grays, never allowing the snow to be beautiful, always bringing the color temperature down as low as possible.

In addition to his fears about language and space, el Super suffers from living in suspended time. He is beginning to doubt his dream of returning to Cuba and knows that his friend Pancho's obsession with military operations against Castro is a bad combination of bravura and delusion. A quarter of his life has passed just in waiting. His decision to go to Miami announces that he wants to reenter, in one way or another, a temporal matrix that has alternative futures, some of which may not be in Cuba itself. This healing matrix takes into account the possibility of finding a space for healing without denying the trauma of historical rupture, and this leads to the climactic irony of the going-away party that he and his wife give. Here they re-create through food, music, dance, and the presence of friends the sense of community that they lost by going into exile, signaling the possibility of partial recovery. Miami will be a second exile creating its own forms of adjustment and its own forms of nostalgia, but it will make possible the reconnection to a larger community so vital to his process of healing. They must now consider that the ten years in New York were more than suspended time, because it can never be suspended. It was part of their lifetime, a time of healing.

If el Super, his wife, and his Cuban friends suffer from an overwhelming nostalgia that they cannot diminish, it is another issue for their children, who suffer the wounds of exile in profoundly different ways and must develop restorative modalities appropriate to their own circumstances. This issue of recovering a heritage that has been lost or rejected in transit receives a rich, comic treatment in *I Like It Like That* (USA, 1994), directed by Darnell Martin. The film's two protagonists, Chino and Lisette Linares, are a very young married couple of Hispanic descent who have too many children and too few prospects. What is surprising about the film is not so much its choice of characters, although working-class Latinos who are not gang members are a rare presence in American cinema, but its treatment of their struggles in a comic mode rather than in a tragic or sociological one, demonstrating, in the process, that laughter is perhaps the best medicine.

Immature, undereducated, underpaid, and overextended, they nonetheless bring an enormous exuberance to their lives. Initially, it is without useful direction. Chino measures his success by the duration of his lovemaking with Lisette. She, in turn, begins essentially without goals. Once Chino is jailed on minor charges, she must find a way to support her children. The remainder of the film portrays them developing goals that will serve themselves and their children better. Lisette strikes out into the music business, where she finds a job as an assistant. There she discovers new confidence but also new forms of sexism. Her boss does not understand why she minds that he answers the telephone while they are having sex. Once released from jail, Chino must find a new job, fend off the advances of a young neighborhood woman who proclaims that she is bearing his child, and learn to accept the changes in Lisette that her new experiences have promoted. The film ends with a tentative reconciliation that may lead to other steps.

How is that outcome possible? The answer lies in the film's representation of the Caribbean culture that infuses their lives. They may not know it, but they live against a background of a *new urban baroque*. While the film's narrational system keeps an ironic eye on Chino and Lisette, it also shows the spectator a city where new hybrid forms of experience can issue from the humblest of materials. Three features of cinematic style contribute, above others, to this image of the city. Extended, sweeping camera movements suggest a vitality that lies in the social process of the streets. The editing fragments, reveals, and reassembles spaces that would be first considered of no interest, markers of nothing more than urban poverty. This is closely linked to the film's uses of music for commentary and celebration. Lisette, for instance, isolates herself in the bathroom trying to think her way through to new options as she listens to Celia Cruz. The film's theme music—"I Like It Like That," performed by Tito Nieves—sets a tone of comic festivity even as it questions what "it" is. Chino and Lisette benefit from the resources of a cultural heritage that they understand only slightly better at film's end than at its beginning. But that does not mean that a spectator cannot know what they only intuit.

I Like It Like That is a recent example of a tradition that reaches back over twenty years. In two films Trinidadian director Horace Ove deals with West Indians in the United Kingdom: *Pressure* (UK, 1976), written by Samuel Selvon, has been compared to Spike Lee's *Do the Right Thing; Playing Away* (UK, 1986), written by Vijay Amarnani and Caryl Phillips, pits country villagers against West Indian immigrants in London in a cricket match that reveals the fears and foibles of both cultures. The Latin music cultures of New York regulate the beat of three films about "making it" in the city. *Crossover Dreams* (USA, 1985), directed by León Ichaso, explores the balance of assimilation and cultural compromise as a singer tries to move beyond the circuit of New York salsa clubs. *Hangin' with the Homeboys* (USA, 1991), directed by Joséph B. Vasquez, explores a night on the town with four young men who think leaving the Bronx is tantamount to emigrating. *Nueba Yol* (USA/Dominican Republic, 1995), directed by Angel Muñiz, gives a seriocomic look at the massive migration of Dominicans to upper Manhattan.

In addition to these works of controlled creativity by artists of Caribbean descent, there is now a substantial body of films from the 1990s that portray the Caribbean diaspora from numerous perspectives and have artists of Caribbean heritage as important components of their creative teams. While the accomplishment of these works is far from even, it would be a mistake to dismiss them out of hand. Above all else, they raise the issue of how texts may be hybrid in their voices and claims to artistic authority—testimony, in the process, to an adaptability and creativity deeply connected to forms of understanding culture, community, and the narrative of history which these films portray as vital elements of Caribbean healing and recovering practices. Among interesting examples are *Q & A* (1990), directed by Sidney Lumet and based on a novel by Puerto Rican writer and New York Supreme Court justice Edwin Torres; *The Mambo Kings* (1992), directed by Arne Glimcher and based on the Pulitzer Prize winning novel by Oscar Hijuelos; and *The Perez Family* (1995), directed by Mira Nair and scored musically by Arturo Sandoval. Even if one dismisses all of these films as betrayals of better motives or forms of communication, their very existence attests to the imaginative hold that the Caribbean experience has over those who wish to make movies, those who wish to offer the "film cure."

Chapter 10 ▨

The End of the Line: Africa, Death, and Freedom in Caribbean Cinema

Ernesto R. Acevedo-Muñoz

Comparisons between different traditions of "Third Cinema"—that predominantly political cinema, thought to be proper to Third World contexts, committed to offering an alternative to the dominant cinemas of Hollywood and western Europe—are often approached from a limited number of perspectives. Latin American, Caribbean, and African cinemas are more often than not discussed in the context of their shared colonial/historical background, their political content, and conditions of underdevelopment in terms of industry, distribution, and markets. There is, however, an even closer and more vital link among these traditions of filmmaking: common narrative themes and a sensitivity toward representations of magic, life, and death.[1]

In the Caribbean, the African cultural legacy combined with the native and European heritages to create a kind of regional cultural supersyncretism, which, in art forms such as cinema and literature, led to the fusion of Africa and the Caribbean as self-completing parts of a single cycle of life. For example, the trauma of the African diaspora in Caribbean cultures often takes the shape of a travel narrative in which the protagonist is displaced from her/his roots into a foreign land to experience exploitation, cultural assimilation, and eventually death. The Caribbean experience serves as a transitional stage between "life" and "death," the ultimate liberation from physical, psychological, and emotional pain. In African movies such as Ousmane Sembène's *La Noire de . . .* (*Black Girl*, Senegal 1966) and Caribbean films like Euzhan Palcy's *Rue cases negres* (*Sugar Cane Alley,* Martinique

1984), Tomás Gutiérrez Alea's *La última cena* (*The Last Supper*, Cuba 1976), and Haile Gerima's *Sankofa* (Jamaica 1993), Africa functions as the mythical place of origin and liberation, the road to which is represented by the death of the physical body, which in turn leads to the unmistakable healing of the soul. Cultural practices portrayed in these films (oral storytelling, the use of ceremonial masks and other amulets and fetishes, traditional medicine, magic spells, zoomorphism) serve as progressive stages that prepare the displaced physical body (always in pain, aging, ailing, and/or confined) for the final experience of the soul's liberating mythical return to Africa.

❖   ❖   ❖

I would like to start by distinguishing the use of the term "Caribbean," not in the context of a geopolitical/societal space, but rather as a "sensitivity": in these movies the Caribbean is more a way of thinking than a region drawn on a map or the ground lying under a national banner. I prefer to use the term "Caribbean" in a rather inclusive sense: in the spirit of Antonio Benítez Rojo's *The Repeating Island*, in which the Caribbean region includes not just the islands of the Antillean archipelago but also the terra firma of the Caribbean basin, including Panama and Yucatán, the northern South American coast, and the points of dynamic Caribbean cultural activity of the south and the east coast of the United States: New Orleans' French Quarter, Miami's "Little Havana," and New York's barrios. The Caribbean is a dynamic idea, "constantly defining itself," says William Luis, and in some way its dynamism, its anti-inertia, which expresses itself in the forms of migrations, displacements, and the instability of constant change, is a defining characteristic of the Caribbean peoples and cultures. The syncretic mélange of African, European, and Native cultures—and the power relations between those groups—is what is most homogeneous about Caribbean nations.[2]

Sidney W. Mintz proposes as the common denominator of Caribbean identity the plantation system, which has undeniably determined the economic and social relations of classes and races since colonial times. While Mintz's model is useful in terms of economic integration, it subordinates the question of culture to the outcome of the plantation economy and its resulting social archetype. Mintz rules out cultural identity as a unifying factor in the Caribbean, describing the area as "a very heterogeneous cultural picture," suggesting that its heterogeneity is a separating rather than a unifying trait.[3] In *The Repeating Island* Benítez Rojo proposes a theory of Caribbean literature and culture identified by a set of common characteristics (cultural syncretism, Africanism, slavery, rhythm, gastronomy) marked, or "branded" by the plantation economy, the psychological burdens of slavery, and the weight of colonialism. Benítez Rojo's attempts to discover a common denominator that defines Caribbean culture despite its diversity leads to his conclusion that "within [the] chaos of differences and repetitions, . . . there are regular dynamics that coexist, and which, once broached within an aesthetic experience, lead the performer to recreate a world without violence. . . ."[4]

Benítez Rojo's basis on chaos theory serves to explain the unpredictable nature of living things: chaos dictates that there is a pattern, a rhythm, an inevitable dynamism to every natural process, and the constant (r)evolution of matter suggests the cyclical structure of life, because every process is the result and part of the infinite web of relations of natural phenomena. This idea proposes that dying is the ordinary outcome of nature's way and that death can be "neutralized" with culture the way violence can be absorbed by "aesthetic experience" and performance. Animistic beliefs, healing and religious practices of the African component of Caribbean cultures, helped to neutralize the unnatural trauma and violence of the Middle Passage, of slavery, rape, pain, and even death of the physical body. With chants, prayer, and storytelling, Afro-Caribbean culture could be removed from the immediate context of slavery, it could be restored to the safety of the African homeland, healing the broken portions of the circle, as we will see below in my discussion of the films *The Last Supper, Sugar Cane Alley,* and *Sankofa.*

The narrative theme of death as resurrection is identified in African films particularly in the treatment of Africa, animistic beliefs, and magic. The idea of the enslaved African body and soul in pain that can be healed through death comes to us first in the cinema of Ousmane Sembène, the Senegalese novelist who in the 1960s, searching to reach larger, illiterate audiences, started making films. Sembène, a politically active figure, educated in Europe and the Soviet Union, made his (and Africa's) first feature film, *Black Girl,* in 1966. The movie tells the story of a young Senegalese woman, Diouna, who is hired as a nanny by a middle-class French couple and shipped to Nice. In France, Diouna is constantly humiliated by her employers, treated as an exotic curiosity for the couple's friends to see, as one of the many African art objects that decorate their apartment. One of these objects, a traditional ceremonial mask, was given to them by Diouna upon her being hired, as a gesture of appreciation. Soon enough, however, desperate and cut off from her family, Diouna fantasizes about her lost life in Dakar, caressing memories of her family and loved ones. She soon becomes physically ill and refuses to work or eat. Diouna packs all of her belongings in the same single suitcase with which she arrived in France. The last thing she packs is her mask, after removing it from its strictly decorative function of hanging on a wall. Diouna finally locks herself in the bathroom and takes her life in a bathtub full of water. Instead of a closure, Diouna's death, especially the gesture of carefully and neatly packing her few belongings, denotes her intention, or her belief, that she is returning home; the liberation from her physical body allows for her soul, her spirit, to in fact do so. When her former employer goes to Dakar to relate the news to her family, he is haunted by the ceremonial mask, which a young relative of Diouna's puts over his face before chasing the French intruder away. Diouna cannot bring her actual life with her when she is exported to France, but she brings her beliefs and an object that confirms the immediacy of her spiritual link to Africa, an artifact she symbolically wields in the hands of her young relative when her soul returns home. The younger relative in a way symbolizes Diouna's successful passage back home when he turns her mask into a sign of rejection of her traumatic experience in France. Sembène's film suggests the liberating power of belief, since it does not portray Diouna's death as a defeat, but as the triumph of her soul over physical and psychological confinement.

The narrative of a "return" voyage foregrounds the theme of the circular quality of time as perceived in African oral literature and cinema, and in Caribbean narrative and films as well. In the 1987 film by Malian filmmaker Souleymane Cissé, *Yeelen* (*Brightness*), now recognized as a masterpiece of African cinema, the protagonist Nianankoro is an apprentice sorcerer who embarks on a long trip to encounter his father Somo Diarra, also a sorcerer, but one who employs the negative powers of magic. The film follows the young Nianankoro in his long voyage tracking his father while learning with every step of the way a new lesson on the powers of magic and nature and their traditional uses. Somo Diarra and Nianankoro must inevitably face each other, for only one can guard the magic secrets. Their rivalry, however, is somewhat contradictory, since, as African film scholar N. Frank Ukadike points out, traditionally this type of knowledge would in fact be passed down from fathers to sons. Yet, at the explosive climax of the film, Nianankoro enters into a duel with his father in which they produce the blinding brightness (or *yeelen*) that purifies, destroys, and allows for a new cycle to begin. In the final scene, after the fade to white symbolizing the "brightness" of the two brands of magic, we see Nianankoro's son walk on the desert sand, presumably where the encounter took place, and unearth two big orbs whose oval shapes suggest the reinitiation of the cycle of life, of a self-renewing order.[5] Like its narratively simpler predecessor *Black Girl, Brightness* tells the story of a return to the source of one's origin (Africa; the father), and of a purifying rite (Diouna with water; Nianankoro with fire) in which one's physical existence substitutes for another more permanent promise of life. Significantly, this scenario is very much repeated in Caribbean cinema; in *Sugar Cane Alley, Sankofa,* and *The Last Supper,* the return to Africa is a sign of spiritual liberation denied to the slave's physical body.

In his essay "Cultural Identity and Cinematic Representation" (1989), Stuart Hall theorizes the "unstable" character of cultural identity in the

Caribbean.[6] Hall argues that each Caribbean island is defined in relation to what it is as much as to what it is not. Yet every island's cultural practices (in music, narrative, art) help to identify it in terms of the African "presence" in its cultural expressions. In other words, regardless of the character of a Caribbean island as far as its Spanish, French, British, or Dutch component, the most defining constant, even when historically variable from region to region, is the African presence. Hall explains that since the 1970s, Caribbean cultural production has actively negotiated or "come to terms" with the African presence in its identity in part by "imagining" (in the Benedict Anderson sense of the term) a historical connection to Africa that has, in fact, been severed by the Caribbean's binding ties to European colonialism for four hundred years. Hall concludes that:

> The Diaspora experience . . . is defined, not by essence or purity, but by the recognition of a necessary heterogeneity, diversity; by a conception of identity which lives with and through, not despite difference, hybridity. Diaspora identities are those which are constantly producing and reproducing themselves anew, through transformation and difference.[7]

Hall argues that this is "the vocation of a modern Caribbean cinema: "allowing us to see and recognize the different parts and histories of ourselves."[8] I would argue, however, that another alternative for the negotiation of the troubled diasporic identity in Caribbean films is to stress the spiritual connection to Africa and "treat" the Caribbean step of the cultural identity ladder as a detour; instead of discovering the "African presence" in Caribbean life, there is a search for a direct connection to Africa, for an *être Africaine* or "African being." In a sense the claim for an African being solidifies the link of Caribbean cinema with such African films as *Black Girl* and *Brightness* specifically by referring to Africa in the present tense and by portraying slavery and colonialism in the Caribbean as a broken joint, or a severed body part that can in fact be fixed with stories, with music, and ultimately by reaching the natural outcome of life: death.

Recent Caribbean films, often largely influenced by the region's literature, serve as examples of the articulation of the "African being." Cuban director Tomás Gutiérrez Alea's first venture into the topic of Afro-Caribbean cultural issues was his little-known 1966 film *Cumbite,* based on Haitian author Jacques Roumaine's novel *Masters of the Dew,* which dealt with the search for an elusive life-giving "source," a water spring.[9] His 1976 film *The Last Supper* tells the true story of a Holy Week slave revolt in a sugarcane plantation near Havana in the late eighteenth century. The master of the plantation is a devoted Catholic Spanish count. In a Holy Week visit to his plantation, he enacts the Catholic ritual of the washing of feet that Jesus

Christ is said to have performed on his disciples on the evening of his last supper. The count's misguided gesture serves only to baffle the twelve slaves he chooses to sit at his table, as the men find it difficult to understand the count's devotion to an afterlife without masters or slaves, in spite of his economic and social position in "the kingdom of this world." In his drunken stupor after dinner, the count promises the twelve slaves at the table that they shall have the following day, Good Friday, off from plantation duties so that they can attend the day's religious ceremonies. When the next day the mulatto overseer refuses to honor the holiday, and the count ignores his own promise of the previous evening, the slaves revolt and kill the overseer and his wife before being caught, cruelly punished, and publicly decapitated.

The intellectual leader of the revolt, an imported slave named Sebastián, has attempted to escape the plantation three times before and is believed to have magical powers. Like the legendary, lycanthropic Makandal of the Haitian slave revolts that led to the country's independence in Alejo Carpentier's novelization of those events, *El reino de este mundo* (*The Kingdom of This World*, 1949), Sebastián possesses a similar power that allows him to survive in the woods (*el monte*): his magic powders give him the power to turn into animals and natural elements in order to evade capture and gain his freedom. He tells his coconspirators: "This time Sebastián will be able to escape. . . . These are my powers, with this [powder] Sebastián becomes a tree in the bushes, a fish in the river, a stone, a bird. . . . I fly and nobody can catch me, nobody can kill me." (Like Makandal, Sebastián's belief that the body can be contained and damaged but that the soul can be liberated is reminiscent of the story of Esteban Montejo in Miguel Barnet's 1966 oral history, *Biografía de un cimarrón* [*Biography of a Runaway Slave*], in which the former slave tells stories of flying spirits and of knowledge of plants and improvised drugs that helped the runaways evade capture.)[10]

Before his liberating transubstantiation in *The Last Supper*, Sebastián's body is locked in shackles, whipped, and persecuted in the woods until, the film clearly suggests, he in fact becomes one with nature, succeeding in remaining a runaway, a *cimarrón* (maroon). The last visual images of the film are of the elements and animals into which Sebastián changes—a bird in the air, a fish in the water, a stone rolling down a cliff, a horse running in the prairie, a tree in the bushes. Aided by the experience gained previously in his attempted escapes, Sebastián, like the Haitian Makandal in *The Kingdom of This World*, who flies away to freedom seconds before being burned alive, is abetted by the belief of both friends and foes in his magical powers.[11] In Caribbean, Latin American, and African narrative and films, magic is not necessarily an extraordinary event but a part of everyday life, and may even be a way of understanding history, as Alejo Carpentier argues in his essay "Lo real maravilloso de América" ("The Marvelous American Reality"), the famous prologue to *The Kingdom of This World*. Thus Sebastián in *The Last Supper* is not an anomaly, but a character well founded in the Afro-Caribbean tradition that portrays history as fiction and magic as ordinary and that includes Makandal and Esteban Montejo among other characters, some real, some legendary, some imaginary.

The Jamaican/African movie *Sankofa* and the Martiniquais film *Sugar Cane Alley* underscore the weight of African cultures in the Caribbean by portraying European influences as disruptive and ill-adapted. The trauma of the African diaspora in these films takes the shape of a "travel" narrative in which a protagonist is (in actuality or in her/his imagination) displaced from her/his roots or time frame and thrown into a foreign land or alternate temporality to experience exploitation and cultural assimilation. Eventually for this character, her/his connection to Africa is solidified with the help of a mentor or formative figure and/or by the passing on of knowledge, culture, and religious practices.

Euzhan Palcy's 1984 film *Sugar Cane Alley* deals with the negotiation of the trauma of indentured servitude as an offspring of slavery in 1920s Martinique. Based on the novel by Joseph Zobel, the film looks at the small community of "Sugar Cane Alley" (or "Black Shack Alley" from the original title *Rue cases negres*), composed of three generations of sugarcane workers who appear destined to die working for the powerful French-owned local sugar mill. The protagonist, José, is a boy around ten years old who lives with and is being raised by his grandmother, M'Amantine, one of the community's wise elders. M'Amantine wants José to fulfill his (Western) education to become, perhaps, a schoolteacher so as to avoid his apparent fate of becoming a sugar mill worker. Thus, José receives a classical colonial education at school ("Our ancestors, the Gauls . . .") and a traditional education at home from the neighborhood griot, Medouze.

The most important part of Medouze's training is that of oral story-telling, through which is expressed the knowledge of and respect for the natural world, the spirits of the forest (*el monte*), and the religious/spiritual knowledge of the elders' belief system. Through oral stories told during frequent meetings with Medouze, José learns about his African ancestry, the history of slavery, Medouze's genealogy, religious objects and fetishes, and the destiny of the souls of dead slaves. José learns that death is, in fact, a liberation, and that although Medouze himself, born on the plantation, has never been to Africa, that is where his soul will "return" after the death of his physical body. The interest José shows in learning from Medouze, his happiness, his rapport with the old man, contrasts with José's formal education at Sunday school—learning the Catholic doctrine of heaven, hell, and purgatory recited in a tedious monotone by the distracted children—and with his mastery of useless knowledge about, say, Europe's navigable rivers. Significantly, as with his relationship with M'Amantine, José's relationship with Medouze skips one generation; with no parents, José is formed by grandparent figures, much in the way Télumée, the female protagonist of Simone Schwarz-Bart's 1972 novel *The Bridge of Beyond (Pluie et vent sur Télumée Miracle)* holds closer formative ties with her grandmother and surrogate figures, Toussine, Queen-Without-A-Name, and Ma Cia.[12] Cultural, spiritual knowledge thus skips a generation, leaving the middle generation—that to which José's parents belong—seemingly maladjusted: in the movie, they drink, fight, get into debt with the company store, and seem somewhat lost in the limbo of indentured servitude. In stark contrast, José, like Telumée Miracle, is initiated into a spiritual knowledge that gives him the advantage to loosen the trauma of slavery by connecting to the mother continent, reducing the Caribbean experience to a physical/transitional phase.

When Medouze feels he is ready to die, he retreats to the woods where José knows he can be found; Medouze goes to die in his element, in the safety of the woods, and José quickly recognizes that Medouze's liberated soul returns to Africa. Medouze's death may be sad, but not traumatic. Similarly, when an ailing M'Amantine dies, José's gesture of washing her feet in the final shot of the film, as if readying her for a trip, symbolizes his acknowledgment of the rite of passage of death as a cleansing, a healing response to the trauma of servitude and the pain of the Middle Passage. Like Medouze, M'Amantine is freed in death, liberated and healed from the torments of "the kingdom of this world." Neither Medouze nor M'Amantine are interested in the powers of Western medicine. They face death as inevitable, as the end of their lifetime of semislavery, yet not as an unhappy ending. Life in the Caribbean plantation system is transitional, perhaps unstable for these characters; it is the midway point, the "line" that separates the point of departure—the Africa of their ancestors—and the final liberation of generations of slaves and servants: the spiritual Africa where souls return to regain their freedom and live forever. Life is thus a circle, which, like time, always returns us "back to the source," as in Alejo Carpentier's 1944 story "Viaje a la semilla" ("Journey Back to the Source").[13]

Life, death, magic, and the circularity of time are the themes that surround Ethiopian director Haile Gerima's film of slave life on a Jamaican sugar cane plantation, *Sankofa*. A coproduction financed by producers from the United States, Jamaica, Ghana, and Burkina Faso, *Sankofa* is a story of slavery and traumatized identity, but it is also a tale of the Afro-Caribbean struggle to "return to the source," to find the spiritual connection to Africa that colonization and slavery, time and assimilation, have debilitated. Like the protagonists of the works mentioned above (and more recently Oprah Winfrey's portrayal of the former slave Sethe in Jonathan Demme's 1998 film version of Toni Morrison's *Beloved*), *Sankofa*'s main character must endure the humiliation of the body in order to free her spirit through the healing processes of cultural awakening. The innovative formal and narrative structure of *Sankofa* directly addresses the issue of cultural identity in modern-day Jamaica.

Sankofa, the story of the house slave Shola, is strategically framed by two modern-day segments that emphasize the circularity of time and history, the recurring impact of colonization, and the continuity of cultural practices. A ceremonious-sounding off-screen voice introduces the opening modern-day segment, creating the impression of a distant past tense. The narrator utters the call: "Spirits of the Dead, rise up and posses your vessel. . . . Come out, you African Spirits, come out and free your Spirit. . . ." While the words are spoken against a background of drum music, we see in successive inserts the images of a vulture, a rocky coast, and an eighteenth-century military fort, all of which appear to exist in an atemporal space. The drummer, taking the place of narrator, says: "The Almighty created the . . . divine drummer"; his image in close-up is juxtaposed to that of a black woman, presumably a model, posing for a white photographer in a bathing suit in the fortress yard. When a group of white tourists appears in the scene, the time frame is unified and explained: the model, the drummer, and the fortress coexist. She wears a blonde wig, the drummer wears traditional ceremonial makeup. The drummer, apparently acting as griot, confronts the woman, named Mona, and tells her to "return to [her] source," specifically warning her against the violation of the fortress, which, he tells her, "is holy land [because] blood has been spilled here." The griot, we soon learn, calls himself "Sankofa." The meaning of the name, "One must return to the past in order to move forward," stresses the symbolic position of the drummer as griot, a storyteller and traditional historian whose responsibility is to tell, preserve, and pass on to younger generations the history of a tribe or nation. In African oral tradition, the griot is "a community educator and historian," a role that is "reflective of the great value placed on oral narrative . . . [a] crucial educational form."[14] African film historians Manthia Diawara and Nwachukwu Frank Ukadike have observed the key role of the griot in the development of a specific African narrative and formal structure in the continent's cinema from Ousmane Sembène's early films of the mid-1960s and early 1970s (*Borom Sarret* and *Xala*) to contemporary films by Ababacar Samb-Makharam (*Jom, ou l'histoire d'un peuple*), Gaston Kaboré (*Wend Kuuni*), and Souleymane Cissé (*Yeelen*).[15] In Caribbean cinema the griotlike characters of a slave in *The Last Supper,* Medouze in *Sugar Cane Alley,* and the title character in *Sankofa* help to establish the indissoluble quality of the cultural connection of the Caribbean with Africa that in all these films is presented as the "cure" to the diaspora's psychological and even physical trauma of slavery.

In *Sankofa,* after the introductory historical continuum with the griot and the tourists, Mona gets lost in the depths of the fortress. There, by virtue of the griot's summon of the "Spirits of the Dead," Mona finds a number of slaves in shackles, branded and held captive, establishing the fortress as an apparent port of entry of imported slaves. Mona becomes one of them. She experiences a spiritual flashback and is promptly seized, chained, disrobed, and branded with an iron. Tellingly, director Gerima chooses African American spiritual music as the background for Mona/Shola's branding scene, establishing again the historical link between contemporary black experience and slavery, as well as playing creatively with the structural circularity of time. This formal device disallows limiting Mona/Shola's story to the past tense; the music's tone and lyrics add a certain soothing quality to contrast the brutal horror of the scene, acting as a healing element. Drumming and chanting, proper to Afro-Caribbean culture, are used for a similar purpose (of "neutralizing" violence) in *The Last Supper, Sugar Cane Alley, The Kingdom of This World, The Bridge of Beyond,* and numerous other Caribbean film and literary works.[16] Gerima's addition of an African American musical practice—Christian spiritual songs—to the branding scene in *Sankofa* renders music (as culture) a universal spiritual pillar of the African diaspora, be it in the Caribbean, where the movie takes place, or in the United States, where the film was an unexpected art-house success. In *Sankofa,* as in *Sugar Cane Alley,* slavery is a malady; culture, here in the form of music, is a healing and liberating alternative practice.

The scene of Shola's branding dissolves to the formal flashback narrative of the sugarcane plantation, where, under the sounds of a cracking whip and the gaze of the mulatto overseer, we see the men and women slaves cutting cane. Shola then takes on the main narrative agency by becoming the de facto first-person narrator in voice-over. Throughout the flashback narrative, Shola gradually becomes involved in a rebellion plotted by the field slaves. During their brief rest pauses, the slaves gather to listen attentively to oral histories of their African ancestors told by the woman Nounou, who, as it turns out, is also the slaves' midwife. Traditional historian, healer, and midwife, Nounou consolidates ancestral forms of learning, teaching, and medical practice. In one particularly symbolic scene, a pregnant woman is tied to a pole and brutally whipped after attempting to escape the plantation. One of the slaves is forced to commit the whipping, during which, to everyone's horror, the woman gives birth. The baby's cries reaffirm the promise of life emerging from such violence, as the pain of giving birth counterbalances the pain of brutal punishment. Nounou, the griot/midwife/healer slave, was imported directly from Africa, and thus experienced the Middle Passage. Raped and having given birth to the bastard son of one of the plantation owners, she is one of the leaders of the planned rebellion. Shola, by contrast, was born on the plantation; it is she who needs to be educated, initiated, and recruited. Haile Gerima's *Sankofa* stresses the cohesive power of oral story-telling, the alienation of the Jamaican-born from the preceding generation of African-born slaves, and the power of traditional cultural practices in bridging that gap and sheltering both generations under a coherent sensibility. After Shola is caught consorting with the plotters, she is beaten, raped, and humiliatingly forced to renounce African deities and proclaim her belief in Catholic dogma, as a result of which she joins the rebellion.

The turning point in Shola's life is when she is healed of her physical wounds by her friend Shango, another one of the plotters with knowledge of medicinal plants and traditional prayers. Shango's name is, of course, significant in the context of Afro-Caribbean religions. Shango is a much venerated deity of the Yoruba culture and of its Caribbean branches, Cuban Santería and Jamaican Shangoism. In "La Regla de Ocha: The Religious System of Santería" (1997), Miguel Barnet writes that according to the original African Yoruba myth, Shango, warrior god of music, thunder, and lightning, has the power to dematerialize and disappear in the face of defeat, as Makandal did in *The Kingdom of This World*.[17] In *Sankofa*, Shango's healing and formation lead to Shola's final cultural and spiritual liberation. Shango, acting as a formative figure, tells Shola a story that helps her come to terms with the life-affirming, healing power of her cultural heritage. As Shola weeps disconsolately in bed, Shango speaks:

> Go on Shola, run. . . . We're not going slave no more, just go on running. Shola, I did have a little sister who ate mud and dead. And up to this date I couldn't understand which part she go. I could only see her body. Then, long after, my father go dead and that is the time I get more confused; I couldn't really understand what did really go on. You know, my father dead . . . my sister dead, all I could see was them body. . . . I realize this was a kind of different thing. . . . I had a friend name Jake. He was the first one tell me 'bout people like me who live up in the hills like normal human beings. . . . We use to sit down and plan up our escape. One morning I wake up and I see Jake hang from a tree. That was the time when I realize say be better if I dead . . . because if I dead, I'd only go to the people who I love: my father, my sister, and Jake.

In his quality as storyteller and healer, Shango wins Shola's trust, and she, from that point, recognizes herself in the community of field slaves. Shango gives her an amulet, a "sankofa" bird carved in wood, like an orisha that can be represented by a paternal heirloom, and Shola tells us that "this sankofa was passed on to [Shango] by his papa. After that I became a rebel. No longer was I afraid of being flayed, burned . . . even death didn't scare me." Thus, traditional medicine heals Shola's body.

Words, tradition, and a belief in the invincibility of her community help her consolidate a cultural identity—symbolized by the wooden amulet—and confirm her conviction that death itself is but a transitional phase; upon dying, she too will "go with the people she loves."

The field slaves, as Shango's story suggests, have been establishing a *palenque* in the nearby hills, and they promise to take those who want to join them, one by one, to live free in the settlement. In Jamaica, *palenques,* or Maroon settlements, were common since the island had been taken from the hands of Spain by the British in the mid-seventeenth century. Clandestine Maroon settlements in Jamaica were an instrumental part of the successful maintenance of African religious beliefs, tribal political organization, and traditional cultural practices through generations.[18] In *Sankofa,* the strength of the Maroon settlement upsets the plantation, where Nounou's son burns down the Catholic chapel with his mother in it, finally instigating the climactic rebellion. In her quality as narrative agent, Shola tells us that after the church fire, "Nounou's body was never found. Nothing but ashes. Some believe to this day that she never died. They saw a big buzzard swoop down and fly her back to her Africa." Shola, after joining the rebellion, kills the plantation owner's son, who had consistently raped her. As she tries to escape with the plantation guards chasing after her, Shola repeats Shango's healing words: "Keep on running. . . . Next thing I know, I'm in the air going up, and up, and up, and this miserable earth is getting smaller and smaller, just like Shango said." Shola's flying here suggests that she was, in fact, caught and killed by the guards. However, as in the case of their fictional and historical predecessors—the elusive Makandal, Sebastián, Medouze, M'Amantine, and even the mythical Shango of Yoruba culture—Shola's and Nounou's physical deaths in slavery are a liberation, an affirmation of life, a "return to the source" guaranteed by faith in the power of traditional spiritual beliefs that defy Western historical explanations.

In the film's epilogue, the narrative returns to the framing modern-day scene. Because time is circular, Shola is reconverted into Mona, the model, emerging from the dungeons of the fortress, her body bearing visible signs of physical abuse and exhaustion. She joins the modern-day griot, Sankofa, in the re-creation of a traditional ritual under the attentive gaze of other modern Jamaicans in traditional African garbs, Nounou among them. The return to the film's origins before Mona's spiritual flashback as Shola demonstrates that she has, in fact, "returned to the past" in order to "move forward." The drummer Sankofa is a further reference to Shango, god of music, and he contributes to Mona's experience as she reconnects her spirituality with a past that thus far she had been unable to experience. The last image of the film is that of the ocean seen from a bird's eye view, presumably Shola's spirit flying "back" to Africa and freedom. But as she was not born in Africa, the final reconnecting to a space and symbolic origin interrupted by several generations also represents Shola/Mona's "move forward," her overcoming or casting off of three centuries of slavery.

Caribbean films dealing with slavery or the pseudo-slavery of the sugar-cane plantation in the first decades of the twentieth century stage a "return to the source" that exorcises the trauma of slavery, purifying the violated body of the slave by combining traditional curative practices with oral storytelling and the conviction that, through death, slavery is erased and overcome. Africa does not have to be looked for or "found" by the characters in these films even after generations of displacement, because it is the natural completion of "the passage." The strength of tradition and spirituality "neutralizes" the violence against the physical body that, metaphorically, represents a threat to cultural identity. In this way, through these characters, Caribbean films reclaim, restate, and rearticulate the indelible power of the Caribbean's Africanness.

Chapter 11

A Writer/Healer:
Literature, A Blueprint for Healing

Opal Palmer Adisa

she received the	words
took them in her	head
let them sit there	untouched
they bounced like ping-pong	balls
she had to do	something
to quiet the chatter	
they gave her no rest	
let us speak they said	she wrote them
their symbols blood on the	paper
where they became	ghosts
she let them	out
and the story still	continues

In the world in which we live, sickness is considered a *normal* part of many people's lives. In fact, the more we seem to advance technologically, the sicker more people are becoming. New diseases and aches, linked to social and psychological factors, are increasing; more people in modern, metropolitan societies are seeking alternative remedies. What can we do when we are sick? What do we ask for? Who will minister to us? What do we give ourselves? I say look to the power of words.

the writer carried the words	
in her breasts	sweet with milk

she hadn't been   taught
how to make music from the noise she heard
she did not yet   recognize
the tips of her fingers
stained with   fire
nor the odor of her breath that always reeked
                            of garlic

I will use a song, says the singer. I will pray, whisper the devout. As a word-smith, I believe in the magic and healing power of words. I know and understand miracles. I know literature is a balm, poultice, medicine, and cure. I will use words to remind us to be well. Literature is one vehicle of healing and wellness.

the story was trapped in a pool of   puss
overcome by the rotting   flesh
the writer   reeled
what tools had she   to combat
this disaster
did words have   a value
beyond the sound they   communicated
the writer grasped until her hands   held them
held them and wouldn't   let go
words as curing as baking soda on   sore gums

Healing is the art of transforming our lived reality to be in harmony with our needs. Healing means living free from pain, is saying no to pain, is forgiving the past and learning from it. Healing is about the act: breathing in the moment to experience enjoyment. Healing implies connecting to your purpose, joining forces with the social, physical, and spiritual worlds to find your path and be at peace with yourself. I heard the words and came to know where I must go. When I saw the words on the page, I felt as if a lump that had been restricting my breath dissolved, and I found I could sing again. I found my voice.

she does not ask the intention
she knows in every syllable
there is a healing agent if called with sincerity
the writer called the words

I cannot say with any amount of certainty that healing was Alice Walker's agenda when she gave us Celie of *The Color Purple* (1982), or if it was Paule Marshall's goal in presenting us Avery Johnson of *Praisesong for the Widow* (1983), or Erna Brodber's desire in sharing Ella of *Myal* (1988), or even how conscious it was for me, Adisa, in presenting Miss Cotton and Arnella of *It*

Begins with Tears (1997). However, the works of these four writers have helped to move and heal many black people from the amnesia and brutal, historical pain in which so many of us were and are still drowning. And the secret words of childhood abuse and pain were written on the page.

> the writer lost herself in the semicolons and commas
> the latter was abundant confusing the subject from
> their action
> exceptions could always be made for the quotations
> but the writer refused to hide indefinitely in fear

In *The Color Purple,* Celie, a sexually abused child, devoid of any parental love or guidance, begins writing letters to God after she is forcefully separated from her sister, her only friend, source of love and the only one who encourages her to smile and stand up for herself. In this work, Alice Walker develops Celie from an abused victim to a woman who, through writing and her friendship with Shug—a brash, free-spirited singer, her husband's lover who in time becomes Celie's lesbian lover—rises above her lot of poverty and abuse to become a whole person, capable of defending herself. This move of recovery, of being healed of the pain that was a constant shadow of her life, results in Celie being reunited with her sister and meeting the children who were taken from her when she was a teenage girl. In this groundbreaking work, written in letterform by Celie—semi-literate, black vernacular—Walker demonstrates resilience, which has always been and remains a trademark of black survival in the New World. And the words of dreams and buried memories of people returning to Africa came to her like a film of cobweb that she walked through.

> instructed to keep her own counsel
> the writer practiced silence
> dug through memory
> and found the stone on which was written
> another chance   she smiled

In *Praisesong for a Widow,* Paule Marshall's Avery Johnson is also a New World survivor, but Avery's station in life is markedly different from Celie's. Having successfully climbed the ladder from struggling working class to comfortable middle class, Avery Johnson is a middle-aged widow of means who yearly goes on a cruise with her women friends. Her life is banal and for the most part purposeless. Avery's world is turned upside down, however, as she is made to experience the Middle Passage in reverse. Her personal history reels before her, forcing her to remember the past, the thread that connects her to her great-grandaunt Cuney and the Tatem community of her childhood. As a child Avery was connected to her history, and learned about Ibo landing where her African ancestors allegedly turned away from slavery and walked on the water straight back to Africa. Similar to Celie for whom Shug is a guide who helps claim Celie's life and relinquish her pain, Avery is guided back to her roots by Lebert Joseph, an Elegba/Esu figure who liberates her from the meaningless sterility of middle-class existence. Words made a buffoon of her life; she must return home and shift through the nursery rhymes to learn the truth.

> the writer hadn't suspected
> that one day she would literally
> have to jump   that jumping
> would be an opportunity to discover
> that she would have to fly
> if he she planned on walking again

Transporting us to another area of the African diaspora, Erna Brodber, Jamaican sociologist and writer, offers us *Myal,* in which readers meet Ella O'Grady Langley, victim of spirit thievery by the white American husband who weds and removes her from her homeland. In the United States he makes a minstrel show of her life, rendering her voiceless. Left to languish in North America, disconnected from her people, Ella's path seems doomed, until she is summoned home by a group of subversive interlopers. With the goal of discarding the cloak of colonialism, they begin by dissecting the educational system. Upon Ella's return home, the fog of her North American experience still covers her eyes; she gradually comes to perceive her role in this endeavor, however, and begins to reinterpret the texts with which she is asked to instruct her pupils as subjects. In this revolutionary work, Brodber takes on the colonial project and speaks directly to the scribes, whose role she sees as essential to the dismantling of neocolonialism. However, as this is such an all-encompassing project that requires the efforts of many, Ella's guide, unlike Celie's and Avery's, is not an individual person but rather a community of people, all of whose roles are vital to the implementation of change. And the words swim in the spiritual realm, appropriating folkism and harkening harmony.

> now is the only time   the writer heard them say
> ready or not   except this was not a child's game
> of seek and find   a life   many lives
> were on the line and she had to make a path
> she held open her hands and they spilled like beans
> these words that looked like aspirins

Adisa's novel, *It Begins with Tears,* also set in the Jamaican landscape, examines healing from a more secular perspective. When Monica, a whore, returns to Kristoff Village, her childhood home, and becomes the prey of jealous wives, plunging the entire community into chaos, Miss Cotton, Arnella, and the other seers of the community unite to purge the village of this wrong that tests its balance. Whereas with Celie, writing letters serves as the tour de force and vehicle of transformation, in *It Begins with Tears* the river, the natural body of water, is the site of change. It is here where the "real" healing takes place: the past is remembered and honored, and the present is allowed the freedom to admit wrong, ask forgiveness, and walk with confidence into tomorrow.

> the writer wasn't sure
> what to do with her hamper of words
> they were too heavy to carry on her head
> yet she knew people awaited them
> hungry in their pain
> they were the *body* and the *blood*
> these words   the miracle
> from which all life is conceived

In all the novels, the healing that occurs is only possible after the characters have confronted the past, tangible and alive in their memories, and made peace with it, for, as the writer Marlene Nourbese Philip poses, "Without memory can there be history?"[1] All four writers, working through different lenses, examine the oppressive, colonial experience of black people in the New World, which has disrupted their lives, thwarted their personal and collective goals, ruined the family structure, and disempowered individuals, leaving them voiceless, empty vessels of pain. Walker, Marshall, Brodber, and Adisa all seem to declare, however, that the pain must cease and that for this to be accomplished one must begin by confronting the past, thereby making space for healing to take place. In these texts, healing is inextricably linked to an embracing of family-community values and a reconnecting with African traditions for the wholesome survival of black people.

All these writers, in varying degrees, integrate folk remedies and an embracement of the past. Memory is key to the various characters' recovery; in all, one or more persons are there to assist. All the characters experience physical trauma that serves as the in-road, the throwing off of the burden of pain, which in these works is rendered as a physical entity that rides the characters' backs, making them weak, forcing them from their feet. And the words spoken assume a life, tracking their voyage until they too hear the words of healing.

> the meeting always occurs
> first inside the head
> the writer found Celie tighter than a drum's head
> so that the every effort to beg out the words
> were as a chisel used in hammering shape
> into/out of a rock

Although Celie begins to find herself after meeting Shug, who, reluctantly at first, befriends her, it is not until she relates her rape and subsequent pregnancy by her stepfather at fourteen that Celie can begin to come to terms with what was done to her, moving beyond the victim mode into one of choosing to be well, throwing off the trauma of the past, taking steps toward healing. Of course, Celie's healing is predicated on her learning to love herself and accepting being loved, in this case by Shug.

> It hurt me, you know, I say. I was just going on fourteen. I never even thought bout men having nothing down there so big. It scare me just to see it. And the way it poke itself and grow.
>   Shug so quiet I think she sleep.
>   After he through, I say, he make me finish trimming his hair.
>   I sneak a look at Shug.
>   Oh, Miss Celie, she say. And put her arms around me. They Black and smooth and kind of glowy from the lamplight.
>   I start to cry too. I cry and cry and cry. Seems like it all come back to me, laying there in Shug arms. . . . [2]

Shug provides Celie with a safe, nonjudgmental space where she can confront the past and admit the hurt of being raped by her stepfather, a violation the burden of which she felt had to remain secret. As the novel develops, Shug becomes Celie's window to the outside world, as do the discovery and reading of Nettie's letters from Africa, letters obtained thanks to Shug's relationship with Mr. and her subterfuge. These letters, along with Shug's love, are Celie's medicine. As a result of reading Nettie's letter, Celie discovers the welfare of her children and learns that the man who had raped and impregnated her is in fact not her real father but her stepfather. The letters, the words, free her from the negativity of the past. Learning that her sister is alive, Celie is reunited with a positive aspect of her past; the letters allow her to redirect the object of her words from God to the person who has always loved her.

> Dear Nettie,
> I don't write to God no more. I write to you.
> What happen to God? Ast Shug.

Who that I say.

She look at me serious.

Big a devil as you is, I say, you not worried bout
no God, surely.

She say, Wait a minute. Hold on just a minute here. Just because I don't
harass it like some people us know don't mean I ain't got religion.

What God do for me? I ast.

She say, Celie! Like she shock. He gave you life, good health, and a good
woman who love you to death.

Yeah, I say, and he give me a lynched daddy, a crazy mama, a lowdown dog
of a step pa and a sister I probably won't ever see again. Anyhow, I say, the
God I been praying and writing to is a man. And act just like all the other
mens I know.[3]

In this feminist-centered text, author Alice Walker, as evident from the
above passage, breaks with the patriarchy—God as icon—and surrounds
Celie in a woman-centered world where she can be healed from the scars
imposed by men and a male-centered social, religious, and economic ide-
ological framework. With Shug's love as the balm and Nettie's letters as
medicine, Celie grows into her own, discovering and claiming her sexuality, her artistry, and her life. Armed with a sense of self, with the knowledge that who and what she is are important, and with the sense of being
loved, Celie is no longer a victim of geography or gender. For the first time
she is free and is able to make choices about the future of her life. The language of truth heals her wounds. Despite the adversities she still must face
(the fact that Shug, her love, leaves her and goes off with a younger man,
and learning that Nettie and the children may have drowned when their
boat from Africa sinks), Celie does not revert to her prior state. Her transformation and healing are not momentary phases. In a long letter to Nettie, whom she presumes is dead (but her gut instincts tell her otherwise),
Celie writes:

Well, your sister too crazy to kill herself. Most times I feels like shit but I felt
like shit before in my life and what happen? I had me a fine sister name Nettie. I had me another fine woman friend name Shug. I had me some fine children growing up in Africa, singing and writing verses. The first two months
was hell though, I tell the world. But now Shug's six months is come and gone
and she ain't come back. And I try to teach my heart not to want nothing it
can't have.[4]

Celie is finally able to cope with difficult experiences without internalizing
them. Her choice to live, her healing, manifests in her refusal to be the victim of any given circumstances.

I will be a healer, a healer. Lay down your troubles and I will make you strong. Surrender and I will direct you to another path. Have faith and I will see that you walk safely through the wilderness. Hold steadfast to the past as a torchlight and guide. Come home and I will heal you, heal you, make you well even when you are not aware that you are ill.

> she never wanted to be a writer
> knew it was a thankless job
> everyone would be needing some of her
> but few would know what they needed
> she had learned that knowing
> didn't mean speaking
> the heart was not merely an organ but words
> well now   that was a subject all together different

Avery Johnson of *Praisesong for the Widow* goes about her life as if amnesia is reward, seemingly oblivious to the sickness that has been lurking at her door, so determined is she to maintain economic difficulties firmly in the past where she left them. However, Marshall suggests that healing will occur sometimes even when one is as unwilling as Avery. She literally has to be knocked off her feet and forced to experience the journey—the Middle Passage—that brought her people to the New World in order to realize the depth of her sickness and allow herself to be nursed to wellness.

> She vomited in long, loud agonizing gushes. As each seizure began, her head reared back and her body became stiff and upright on the bench. She would remain like this for a second or two, her contorted face giving the impression she was cursing the sky, which was the same clear impeccable blue as before despite the turbulence of the sea. Then, as her stomach heaved up, she would rock forward and the old women holding her would have to tighten their grip as the force of the vomiting sent her straining out over the railing, dangerously close to the water.[5]

Unlike Celie whose illness is precipitated by a sick stepfather, himself a victim of racism and classism in the southern United States, Avery's illness is more self-imposed by a desire to escape a life of poverty. So resolute are Avery and her late husband, Jay, to put the past behind them that she literally has amnesia about her past until the above voyage teases out her memory. Marshall goes about the healing by weaving several different yet related threads together. Because the work that Avery will eventually undertake has such far-reaching implications, and because it is not simply about her own recovery but involves the passing on of history, the recovery of a people's past, Avery Johnson's healing must take place in a community that is conscious of its place in life and that actively, regularly ritualizes its connection to the past through the yearly "Beg Pardon" ceremony. And as the character Lebert Joseph declares, "'*when you see me down on my knees at the Big Drum is not just for me one . . . Oh, no! Is for tout moun'*. And his little truncated arms had opened in a gesture wide enough to take in the world."[6] Avery Johnson's healing is predicated on its rippling effects and impacts more than herself.

> the writer had been instructed
> to respect her elders
> Avery was a woman growing in wisdom
> it would not be wise for
> the writer to discount her
> like life itself
> wisdom had to be nurtured

Praisesong for the Widow is a double tribute to middle-aged women in a society that renders them invisible. It moves beyond recovery to action, and reinvests the elders with the full honor and responsibility of teaching the next generation and continuing the tradition. So when Avery seeks shelter from the burning sun after she jumps ship, she finally recognizes and accepts her invisibility.

> There was no indication that the man had heard her or, for that matter, that he has even seen her—really seen her—as yet. Because although his dimmed gaze was bent on her face and he was looking at her, it clearly hadn't registered with him that she was a stranger.[7]

Although she projects her invisibility onto Lebert Joseph, it is his role and presence that allows her to recognize her individual and societal absenting. Avery Johnson has been absent from life; she has abdicated her responsibility in lieu of a comfortable, insignificant job, traded her memory for material things. She becomes no more than a mirage, or at the most a possession, until "a laying on of hands" awakens her memory and results in her healing.

The journey that Avery Johnson makes from her luxurious cruise to the small island of Carricou, where she is welcomed into a community of elders and upholders of the tradition, is a necessary one, a retracing of one's steps. In this work, Marshall collapses several African and New World traditions: Elegba, the Orisha of the crossroads, is manifested in Lebert Joseph and Avery's awakening from the middle-class stupor into which she had fallen suggests a connection to the Akan symbol *sankofa,* which literally means to return and retrieve something lost. In this case, it is the importance of the past, as Avery discovers when she allows herself to remember it. Marlene Nourbese Philip's poem aptly speaks Avery's desire:

> Hold we to the centre of remembrance
> that forgets the never that severs
> word from source
> and never forgets the witness
> of broken utterance that passed
> before and now
> breaks the culture of silence
> in the ordeal of testimony;
> in the history of circles
> each point lies
> along the circumference
> diameter or radius
> each word creates a centre
> circumscribed by memory . . . and history
> waits at rest always
> still at the center[8]

As a result of hearing the words, Avery realizes that it all is not struggle; there is laughter and dance too, vital medicine for the soul. So whereas Celie's crossover is individual and largely outside of a wider community, Avery's is group identified, witnessed and enabled by a community whose agency in its own continuity is vigilant. After Avery Johnson responds to the rhythm that identifies her ancestral connection and joins the circle of dancers, she understands and is able to think-speak her healing.

> She had finally after all these decades made it across. The elderly Shouters in the person of the out-islanders had reached out their arms like one great arm and drawn her into their midst.
>
> And for the first time since she was a girl, she felt the threads, that myriad of shiny, silken, brightly colored threads (like the kind used in embroidery) which were thin to the point of invisibility yet as strong as the ropes at Coney Island.[9]

And indeed all the threads, the varied aspects of Avery Johnson's life, have come together to greet and celebrate her recommitment to lineage, to history, to continuity. And the drum and the dance shall begin the ceremony; without them there is no space for healing.

> struggling always
> not to be the soothsayer
> the writer spins around like a top

> but lands nonetheless
> the words strewn at her feet

In both *The Color Purple* and *Praisesong for the Widow*, healing of the protagonists, Celie and Avery, occurs on multiple levels, but fundamentally it is their perceptions and minds that are mended. Once they are able to claim without shame their own life experiences, they find their voices and begin to live more fully, more meaningfully. While the characters' recovery has different implications for their respective communities, both Walker and Marshall render their physical and psychological pain in words that permit the reader to participate in the healing process as well. The words are like the breeze of a fan that cools all within its path.

> the writer shuffled the words like a deck of cards
> spread them face down on the table
> she vowed not to touch them
> but they burned into her psyche
> and she had no choice but to entertain them
> after all Ella was there   left in limbo

In *Myal*, writer Erna Brodber's agenda, like Marshall's, has far-reaching implications. Brodber focuses on Ella, a young biracial woman whose role is to teach the new generation. In the context of a postcolonial country such as Jamaica, in which the novel is set, the Ellas of the society must find a new way to educate the youth and prepare them for true independence. Ella's situation—having been married and taken from her homeland to North America by a husband who had then proceeded to make a mockery of her life—represents the masses of people whose spirits have been robbed by a colonial power that belittles their ethos. Similar to Marshall, who forces readers to witness the Middle Passage journey through Avery's trip to Carricou, Brodber has the reader observe Ella's passage to the United States, where she is isolated and exoticized and finally suffers a nervous breakdown precipitated by hallucination.

> "It didn't go so," she said under her breath. And these were the last words that escaped her lips for some time. But long conversations between her selves took place in her head. Mostly accusation.[10]

The reality of her life becomes so painful, her husband's deception and his inability to understand her life so overwhelming, that Ella withdraws into her own head. How then does she get home and do the work that awaits her?

It is at this juncture that Brodber evokes and inserts the collective power of a community tapped into each other's psyche to rescue Ella, the foundation of which has already been laid for her in the form of a master plan prepared by a group of subversives. Their dialogue on the spiritual plane offers much insight:

—Yeah. Planning a strategy. To beat back those spirit thieves and make our way home.—
—To beat back those spirit thieves and make our way home?—
—Get in their books and know their truth, then turn around ship and books into the seven miles of the Black Star line so desperately needed and take who will with you.[11]

Brodber collapses two historical periods, colonial and postcolonial, in the dialogue quoted above. Although she references Marcus Garvey and his repatriation movement envisioned by the purchase of ships, the Black Star Line, Brodber is not advocating a return of Jamaicans or other black people throughout the diaspora to Africa; the return is a mental one, through what some might call an Afrocentric education and philosophical outlook, which she implies is the only antidote to cure the ex-colonized of the traps of colonialism. Expanding on Frantz Fanon's *Black Skin, White Masks,* in which he examines the warping of the colonized minds as a major strategy of the colonizer, Brodber regards the former subject not as victim but rather as agent of her/his own transformation. One will not and cannot be cured unless one acknowledges one's illness and makes an effort to be well. Wellness occurs, Brodber also seems to suggest, not in a vacuum but as a collective generating force, tapping into the same field of energy or ancestral memory. Percy and Willie, Dan, Parson, and Maydene all tap into the Ole African psyche that acts as the spiritual guide force. For, as Mass Cyrus astutely notes, "Curing the body is nothing. Touching the peace of those she must touch and those who must touch her is the hard part. The family will have to come too."[12]

Brodber then adds another dimension to healing absent in Walker and Marshall (although the reader comes to understand that neither Celie's nor Avery's recovery is without its trickle-down positive effect on the people around them). Brodber focuses on an entire community and as such emphasizes the interdependent relationship among people in order to effect any long-lasting, far-reaching, and fundamental changes in the society. Whereas Celie's healing, and even Avery's reconnection, can be read as that of an isolated individual, the same cannot be said of Ella, who has no place without a community. As a result of various conversations with different members of the community, Ella comes to understand the challenge that lies ahead for her. As Reverend Simpson puts it: "Now listen," he said to her. "You have a quarrel with the writer." He wrote, you think, without an awareness of certain things. But does he force you to teach without this awareness? Need your voice say what his says?"[13] This is the crux of Brodber's message to educators and scribes: Deconstruct and interrogate the text, realize its omissions, and teach from that place of understanding. Once Ella understands that the words in print conform the colonial instruments to subject and subordinate, she is then able to not only free and develop her own thoughts, but provide her students with a fuller and true understanding of themselves.

By reinterpreting the basic primer reader that was used in Jamaica prior to independence, in which the docile farm animals correspond to the colonizer's image of the people, Brodber accomplishes at least two of her agendas. She questions the credibility of the printed word, and demonstrates the significance of perspective and allowing a people to speak for themselves. Because as Mr. Dan says, "My people have been separated from themselves, White Hen, by several means, one of them being the printed word and the ideas it carries."[14] Brodber uses the very medium that she is criticizing to critique itself, and in writing *Myal*, which means healer, she is erasing and thereby healing the community's oppression and entrapment by words. She is not calling to abandon words, however; to the contrary, she advocates using them, but being mindful of their consequences.

> the writer did not know
> could not begin to say when
> the words were fashioned into a chain
> she wore around her neck
> but she knew she often fondled them
> in moments of great introspection
> and the weight of them was as a ton of gold
> as the village would be to Miss Cotton

In *It Begins with Tears*, Adisa, similar to the other writers, is conscious of healing, and like Brodber, pulls together several members of the community to bring about and participate in a ritual in which this can be realized for many of the central characters. Adisa's text is grounded in Afro-Caribbean spirituality, a syncretization of African cosmology and Christian doctrines. No one person holds the key; without the collective participation of the group, there is no ritual, and hence no healing.

> Monica's tears paled in the streaming water; her body danced and shook. Miss Cotton and Arnella signaled the women to cease spraying water, and they freed Monica from the glass in which she was trapped. They spun her around, then Miss Cotton stood to one side of her and Arnella to the other.[15]

In this text, the women of the community initiate the healing, led by the seer among them, Miss Cotton. The modus operandi for Monica and the other characters of this novel is comparable to Celie's in that healing can begin only by naming and then releasing past wrongs, ushering in forgiveness, which in turn makes space for healing.

Monica is not the only one who experiences release at the river, the site of cleansing. Several of the other characters who have been carrying their pain like glass dolls also have the opportunity to shed, to leave behind old baggage, to forgive themselves. "Althea felt ashamed for her mother and for herself. Since her mother was unable to ask forgiveness for herself, Althea knew the responsibility fell on her as the only daughter."[16] Adisa understands that people are not always able to ask forgiveness for themselves, but that does not prevent the healing from taking place if another asks in their place. Because the novel is not about one individual, Monica, but rather about the entire community and their interdependence, everyone, willingly or not, who needs to be healed is welcomed and encouraged into the circle. "Beryl was not prepared to shed the tears, but they came, falling directly from her eyes into the ground. Monica reached over and touched her. 'Is your time now.'"[17] It is not only the right time and moment for Monica and Beryl but also for Althea, Angel, and all the other women present.

In *It Begins with Tears,* healing occurs on many different levels, beyond the individual characters' physical and psychological ailments. The environment and the connecting of past rituals with present ones—as evident in Arnella giving birth outside, following the example of her maternal ancestors years earlier—is also an act of healing. Folk wisdom is elevated in this text and serves as the source or the medicine for the cure. By weaving Afro-Caribbean cosmology, juxtaposing different plains of reality—Kristoff Village and Eternal Valley—Adisa is suggesting that an integration of several realities is a necessary prerequisite for healing.

> They couldn't hear anything but words, so they needed her. One told two, two told many, and they spilled into the congested yard. She told them which bush to boil, what colours to wear, where to walk, who to talk to, and they believed her. They heard their own knowledge and their life changed, improved; but still they thanked her, believed she had created the miracle that was inside themselves.[18]

The villagers are unable to hear their own wisdom because they are fragmented; they need someone to speak the words until they are able to speak and hear them themselves. As Marlene Nourbese Philip profoundly notes, "Words collect emotional and physical responses."[19] They also project these responses. When a reciprocal response is established among the speakers, words release the heart to accept the blessing and healing.

Walker, Marshall, Brodber, Adisa, and Philip all understand the power of words and thus wield them in their journey through the brutality that is an integral part of the lives of all people of African descent in the New World. Each writer seems to realize that in order for black people in the diaspora to throw off the burden of their history and forge a new reality, they will have to tackle the past, perhaps even re-experience it like Avery, in order to be free to shape the future. While there is no blueprint for how to accomplish this, these four writers have armed themselves with a hamper of words and have begun the work.

I will become a healer of my people, I said to myself. I will cure the illnesses. I will find remedies. I will restore us to a state of wellness. I will write a book that is a guide, a path to salvation, to health. I will become a healer. As a writer I can say categorically that I have to write whether or not I get published. I don't have any choice about writing if I want to remain sane and be coherent. I must write. I can choose to write something frivolous and narcissistic or I can use my writing as a cure to create miracles that are not extraordinary occurrences, but rather the small steps that we take daily. By writing I make myself well. In writing I am healing.

> the writer bowed
> acknowledged timidly the praises
> she was after all an apprentice   still learning
> to read the medicine in each word
> and estimate the correct dosage
>
> write they said
>   write and heal and eradicate illness.

Chapter 12 ▧

The Great Bonanza of the Antilles[1]

Mayra Montero

I t is not a coincidence that I, a Cuban writer, should have chosen for the title of what was originally my first lecture in Italy that of a short story by Italo Calvino, a Cuban-born Italian writer. It is a phrase that encompasses at least two possible readings.

On the one hand, the "great bonanza" is that period of tranquillity in the open seas—in our countries we call it *calma chica*, or dead calm—that threatening stillness, intense and suffocating, that paralyzes the boat and its crew and convulses with impatience the mysteries, the so-called *loa*, the legion of saints. A paralysis that portends everything but saneness; that provokes everything but joy; that vanquishes everything but sadness.

A second reading evokes prosperity: the bonanza of galleons loaded with gold and spices; the clamorous resplendence of the Caribbean ports with their cargo of sacks of coffee; their bales of tobacco leaves; their barrels overflowing with aged rum, dark and bountiful; bunches of green plantains piling up on the docks and enormous baskets bursting with pineapple and papaya. Moving and organizing the cargo, there is a small army of mestizo men and, barking orders and cursing distant mothers, a mulatto foreman wearing a Panama hat, a gun at the belt, and the shiny riding boots with which he can ride himself into only a rage. Nearby, under an improvised sun canopy made with palm leaves, three placid and heavy-breasted negresses sell their cargo of nutmeg for seasoning, of wild cinnamon to arouse men, and pulp of mamey to thicken the blood.

It may be for that reason that the Antillean bonanza, in its most subtle context, is rooted in the richness and variety of its smells, in the unimaginable profundity of its effluviums: the Caribbean smells of sweat, of overripe fruit, of French perfume, of bitter cassava fritters, fresh gunpowder, and raw fish. The stench of lard, a rancid and turbid pork lard, with residues of ancient fritters, traverses just as well the Boulevard Allégre in Fort-de-France as the Calle de la Luna in Old San Juan; it pervades the Paseo del Conde in Santo Domingo and the Rue de la Marine in Pointe à Pitre; it floats through the Jamaican alleyways of Trenchtown and arouses, or I should say, used to arouse, the Habaneros that strolled among the breezes of the Alameda de Paula.

My first memories revert precisely to those smells: sour milk, for example, and ripe guava, too ripe, perhaps even rotten. I don't believe there's any other place in the world in which milk goes sour as abruptly and mysteriously as it does in our Caribbean islands; nor do I believe there exists another fruit that decays with the lassitude, the voluptuousness, and the carnal texture of guava.

Together with the smells—or perhaps as a consequence of them—a savory percussion and an implacable chakachá of maracas gravitates over us. On our islands we have been, and still are, not only the kings of mambo, who play songs of love every hour of the day, even at the hour of our death, but also the kings of salsa, of the bolero played to the beat of our disenchantment, and of the monumental guaracha.

We were born for the beat, our waists sway with ease—more or less with the same ease that we fly off the handle—the rumba and the undulation of hips comes naturally; even our gods, when they descend to mount us, that is, when they decide to take possession of our bodies and our souls, arrive ablaze by the nocturnal beat of some ritual drum, seduced by that hot and tight rhythm that is also a part of our elementary bonanza. Good-natured and terrible, by the way, are the spirits that govern us, those who open and close paths for us, those who mold our characters and fix the routes we must follow.

I was born in Havana and grew up in the City of the Columns, as Alejo Carpentier so aptly named it, but as far back as my memory can reach, since I was a girl, since forever, I yearned for the balconies of an old mansion in Port-au-Prince; the cacophony of cries, yells, and bellows of the markets of Cap Haitien; the never-ending ceremonies in honor of Damballah celebrated in the farms of Artibonite, and the beats of the Vodou drums that greeted Baron Samedi, indisputable master of the cemeteries.

Madame Loulou, the old woman who left such a deep mark on my childhood, was born in France but was taken to Haiti when she was barely a few months old. It was there she grew up, there she was free and miserable, there she learned the secrets of the hills—she would lower her voice when she mentioned the Mont des Enfants Perdus—and there where she slept under the tree of death. She was a light-skinned mulatto, almost white, first cousin to that other brilliant Caribbean mestizo, Paul Lafargue, who in turn was son-in-law and collaborator of Karl Marx. During school vacations, I spent nights of terror lying next to this woman, obsessed by her spirits of love and vengeance.

It was she who taught me the names of Legba, Agwé Taroyo, of the Marassa twins, Erzulie Frieda, Papá Lokó, and so many other mysteries or loa belonging to the Vodou pantheon. It was from her lips that I heard my first tales of zombies and *bokors,* of *houngans* and mambos, of violent possessions that left in their wake a trail of rancor and blood.

In her hands I saw the first wangas (evil preparations to cause harm); I saw my first "packets" (made in the shape of onions and filled with magical substances that protected from harm and cured the ill); and I saw my first bottles of *acassan, tafia*-rum, and *clairin,* quasi-sacred liquors of Vodou ceremonies.

It was this unforgettable old woman who placed around my neck my first ceremonial necklaces, and it was she, in the long run, who taught me that Haiti was the land of adventure, an adventure that the eyes of the tourists could not see, nor could those of hurried anthropologists, an adventure that simmered in secret, for the use and abuse of the few chosen ones, for their glory and sometimes also for their perdition.

Already middle aged, and after suffering many misfortunes, Madame Loulou emigrated to Cuba, where she lived for more than thirty years until her death, which took place at the beginning of the 1980s. She never knew that even in her moments of greatest rancor, in the clamor of her most powerful narratives of hatred against Haiti, a thread of love and nostalgia betrayed her. It was the thread I pursued, much later, to narrate my own stories.

Apart from the interest in Haiti and the Vodou cult, around that same period of my childhood and adolescence, I began to have increasingly more frequent contacts with the beliefs, liturgies, and poetry of Cuban magic-religious systems. Even though I studied in a rigid school run by Spanish nuns, all I had to do was to go out for a stroll on the streets of Old Havana, or go into the Colón Cemetery, or venture with my schoolmates into the neighborhoods near the port of Havana to stumble at every turn into the most varied, enriching and hallucinating examples of popular religiosity. No wonder Alejo Carpentier himself sustained that he had never been very impressed by the exhibits of poetic objects organized by European surrealists at the height of their movement, for the simple reason that those very same objects, their magic and poetry intact, had since time immemorial been present for us in Cuba, at our fingertips, in almost every Santería altar.

I suspected in some way, even at that early age, that there was a philosophy in the cults of Ocha, Palo Monte, Vodou, and Espiritismo de Cordón that in one way or another expressed an integral conception of the world—a concept of man and of his organic relationship with the world. As Roger Bastide accurately assessed, African mysticism is a passionate, complex, and beautiful form of mysticism—a fountain in which thirsty souls can quench their thirst and drink heaven. Concepts aside, it was rare to find a Havana home in which, in addition to the traditional Catholic images, there were no visible representations of one of these cults, the image of some Orisha, for example. The Orishas are the deities of the Yoruba pantheon who rule the Regla de Ocha, as Cuban Santería is known.

In my own home in Havana, in a corner away from the door (so as not to attract the curiosity of visitors), there was always an image of Babalú Ayé, also known as St. Lazarus. He is a *santo* who does not have a concrete equivalent among Catholic saints, since he is not the St. Lazarus who was bishop of Milan, nor the monastic Lazarus, nor that St. Lazarus who was bishop of Marseilles, even though their feast is celebrated on the same day, the seventeenth of December. The image of the bishop of Marseilles is that of a healthy and strong old man, richly dressed, while the image of the St. Lazarus of Cuban Santería is that of a sad and frail old man, dressed in rags, who helps himself along with crutches (as the Papa Legba of the Vodou cult) and who is always surrounded by three or four dogs licking his wounds. In my house, Babalú Ayé was always offered a glass of rum and a Havana cigar, purple candles and yellow flowers, the darkest coffee and some blackened one-cent coins.

I also remember that we kept in each room, equally hidden from indiscreet gazes, a glass brimming with fresh water, following the suggestion of babalaos and iyalochas, priest and priestesses of Santería, whose opinion was that water so placed "cleared" the environment and soothed the souls of our dead.

If by chance we boarded the launch to visit the small village of Regla, a very popular outing back then, since we had to cross the Bay of Havana, we were given several cents to throw into the sea during the crossing, thus paying a tribute to Yemayá, the deity who ruled the seas, and whose counterpart in the Catholic ritual is precisely Our Lady of Regla.

Every Sunday my sister and I were adorned with our lace mantillas and taken to the ten o'clock Mass and, in the exquisite Gothic Church of the Sacred Heart we went to confession, took communion, and sang our praises to Mary. There was not the slightest glimpse of guilt or doubt in any of us; we carried syncretism in our blood.

At the same time that those nuns from Asturias were teaching us to speak correct Castilian, outside in the street we heard and appropriated many of the words spoken by the *ñáñigos,* the members of the Secret Abakuá Society, an important organization, very influential in the culture and society of Cuba, founded by Carabalí blacks in the nineteenth century. This is why we started to call everything that was pleasant *chévere;* we said *subuso* when we wished to keep a secret; our male friends called their best friends *ekóbios,* and we referred to a *koriofó* when an important group of people congregated. Without realizing it, in an almost instinctive way, we were integrating terms of Abakuá origin into our everyday speech. There still has not been a linguistic study that does full justice to the influence that the Abakuá dialect has had on the Spanish spoken not only in Cuba, but also in other Caribbean countries, such as the Dominican Republic, Puerto Rico, and Venezuela.

What I have tried to emphasize is that the fact of having been born in Cuba, the fact of having grown up there, gave me a broad and I suppose rather unprejudiced view of my own Caribbean identity. I was exposed to phenomena of syncretism as singular as that of Chinese Santería, and I visited, in the legendary Calle de Zanja, crucial heart of the Chinese barrio of Havana, altars in which the African Orishas blended with the improvised Orishas of Asian origin, such as the very miraculous San Fan Con, who derived from the mythical warrior Cuang Con. It was said in Cuba that Chinese Santería—that is, the cult of Ocha with its typical Yoruba deities but duly transculturated and adapted to Asian idiosyncrasies by Chinese-Creole *paisanos*—was infallible in the accomplishment of certain types of magic.

All this, united to the fact of migration, which brought me to live in as complex a country as Puerto Rico, developed within me an unorthodox conception of Antillean reality, something that is present in each one of my published novels. In *La trenza de la hermosa luna* (The Braid of the Beautiful Moon, 1987), a novel that narrates the friendship between an houngan, or Vodou priest, and an impoverished sailor from a schooner who returns to Haiti on the eve of the fall of Jean-Claude Duvalier, I think I begin to formulate what will become a sort of leitmotiv in all my writings: that the Antillean islands, despite their linguistic diversity and different levels of political and economic development, despite their marked sociocultural and even historical differences, can be integrated and turned into a geographic whole in the thoughts and life project of one single man, in this case a humble sailor.

There is something of that also in *La última noche que pasé contigo* (*The Last Night I Spent with You,* 1991), but through very different characters and situations. Here it is a middle-aged couple, paralyzed by routine and apathy—another sort of bonanza, if you like, much more intimate and dangerous—which begins to turn their cherished cruise, their Caribbean voyage from island to island, into this unique maelstrom of discovery and perversion. In Puerto Rico as in St. Thomas, in Martinique as in Guadeloupe, in St. Croix as in Antigua, drama and desire simmer with the same intensity. The protagonists navigate in a circle through what would seem to be one sole territory, butterflies of light attracted by the same flame, smells that reiterate each other to the beat of the same enervating music.

In *Del rojo de tu sombra* (From the Red Glow of Your Shadow, 1994), a novel I consider, above all and despite all, a love story and a reflection on human passions, the misfortunes of the migrants, the way in which they cling to the small scraps of their own identity, evolves, paradoxically, into the most categorical affirmation of a shared destiny.

We move as nomads through our islands, belonging to each a bit, not belonging completely to any. We share the same light; not for nothing the writer Severo Sarduy, upon walking the streets of San Juan for the first time, wept with emotion on perceiving that the clarity, the luminous light that fell on his hands, was the same that shone on Havana. Nor is it strange either that José Lezama Lima had narrated the sensorial details of a voyage by sea to Jamaica—with its smells, sounds, and landscapes—without having moved from his house on Calle Trocadero.

In some way, we are part of the same mirage, we bear with us a sort of natural password—maybe a way of walking, a way of opening our arms, a certain way of returning a gaze—that allows us to recognize each other, and possibly to understand each other better.

Within this context, a question someone asked me some time ago in Santo Domingo, at the occasion of the presentation of one of my novels, returns to my mind: What is a Cuban writer who lives in Puerto Rico doing writing about Haitians who emigrate to the Dominican Republic? The question answers itself, like a serpent biting its own tail. In the middle of the circle traced by the serpent, there is a whole universe of symbols, of certainties and cherished relics.

The last thing I would like, in any case, is to project the Caribbean as an extravagant region in which magic, misery, violence, and death have no other purpose but that of adorning some narratives and exacerbating the imagination of readers. Quite the contrary. Life there, in the barracks of the cane fields of Boca Chica or La Romana, is such as I describe it; the men behave in the same contradictory and obstinate way; and the women, who have experienced every sort of vicissitude, are as dauntless, as lucid, as strong, and at the same time as defenseless as Zulé.

If there is something that surprises, that shocks, or that could seem exotic in my novels, if there is something that produces incredulity, it is due principally to the fact that we are still perfect strangers to a great part of the world. But the fact is that that is how we are, and I must tell it like it is.

What I desire in reality is to put in perspective this supposed inverisimilitude; and to show that despite the isolation and lack of communication that evidently exists among Caribbean peoples, there are defining traits, common elements, and above all, a sincere determination among artists to break this isolation.

In Italo Calvino's tale, Donald Duck's nephews, kneeling before him, beg him to please tell them the ending of the story of what happened in the Great Bonanza. The old man nods off in his armchair and twists and retwists the anecdote without revealing the denouement. Suddenly the nephews give up making the uncle speak and let him sleep. Then they start to tell each other the multiple endings that occur to them, each more amusing and bewildering than the one before, that is, each one more real than the one before. This second part of the story, in which the nephews take over the reins of fantasy, does not belong to Calvino's metaphor, but to that of the Caribbean. While the old masters lie down and dream of their past glories in naval battles, we try to contrive a solution for the contrary ships, a dignified exit from oceanic paralysis, and maybe while we are at it, a remedy for scurvy.

Every once in a while, a gale comes and redeems us.

That is how one writes in the Caribbean—after a hurricane goes by and before the next one arrives, the eye of the heart placed in the crucial eye of the storm, taking advantage of the times of bonanza so that our pages will not blow away.

Translated by Lizabeth Paravisini-Gebert

Chapter 13 🔳

"My Work Is Obeah": An Interview with Poet/Painter LeRoy Clarke

Margarite Fernández Olmos and Heidi Holder

> *My art is Obeah. Obeah is a way, the art of the way to being.*
>
> LeRoy Clarke

For LeRoy Clarke, art is the only way of being, of living, of working. Each stroke of his brush or pen is loaded with the power and conviction of Clarke's philosophy, which is infused with the spiritual magic of Obeah. On New Year's Eve of 1969, Clarke swore an oath to spend the rest of his life creating *De Poet,* a series of paintings, drawings, and poems that Clarke has divided into thematic and consecutive phases or movements, the main subject of which is the neocolonial African. Through each phase of *De Poet,* Clarke attempts to restore the African (the group Clarke believes has fallen farthest among the neo-colonial peoples) to a state of grace and sovereignty. Each stage of *De Poet* mirrors the African experience in the New World—the journey from Africa, the loss of cultural and spiritual identity, and the eventual hope to regain all that was lost. Clarke attempts to heal the neocolonial African through his art.

> Who will rechart the ruins . . . ?
> Who will piece it together
>   in its beginnings . . . ?

> Who will utter the cipher . . . ?
>   —LeRoy Clarke, "Inquiry"

A sixty-year-old, grand, graying figure with an intent, fiery gaze, Clarke is also a philosopher. Trinidadian folklore is the point of departure to an imaginative landscape that informs his worldview and expands his hundreds of paintings and drawings from the realm of art to that of odyssey. In the past, Clarke's worldview was most readily expressed in poetry; among his published works are *Douens* (1981), a collection of poems that form the voice of the images in *De Poet,* and *Taste of Endless Fruit* (1973), love poems. Clarke has produced numerous visual images as well in oil on canvas and in ink and acrylic on paper, corresponding to phases of *De Poet,* a theme that Clarke also explores in public and private talks in movements, which can be summarized as follows.

Fragments of a Spiritual, the first phase of *De Poet,* dating from 1970 to 1973, is based on the idea of a people fallen from grace; the African, stripped of language, religion, family, and self, is left with only fragments of his/her spirituality. By 1974, *Fragments* had evolved into *Douens.* According to Trinidadian folklore, douens are the spirits of unnamed and unbaptized children. For Clarke, the douens are a metaphor for all neocolonial peoples, but specifically the Africans, who also were stripped of their identities. *Douens,* an indictment of the negativity surrounding the African's existence in the New World, evolves into an affirming third phase, *El Tucuche,* named for the second-highest mountain peak in Trinidad, which becomes Clarke's metaphor for man's state of grace, the summit to which his journey points. In the period from 1981 to 1991, new movements emerge: *In de Maze, a Single Line to My Soul,* "dealing with man's choices and decisions; *De Eye Am* approaching the superior self and leaving behind ordinariness, . . . *El Tucuche Approaching Apotheosis,* man's view from El Tucuche where he sees the Godhead of Aripo, which is higher still—a brief ecstatic vision of unity."[1] Another movement, *Utterances,* is followed by *Pantheon,* a transcendental phase in which the now godlike man arrives as a pantheon of entities akin to the Orishas. In Clarke's latest phase, *Revelations I: Movement I Fables . . . Planting Signs in the Dark,* the artist attempts to make words visible, to represent consciousness in pictorial form. The following questions, posed in 1998, offer us a glimpse of LeRoy Clarke's world.

When did you begin your journey as artist/healer? Your work in Douens *has been described as a "spiritual anthology." Is this an accurate description? What exactly do you mean by "douens" and "douendom"? What are the sources of the spirituality described and of your own creative energy?*

It is possible that this thing did not happen to me just so, but rather I am a link in that interminable line or thread or chain or string of beads that informs and preserves the Oríkì,[2] in a specific way, the living idea of Africa and, on the other hand, the living idea of man as world. It was in 1970, while reviewing and redrawing the folklore images that an artist, Alfred Cadallo,[3] left us (this had a profound impact on me in my youth), that I found a symbol for the spiritually defunct state that I feel still pervades African people. That symbol is the *douens.*

I saw parallels in the views of Aime Cesaire's *Return to My Native Land,* T. S. Eliot's *The Waste Land,* Frantz Fanon's *The Wretched of the Earth,* Wole Soyinka's *Idanre and Other Poems,* Wilson Harris' *Palace of the Peacock* and *Tradition, the Writer and Society,* and Christopher Okigbo's *Labyrinths, with Path of Thunder.* At that time too, I became very excited by what was happening in Latin America, particularly in the novels of Juan Rulfo, Miguel Angel Asturias, Gabriel García Márquez, Carlos Fuentes, and Alejo Carpentier, and the poetry of Octavio Paz, Pablo Neruda, and Jorge Luis Borges. Then too, my interest in the "inner time" of calypso, blues and jazz started to swell my insides. By 1972 I entered the house of Orisha. This fired the impetus of my quest to rechart the ruins, to piece it together in its beginning. . . . Eye acknowledged that my house was corrupt.[4]

Among the images in our folklore, the one that I saw as an apt symbol for our decrepitude was douens. Douens are the spirits of children who died before they were christened or baptized. The artist Alf Cadallo provides the only known representations of these spirits. There are no other visual impressions preserved, and so we rely on his descriptions that display these creatures as mischievous, frolicking, little, naked, sexless children, their backward-turned heads and feet; oversized heads under broad-brimmed straw hats that shield them from sunlight; their bloated stomachs and spineless air, their laughter and insectlike feverishness as they nimble with moss and jumbie parasols[5] in murky shadows made for a twilight zone with its citizens of halves!

Douendom is that zone where beings, where lines, are merely half-initiates. A people who suffer from douenophilia, as Dr. J. D. Elder calls it, experience a growth arrest. This sickness is evident where there is self-denial, a denial of our essence, the nature, the origin of one's being, and is the result of massive fracturing of psyche. This is the state of douendom. African people have come to be known as "black people," an invention of those who maintain a "superiority" over them.

How do you react to the idea of the poet/artist as "Obeahman," and art as ritual?

Art for me is a way of becoming. . . . It is a self-creating process. Art is the language of self to the degree that one practices self, and self emerges as that which is noble in humanity—be one a street cleaner, a shoemaker, a carpenter, etc. One is as one's being achieves itself as art. In that sense, one's

Figure 13.1 "How I Carry Myself." Illustration by LeRoy Clarke.

every word, one's everywordness, is an ongoing characterizing of a self, a people; it is that ritual where one's unique spirit is in its perpetual motion of renewing its own identical substance.

Art is a ritual of being for the individual as well as his group. It attempts to envisage life as a ceaseless act fathoming the unfathomable psyche, a perfectioning, so to speak. As an African, mine is the unique task of recharting the ruin, gathering up my dismantled psyche, piece-piece, like reaped moss, piecing it together in its beginning where precision is consciousness of a profound sensing of self in the affirmation of Past-Present-Future. Presencing of self therefore is the degree to which one engages the pendulumic swing through the inner passions of those points in time . . . past, present, future.

My sister, the chanter Ella Andall[6], coins the word "O-be-ah-man" from "Obeahman," evoking the terrifying task of what Eye call stand-up-ness or perpendicularity of self. While Eye do have a great sense of a universal happening, Eye confess that Eye am rebuilding my own house, my word, my being—that which was run asunder by what mother calls "every bitch and dey brother." African people are left splayed in the world, in the involuntary open as "Black People," the accommodation of everyone else but themselves.

My life's work began by presenting Africa as fallen from the grace of being, a dismantled psyche, flagellated, its pieces splayed here, there, everywhere in incoherence. Yet Eye could sense its undaunting spirit, it resides in me!

Where are the Caribbean people today, in terms of their healing process?

Despite what might be observed as successes in our region, there remains, as if untouched, a formidable psychological labyrinth which our efforts are yet unable to penetrate, if only because such an engagement would require of us to become seriously sensitive to the tides of our imagination that so often rise up among us but which are soon swallowed up in the gossip of our numerous sands of indifference. In fact, we are so locked into the spirit of aspiring to be like the other that we have become mere parrots. Mimicry at its best. Ours is a society still unformed . . . uninformed, a light shed from a dream deferred.

Imagination has to be our chiefest rule, pushed forward by a strident courage, making every word an utterance of being lifted from under layers of tourists' spit. With it, if we were to pursue and explore our own bountiful potential, we should be sure to penetrate that which detracts us by being too obvious, easy, and flattering. We may bring to the world at large a far more significant text of liberation, fated, I am sure, to form the basis for a far more authentic expression of our being.

Obeah is that cultural instrument, a practice that begins behind the zero, as if one were to design the compass anew. For behind there is a "hidden life," an "inner time" beyond the reaches of gossip and *mamaguy*,[7] that wait to be evoked and affirmed.

Figure 13.2   "Totem of Utterance." Illustration by LeRoy Clarke.

Having placed our space as one in a prison of suffocating connections vis-à-vis douendom, where life is reduced to mere denial of self with its tendency of redundancy, recurrence, and obedience . . . Eye set out to locate an alternative. That alternative is symbolized by El Tucuche. El Tucuche is the name of the second-highest mountain in the Northern Range of Trinidad. The highest is Aripo. These names may be of Amerindian origin. My own sights were set from douendom—a state of fragments and halves—to ascend the reaches of consciousness of being, an exaltation of purest utterance that, of necessity, will call on my finest efforts.

Surely, such effort will make the greatest demands on not only physical resources but alas, more importantly, on the psychological and the spiritual. To this task I am attempting to reconstruct the idea of Obeah as a force not easily defined by our usual manner, but by an experience of intensifying energy that creates patterns of succession toward a perfectioning of self.

So, simply put, here we have it; douendom and El Tucuche as opposite planes. On the one, defeat, under the feet; on the other, El Tucuche, a liberated voice, affirmation, and a readiness to Apotheosis. That embodiment, and its transcendence of the struggle it takes, is akin to the practice of a faith: Obeah. That is the sensing I bring to my work in art—painting, drawing, poems—which is art as languaging self, the Obeahing of self. As artist Eye am de Obeahman. My work is Obeah.

Notes

Preface

1. Also referred to alternatively as Voodoo, Vodun, and Vaudon. The spelling of this and many other terms of African origin used to describe various practices and beliefs is a constant source of debate among scholars and believers. We have respected the individual preferences of the contributors of this book throughout rather than arbitrarily imposing our preferred spelling.
2. George Eaton Simpson, *Black Religions in the New World* (New York: Columbia University Press, 1978).
3. Joseph M. Murphy, *Working the Spirit: Ceremonies of the African Diaspora* (Boston: Beacon Press, 1994), 6–7. For a more detailed discussion of African-based religious practices, see our book *Sacred Possessions: Vodou, Santería, Obeah, and the Caribbean* (New Brunswick: Rutgers University Press, 1997).

Chapter 1

1. Unless otherwise indicated, the healing recommendations throughout this essay are based on the testimony of the Afro-Cuban folk healers interviewed by the ethnographer Lydia Cabrera in her works *El monte: Igbo-Finda; Ewe Orisha, Vititi Nfinda (Notas sobre las religiones, la magia, las supersticiones y el folklore de los negros criollos y del pueblo de Cuba (The Sacred Wild: Igbo-Finda; Ewe Orisha, Vititi Nfinda. Notes on the Religions, the Magic, the Superstitions, and the Folklore of Creole Blacks and the Cuban People,* 1954) and *La medicina popular de Cuba* (Popular Medicine in Cuba, 1984), and are of the type that might typically be found in botánicas.
2. Michel Foucault, *The Birth of the Clinic: An Archaeology of Medical Perception,* trans. A. M. Sheridan Smith (New York: Pantheon, 1973); Ivan Illich, *Medical Nemesis: the Expropriation of Health* (London: Calder and Boyars, 1975).
3. Byron J. Good, *Medicine, Rationality, and Experience: An Anthropological Perspective* (Cambridge: Cambridge University Press, 1994), 5.
4. Ibid., 5.

5. Arthur Kleinman, *Writing at the Margin: Discourse between Anthropology and Medicine* (Berkeley and Los Angeles: University of California Press, 1995), 23–24. Kleinman notes that the variety of healing practices in suburban America compete in number and diversity with those of other societies: "experts in various massage and dietary therapy, herbalists, acupuncturists, practitioners of many different Asian traditions of martial arts, Christian Science healers, pentecostal healing ministries, charismatic Catholic healing groups, rabbinical practitioners, astrologers, fortune-tellers, iridologists, chiropractors, homeopaths, naturopathic physicians, spirit mediums, self-styled shamans, hypnotists, together with a bewildering variety of lay psychotherapists. . . ." (24).

6. Lydia Cabrera, *El monte,* 4th ed. (Miami: Ediciones Universal, 1975); Michel Laguerre, *Afro-Caribbean Folk Medicine* (South Hadley, MA: Bergin & Garvey Publishers, 1987), 4.

7. Fred M. Frohock, *Healing Powers: Alternative Medicine, Spiritual Communities, and the State* (Chicago: University of Chicago Press, 1992), 2.

8. Hampton Sides, "The Calibration of Belief," *New York Times Magazine,* 7 December 1997, 94.

9. Laguerre, *Afro-Caribbean Folk Medicine,* 16–21.

10. Ibid., 23.

11. Laguerre observes the fact that in Miami, Puerto Ricans can be found buying folk remedies from Cubans, and Bahamians consult root doctors, while in New York, Puerto Rican *curanderos* (healers) treat Cuban patients, and Puerto Ricans in turn consult Haitian folk healers (47). He reiterates the point regarding medical syncretism and pluralism within U.S. medical subcultures in the chapter "Health Beliefs and Practices" in *American Odyssey: Haitians in New York City* (Ithaca: Cornell University Press, 1984), 108–140.

12. Laguerre, *Afro-Caribbean Folk Medicine,* 11.

13. See Zora Neale Hurston, "Hoodoo in America," *Journal of American Folklore* 44: 174 (October–December 1931): 318–417; Holly F. Mathews, "Doctors and Root Doctors: Patients Who Use Both," in *Herbal and Magical Medicine: Traditional Healing Today,* ed. James Kirkland, Holly F. Mathews, C. W. Sullivan III, and Karen Baldwin (Durham: Duke University Press, 1994), 68–98.

14. See for example our work *Sacred Possessions: Vodou, Santería, Obeah, and the Caribbean,* ed. Margarite Fernández Olmos and Lizabeth Paravisini-Gebert (New Brunswick: Rutgers University Press, 1997).

15. Ada Ortúzar-Young, "Lydia Cabrera," in *Spanish American Women Writers: A Bio-Bibliographical Source Book,* ed. Diane E. Marting (Westport, CT: Greenwood Press, 1990), 112.

16. Lydia Cabrera, *El monte,* 10.

17. Eugenio Matibag, "Ifá and Interpretation: An Afro-Caribbean Literary Practice," in *Sacred Possessions: Vodou, Santería, Obeah, and the Caribbean,* 153.

18. Cabrera, *El monte,* 493–94. My translation.

19. Ibid., 11.

20. Among the African-based religious traditions in Cuba, the most widespread are: *Santería,* the Yoruba (in Cuba known also as the Lucumí) tradition, more properly referred to as the *Regla de Ocha* (*regla* meaning socioreligious system), which is derived from the beliefs of the descendants of Yoruba slaves from southeastern Nigeria syncretized with Roman Catholic traditions and is the most widespread of the practices on the island; the *Reglas Congas* (from the former Belgian Congo), among them the *Regla de Palo Monte,* the *Mayombé,* and the *Regla Kimbisa;* and the male secret society *Abakuá* or *ñáñigo,* a *Regla Carabalí,* with origins in the Efik peoples of the ancient Calabar region of Africa. See Isabel Castellanos and Jorge Castellanos, *Cultura afrocubana,* vol. 3: *Las religiones y las lenguas* (Miami: Ediciones Universal, 1992).

21. Indeed, one critic feels that *El monte* is too scientific to be considered a literary work. "The material is carefully documented and transcribed; the notes are presented from an objective point of view; and Cabrera does not attempt to explain or interpret the significance of the date. In short, *El monte* is a scholarly work that would do credit to any folklorist, ethnographer, or anthropologist. Its strengths as a scholarly work, however, underscore its weaknesses as a literary document. It reads like a *medical* journal. It is discursive, rambling, repetitious, and difficult to follow precisely because it is a collection of notes and not a unified or organized work." Miriam DeCosta Willis, *CLA Journal* [College Language Association] 27 (September 1983): 85–86. My emphasis.

22. Cabrera, *El monte,* 234.

23. Ibid., 216–17.

24. Recent economic hardships in Cuba have redirected the focus of its established medical system toward a reevaluation of "green" medicine, or the traditional use of herbs and natural remedies.

25. See Stuart Hall, "Negotiating Caribbean Identities," *New Left Review* 209 (January–February 1995): 3–14.

26. Cuban scholar Fernando Ortiz first described Cuban culture as an *ajiaco,* a steamy, one-pot meal that is a staple of the Caribbean diet (also known as *sancocho*), composed of a combination of diverse local ingredients, each contributing distinctly to its overall unique taste and texture. We add here its popular description as a dish that can "raise the dead" when well prepared and served at appropriate times (i.e., to cure a hangover or a cold).

27. A popular advertising infomercial on U.S. Spanish-language television, Público.

28. Dolores Prida, *Beautiful Señoritas & Other Plays* (Houston: Arte Publico Press, 1991). My translation.

29. Scholars in religious studies such as Anthony Stevens-Arroyo have referred to the botánica as a "temple." "The *botánica* was traditionally a dispensary for curses and spells along with traditionalist herbs; but now it frequently becomes also a temple for worship." Introduction, *Enigmatic Powers: Syncretism with African and Indigenous Peoples' Religions among Latinos,* ed.

Anthony M. Stevens-Arroyo and Andrés I. Pérez y Mena (New York: Bildner Center for Western Hemispheric Studies, 1995), 10.

30. The proliferation of such sites is drawing mainstream attention. Haitian home altars and basement temples created by women, for example, can be found in residential neighborhoods throughout New York City, as noted in Patricia Leigh Brown's "Where the Spirits Feel at Home," *New York Times* 31 December 1998, sec. F1, 5. I. M. Lewis observes in *Ecstatic Religion: A Study of Shamanism and Spirit Possession* (London: Routledge, 1989) that women have played a more important role in religious innovation than has previously been recognized, particularly in marginal possession "cults," which can be considered a form of social protest (26–28).

31. Greek humoral pathology, most agree, was elaborated by the Arab world and taken to Spain during the Muslim period; it then traveled to the Americas via the Conquest. "According to this classical pathology, the basic functions of the body were regulated by four bodily fluids or 'humors,' each of which was characterized by a combination of heat or cold with wetness or dryness (blood—hot and wet; yellow bile—hot and dry; phlegm—cold and wet; black bile—cold and dry). Proper balance of these humors was considered necessary for good health, and any imbalance resulted in illness." See Ricardo Arguijo Martínez, *Hispanic Culture and Health Care: Fact, Fiction, Folklore* (St. Louis: C. V. Mosby Co., 1978), 138.

32. On the therapeutic uses of spiritualism in Mexico, see Michael Kearney, "Spiritualist Healing in Mexico," in *Culture and Curing: Anthropological Perspectives on Traditional Medical Beliefs and Practices,* ed. Peter Morley and Roy Wallis (Pittsburgh: University of Pittsburgh Press, 1979), 19–39. A renewed interest has also emerged in the influence of spiritualism/spiritism within Caribbean culture; see Arcadio Díaz Quiñones, "Fernando Ortiz y Allan Kardec: Transmigración y transculturación," *Latin American Literary Review* 25, no. 50 (July-December 1997): 69–85.

33. Robert T. Trotter, *Curanderismo, Mexican American Folk Healing* (Athens, GA: University of Georgia Press, 1981), 3, 162–63. Interestingly, in "Folklore and Medicine," David J. Hufford notes that the conventional idea that folk medical belief is limited to the isolated, poor, and less-educated segments of the U.S. population is inaccurate: "*All* medical traditions in the pluralistic cultural environment of the United States affect one another deeply and constantly. Health food beliefs have developed from traditions of folk herbalism, Pennsylvania German powwow doctors have been influenced by both Puerto Rican spiritism and chiropractic, and New Age healers explicitly seek out and adopt the practices of Native American shamans. . . . College graduates do seem more likely than others to use folk medicine," in *Putting Folklore to Use,* ed. Michael Owens Jones (Lexington: University Press of Kentucky, 1994), 117, 119.

34. Mercedes Cros Sandoval, "Afro-Cuban Religion in Perspective," in *Enigmatic Powers: Syncretism with African and Indigenous Peoples' Religions among*

Latinos, ed. Anthony M. Stevens-Arroyo and Andrés I. Pérez y Mena (New York: Bildner Center for Western Hemispheric Studies, 1995), 92.

35. Mainstream health practitioners are attempting to keep an open mind on the topic as they examine this belief system's influence on their patients. See Leonardo Alonso and William D. Jeffrey, "Mental Illness Complicated by the Santería Belief in Spirit Possession," *Hospital and Community Psychiatry* 39:11 (November 1988): 1188–91.

36. Mercedes Cros Sandoval, "Afro-Cuban Religion in Perspective," 95.

37. Ibid., 98, 96.

38. Introduction, *Wings of Gauze: Women of Color and the Experience of Health and Illness,* ed. Barbara Bair and Susan E. Cayleff (Detroit: Wayne State University Press, 1993), 20, referring to Wonda Lee Fontenot, "Madame Neau: The Practice of Ethno-Psychiatry in Rural Louisiana," 41–52.

39. Karen McCarthy Brown, "The Power to Heal: Haitian Women in Vodou," in *Daughters of Caliban: Caribbean Women in the Twentieth Century,* ed. Consuelo López-Springfield (Bloomington: Indiana University Press, 1997), 127.

40. "Unlike the categories of standard Western psychiatric nosology, culture-bound syndromes are restricted to specifiable peoples and locales, hence the term 'culture-bound.' Thus their full explications require description not only of the behaviors and experiences that are considered deviant, but also of the ways those behaviors and experiences are embedded in specific social systems and cultural contexts.

   The category of culture-bound syndrome is intrinsically ethnocentric, since the phenomena it lumps together have in common only the fact that they occur someplace other than Western cosmopolitan society and the fact that they are culturally elaborated." Ronald C. Simons, "Sorting the Culture-Bound Syndromes," in *The Culture-Bound Syndromes: Folk Illness of Psychiatric and Anthropological Interest,* ed. Ronald C. Simons and Charles C. Hughes (Dordrecht, Netherlands, and Boston: D. Reidel Publishing Co., 1985), 25.

41. The comments on *ataques de nervios* and Puerto Rican Syndrome are based on a study by Victor De La Cancela, Peter J. Guarnaccia, and Emilio Carrillo in "Psychosocial Distress among Latinos: A Critical Analysis of *Ataques de Nervios,*" *Humanity and Society* 10:4 (November 1986): 431–47.

42. Ibid., 441.

43. Ibid., 423–33.

44. "Viewing a system of psychotherapy as a set of techniques and symbols used by a healer to realign a client's subjective attitudes and behavior with a socially accepted pattern of symbols and activities ... enhances the observer's appreciation of how closely such a system relates to a particular sociocultural milieu and derives its symbols from that milieu ... although the various techniques of psychotherapeutic systems ... are readily transferable cross-culturally, their particular symbolic systems are not." Alan Harwood, *Rx, Spiritist as Needed: A Study of a Puerto Rican Community Mental Health Re-*

source (Ithaca: Cornell University Press, 1987), 200. According to Joan D. Koss, in Puerto Rico "almost everyone knows 'something' about spiritism. An estimated 60% of persons of all socioeconomic classes have visited a spiritist center at some time." Joan D. Koss, "Expectations and Outcomes for Patients Given Mental Health Care or Spiritist Healing in Puerto Rico," in *American Journal of Psychiatry* 144:1 (January 1987): 56. See also Vivian Garrison, "Doctor, *Espiritista* or Psychiatrist?: Health-Seeking Behavior in a Puerto Rican Neighborhood of New York City," *Medical Anthropology* 1:2 (Spring 1977): 65–181; also, by the same author, "The 'Puerto Rican Syndrome' in Psychiatry and *Espiritismo*," in *Case Studies in Spirit Possession,* ed. Vincent Crapanzano and Vivian Garrison (New York: John Wiley & Sons, 1977), 383–449.

45. For a discussion of "culture conflicts" as a result of immigration and geographic dislocation see *Aliens and Alienists: Ethnic Minorities and Psychiatry.* 2nd ed., ed. Roland Littlewood and Maurice Lipsedge (London: Unwin Hyman, 1989).

46. T. Hugh Crawford, *Modernism, Medicine & William Carlos Williams* (Norman: University of Oklahoma Press, 1993), 7.

47. Julio Marzán, *The Spanish American Roots of William Carlos Williams* (Austin: University of Texas Press, 1994), 65.

Chapter 2

1. Erwin H. Ackerknecht, *Medicine and Ethnology: Selected Essays* (Baltimore: Johns Hopkins Press, 1971), 21.

2. See Arie Boombert, "The Arawak Indians of Trinidad and Coastal Guiana ca 1500–1650," *Journal of Caribbean Studies* 19 (1984): 123–88; Peter Hulme, "The Rhetoric of Description: The Amerindians of the Caribbean within Modern European Discourse," *Caribbean Studies* 23 (1990); and Peter Hulme and Neil L. Whitehead, eds., *Wild Majesty: Encounters with Caribs from Columbus to the Present Day* (Oxford: Clarendon Press, 1992).

3. See Eric Williams, *Capitalism and Slavery* (Chapel Hill: University of North Carolina Press, 1944); and Philip D. Curtin, *The Atlantic Slave Trade: A Census* (Madison: University of Wisconsin Press, 1969).

4. See David Dabydeen and Brinsley Samaroo, *India in the Caribbean* (London: Hansib, 1987); and Marian D. Ramesar, *Another Crossing: A History of East Indians in Trinidad, 1880–1946* (St. Augustine, Trinidad: University of the West Indies, 1994).

5. See Alfredo López Austin, *Textos de medicina Nahuatl* (Mexico City: UNAM, 1967); Audrey Butt Colson, "Binary Opposition and the Treatment of Sickness among the Arawaio," in *Social Anthropology and Medicine,* ed. Joseph B. Loudon (New York: Academic Press, 1976), 422–99; George M. Foster, "On the Origin of Humoral Medicine in Latin America," *Medical Anthropology Quarterly* 1 (1987): 355–93.

6. Jan Rogozinski, *A Brief History of the Caribbean* (New York: Facts on File, 1992), 18.

7. See Karen F. Olwig, "Slaves and Masters on Eighteenth-Century St. Johns," *Ethnos* 50 (1985): 214–30.

8. Susan A. McClure, "Parallel Usage of Medicinal Plants by Africans and their Caribbean Descendants," *Economic Botany* 36 (1982): 291–301.

9. Nina L. Etkin and P. J. Ross, "Food as Medicine and Medicine as Food," *Society for Scientific Medicine* 16 (1982): 1559–73.

10. Arthur J. Rubel and Michael R. Hass, "Ethnomedicine," In *Medical Anthropology: A Handbook of Theory and Method,* ed. Thomas M. Johnson and Carolyn F. Sargent (New York: Greenwood Press, 1990), 126.

11. See Adolfo de Hostos, "Plant Fertilization by Magic, in the Taino Area of the Greater Antilles," *Caribbean Studies* 5 (1965): 3–5.

12. Edward S. Ayensu, *Medicinal Plants of the West Indies* (Algonac, Mich.: Reference Publications, Inc., 1981); D. Pedersen and V. Baruffati, "Health and Traditional Medicine Cultures in Latin America and the Caribbean," *Social Science and Medicine* 21 (1985): 5–12; and Michel Laguerre, *Afro-Caribbean Folk Medicine* (South Hadley, Mass.: Bergin and Garvey Publishers, 1987).

13. B. Weniger, "Interest and Limitation of a Global Ethnopharmacological Survey," *Journal of Ethnopharmacology* 32 (1991): 37–41.

14. Lydia Cabrera, *La medicina popular en Cuba* (Miami: Ultra Graphics Corporation, 1984); and José S. Gallo, *El folclor médico de Cuba: Provincia de Camagüey* (La Habana: Editorial de Ciencias Sociales, 1987); and *El folclor médico de Cuba: Enfermedades infecciosas* (La Habana: Editorial de Ciencias Sociales, 1993).

15. See Daisy Carvajal et al., "Pharmacological Screening of Plant Decoctions Commonly Used in Cuban Folk Medicine," *Journal of Ethnopharmacology* 33 (1991): 21–24.

16. See Daisy Carvajal et al., "Pharmacological Study of Cymbopogon Citratus Leaves," *Journal of Ethnopharmacology* 25 (1989): 103–7.

17. Kenneth Bilby, "The Holy Herb: Notes on the Background of Cannabis in Jamaica," *Caribbean Quarterly Monograph* (Kingston: University of the West Indies, 1985).

18. Barry Chevannes, *Rastafari: Roots and Ideology* (Syracuse: Syracuse University Press, 1994).

19. Joseph K. Long, "Jamaican Medicine: Choice Between Folk Healing and Modern Medicine," Ph.D. diss., University of North Carolina, Chapel Hill, 1974.

20. Long, 97.

21. Elisa J. Sobo, "'Unclean Deeds': Menstrual Taboos and Binding 'ties' in Rural Jamaica," in *Anthropological Approaches to the Study of Ethnomedicine,* ed. Mark Nichter (Philadelphia: Gordon and Breach Science Publishers, 1992), 101–26. See also *One Blood: The Jamaican Body* (Albany: State University of New York Press, 1993).

22. Jean Gearing also mentions that the use of "folk methods of abortion included several herbal concoctions" but does not provide any further information in "Family Planning in St. Vincent, West Indies: A Population History Perspective," *Social Science and Medicine* 35 (1992): 1273–82.

23. Sobo (1993), 36.

24. W. Bailey and D. R. Phillips, "Spatial Patterns of Use of Health Services in the Kingston Metropolitan Area, Jamaica," *Social Science and Medicine* 30 (1990): 1–12.

25. Paul Gertler et al., "Determinants of Pregnancy Outcomes and Targeting of Maternal Health Services in Jamaica," *Social Science and Medicine* 37 (1993): 199–211.

26. Carolyn Sargent and Joan Rawlings, "Transformation in Maternity Services in Jamaica," *Social Science and Medicine* 35 (1992): 1225–32.

27. Judith D. Gussler, "Poor Mothers and Modern Medicine in St. Kitts," in *Anthropology of Human Birth,* ed. Margarita A. Kay (Philadelphia: F. A. Davis Co., 1982), 253–66. In some cases ethnopharmacological and other traditional healing regimens are followed because they have cultural value and have proved successful. In other cases they may be selected because alternate choices are too costly, and in still others because anything better is lacking. Whiteford states: "Rural Dominicans face crumbling clinics, missing or expensive medications, and bored or absent physicians. All this results in expensive, low-quality medical care" (see Linda M. Whiteford, "A Question of Adequacy: Primary Health Care in the Dominican Republic," *Social Science and Medicine* 30 [1990]: 221). Patients thus may turn or return to traditional healing. Elsewhere, though, this same author bemoans the fact that during the U.S. military occupation, indigenous healers, folk medicine, and midwives were forbidden, thus creating a void. Would health care have been different if the Dominican Republic had been allowed to develop "its own indigenous system"? (Whiteford, "Contemporary Health Care and the Colonial and Neo-Colonial Experience: The Case of the Dominican Republic," *Social Science and Medicine* 35 [1992]: 1215–23.)

28. Gerald F. Murray and M. D. Alvarez, *Childbearing, Sickness, and Healing in a Haitian Village* (Port-au-Prince: n.p., 1973).

29. B. Weniger et al., "La Médecine populaire dans le plateau central d'Haïti. 1, Étude du système thérapeutique traditionnel dans un cadre socio-culturel rural," *Journal of Ethnopharmacology* 17 (1986): 1–11.

30. B. Weniger et al., "La Médecine populaire dans le plateau central d'Haïti. 2, Inventaire Ethnopharmacologie," *Journal of Ethnopharmacology* 17 (1986): 13–30.

31. Sidney W. Mintz, "Peasant Markets," *Scientific American* 203 (1960): 112–22.

32. Jeannine Coreil and Eddy Genece, "Adoption of Oral Rehydration Therapy among Haitian Mothers," *Social Science and Medicine* 27 (1988): 87–96.

33. Jeannine Coreil et al., "Social and Psychological Cost of Preventive Child Health Services in Haiti," *Social Science and Medicine* 38 (1994): 231–38.

34. Diane Vernon, "Some Prominent Features of Ndjuca Maroon Medicine," *New West Indian Guide* 63 (1989): 209–22.

35. Walter Edwards, ed., *An Annotated Glossary of Folk Medicines Used by Some Amerindians in Guyana* (Georgetown: University of Guyana, 1989).

36. Ibid., 1.

37. Ibid., 5.

38. Wade Davis, "The Ethnobiology of the Haitian Zombie," *Journal of Ethnopharmacology* 9 (1983): 85–104.

39. Roland Littlewood, "From Vice to Madness: The Semantics of Naturalistic and Personalistic Understanding in Trinidad Local Medicine," *Social Science and Medicine* 27 (1988): 129–48.

40. Ibid., 27.

41. Richard Harris, *Local Herbs Used the Chinese Way* (Woodbrook, Trinidad: Traditional Chinese Medical Center, 1991).

42. Noor K. Mahabir, *Medicinal and Edible Plants Used by East Indians of Trinidad and Tobago* (El Dorado, Trinidad: Chakra Publishing House, 1991).

43. See Murray and Alvarez; and Koss-Chioino, *Women as Healers, Women as Patients* (Boulder, Colo.: Westview Press, 1992). See also Alan Harwood, "Mainland Puerto Ricans," in *Ethnicity and Medical Care,* ed. Alan Harwood (Cambridge: Harvard University Press, 1981), 397–481.

44. Georges Chanteur, *Médecine populaire et croyances alimentaires locales* (Fort-de-France, Martinique: Centre Regional de Documentation Pedagogique, 1985); Luis Liriano, *Vivencias de mi campo* (Santo Domingo: Editora Buho, 1988); Christine David, *Folklore of Carriacou* (St. Michael, Barbados: Coles Printing Ltd., 1985); and Portia B. Jordan, *Herbal Medicine and Home Remedies* (Nassau: Nassau Guardian Printing Press, 1986). A very useful study of folk healing in Suriname deals with more than 200 of the most frequently employed plants. See Nellius Sedoc, *Afro-Surinamese natuurgeneeswijzen* (Paramaribo, Suriname: n.p., 1992).

45. I am using "sacred" ritual in contrast to "secular" ritual as used in Brian M. du Toit, *Drugs, Rituals, and Altered States of Consciousness* (Rotterdam: A. A. Balkema, 1977).

46. Jane C. Beck, "Review of *Afro-Caribbean Folk Medicine* by Michel Laguerre," *Journal of American Folklore* 103 (1990): 111–12.

47. Ibid., 112.

48. Karen McCarthy Brown, "Afro-Caribbean Spirituality: A Haitian Case Study," in *Healing and Restoring.* Ed. Lawrence E. Sullivan (New York: Macmillan, 1989), 277.

49. Paul E. Brodwin, "Guardian Angels and Dirty Spirits: The Moral Basis of Healing Powers in Rural Haiti," in *Anthropological Approaches to the Study of Ethnomedicine* (1992), 57–74.

50. Brown, 278.

51. Lydia De Santis, "Health Care Orientations of Cuban and Haitian Immigrant Mothers: Implications for Health Care Professionals," *Medical Anthropology* 12 (1989): 69–89.

52. See Long, 83.

53. William Wedenoja, "Mothering and the Practice of 'Balm' in Jamaica," in *Women as Healers,* ed. Carol Shepherd McClain (New Brunswick: Rutgers University Press, 1989), 76–97. See also W. Penn Handwerker, "West Indian Gender Relations, Family Planning Programs and Fertility Decline," *Social Science and Medicine* 35 (1992): 1245–57.

54. George E. Simpson, *Religious Cults of the Caribbean: Trinidad, Jamaica, and Haiti,* Caribbean Monograph Series no. 15 (Río Piedras, Puerto Rico: Institute of Caribbean Studies, 1980).

55. See Robert O. Williams, *The Useful and Ornamental Plants in Trinidad and Tobago* (Port of Spain: n.p., 1951).

56. Laguerre, 27.

57. Angelina Pollak-Eltz, "The Shango Cult and Other African Rituals in Trinidad, Grenada, and Carriacou and Their Possible Influences on the Spiritual Baptist Faith," *Caribbean Quarterly* 39 (1993): 12–26.

58. Arthur Niehoff and Juanita Niehoff, *East Indians in the West Indies* (Milwaukee: Milwaukee Public Museum Publications in Anthropology, no. 6, 1960).

59. Paul Farmer, "Sending Sickness: Sorcery, Politics, and Changing Concepts of AIDS in Rural Haiti," *Medical Anthropology Quarterly* 4 (1990): 6–27.

60. See Koss-Chioino.

61. Cecil Helman, *Culture, Health and Illness* (Boston: Butterworth-Heinemann, 1994).

62. Merrill Singer and Roberto García, "Becoming a Puerto Rican Espiritista: Life History of a Female Healer," in McClain, *Women as Healers,* 157–85.

63. Koss-Chioino, 77.

64. See also Carol L. Weiss, "Controlling Domestic Life and Mental Illness: Spiritual and Aftercare Resources Used by Dominican New Yorkers," *Culture, Medicine, and Psychiatry* 16 (1992): 237–71.

65. Mario Núñez Molina, "Therapeutic and Preventive Functions of Puerto Rican *Espiritismo,*" *Hómines* 13 (1989): 267–76.

66. Chevannes, 31.

67. Raul Cañizares, *Cuban Santería: Walking with the Night* (Rochester, Vt.: Destiny Books, 1993), 77, 99.

68. Migene González-Wippler, *Santería: The Religion* (St. Paul, Minn.: Llewellyn Publications, 1994).

69. See Cañizares (99) and Gonzáles-Wippler (287).

70. Harry Ramnath, *The Unwritten Laws of Hinduism* (Marabella, Trinidad: Danprint, 1987).

71. Chevannes, 31.

72. Simpson, 188.

73. William W. Dressler et al., "Social Factors Mediating Social Class Differences in Blood Pressure in a Jamaican Community," *Social Science and Medicine* 35 (1992): 1233–44.

74. Lee M. Pachter, "Introduction: Latino Folk Illnesses: Methodological Considerations." *Medical Anthropology* 15 (1993): 107.

75. See Ronald C. Simons and Charles C. Hughes, *The Culture-Bound Syndromes: Folk Illnesses of Psychiatric and Anthropological Interest* (Dordrecht, Netherlands: D. Reidel Publishing Co., 1985); and Roland Littlewood and Maurice Lipsedge, "Culture-Bound Syndromes," in *Recent Advances in Psychiatry* 5th ed. Kenneth Granville-Grossman (Edinburgh: Churchill-Livingstone, 1985), 105–42.

76. Phillip Singer et al., "Learning of Psychodynamics, History, and Diagnosis Management Therapy by a Kali Cult Indigenous Healer in Guiana," in *The Realm of the Extra-Human: Agents and Audience,* ed. Agehahanda Bharati (The Hague: Mouton, 1976), 345–69.

77. Phillip Singer et al. This inclusion of the family in the healing process reminds one of the therapy group, healing village, support of the family, etc. of the African patient. There too the family is present during the diagnosis, the confession, and the healing.

78. Phillip Singer et al., "Integration of Indigenous Healing Practices of the Kali Cult with Western Psychiatric Modalities in British Guiana," *Revista Interamericana de Psicología* 1 (1967): 103–13.

79. Peter J. Guarnaccia et al., "The Multiple Meanings of *Ataques de Nervios* in the Latino Community," *Medical Anthropology* 11 (1989): 47–62.

80. Peter J. Guarnaccia, "*Ataques de Nervios* in Puerto Rico: Culture-Bound Syndrome or Popular Illness," *Medical Anthropology* 11 (1993): 157–70.

81. Maria Oquendo et al., "*Ataques de Nervios*: Proposed Diagnostic Criteria for a Culture Specific Syndrome," *Culture, Medicine, and Psychiatry* 16 (1992): 367–76. See also Michael Swerdlow, "'Chronicity,' 'Nervios,' and Community Care: A Case Study of Puerto Rican Psychiatric Patients in New York City," *Culture, Medicine, and Psychiatry* 16 (1992): 217–35.

82. Gerald F. Murray, "Women in Perdition, Fertility Control in Haiti," in *Culture, Natality and Family Planning,* ed. J. Marshall and S. Polgar (Chapel Hill: Carolina Population Center, 1976), 59–78.

83. Merrill Singer et al., "Culture, Critical Theory, and Reproductive Illness Behavior in Haiti." *Medical Anthropology Quarterly* 2 (1988): 370–85.

Chapter 3

(All endnotes are the translator's.)

1. The orichas are the deities of Santería, or the Regla de Ocha. They are also referred to as *santos* (saints). The cabildos are Afro-Cuban mutual aid/social/cultural organizations. The vodunsi belong to the Arará or Haitian Vodou tradition. Congos is a common name for the Palo Monte tradition or its variant, the Mayombe.

   Cabrera refers to two of the more pervasive African-based religious systems in Cuba: *Santería,* the Yoruba-Lucumí system more properly referred to as *Regla de Ocha* or the belief system of the *orichas,* derived from the beliefs of the descendants of Yoruba slaves from southeastern Nigeria: and the *Regla de*

Palo Monte, Mayombe, or *Regla Conga* tradition, based on the belief system of peoples from the former Belgian Congo area of Africa. She also mentions the Arará cult based on the Vodou traditions of Haiti.

Nganga means both a priest and a consecrated object in the Congo tradition.

2. "Seated," referring to the Santería initiation ceremony wherein an oricha is "seated" or installed inside the head of the initiate.

3. The practitioners of Santería, or Regla de Ocha, are like members of a family, guided by the *babá* (father-priest) or the *iyá* (mother-priestess).

4. Omí Tomí was a woman who worked in Cabrera's home and introduced her to the world of Afro-Cuban religious beliefs.

5. Tutelary Santería deity, master of wisdom and divination, also referred to as Orula.

6. Copper mining town in eastern Cuba, the site of veneration of the patron saint of the island, the Virgin of Caridad (Charity), syncretized with the Santería deity Oshún.

Chapter 4

1. A version of this paper appears in *Healing and Restoring: Health and Medicine in the World's Religious Traditions,* ed. Lawrence E. Sullivan (New York and London: Macmillan, 1989).

2. As will be seen below, there is a sense in which the dead continue to exist; however, none of the living would consider this existence superior to his or her own. Thus immortality does not function as a reward for sacrifices made in the present life.

3. A partial qualification to this characterization exists in the large numbers of homosexual priests who have genuine power and prestige within Vodou. This is somewhat surprising given the extreme homophobia in Haitian culture. However, it is only a partial qualification because many of these priests are more accurately described as bisexuals. They often have traditional families.

4. See William Bascom, *The Yoruba of Southwestern Nigeria* (New York: Holt, Rinehart and Winston, 1969); also Melville Herskovits, *Dahomey: An Ancient West African Kingdom,* 2 vols. (Evanston: Northwestern University Press, 1967).

5. Marriage to a Vodou spirit—a ritual complete with marriage license, an exchange of rings (wherein the spirit is represented by his or her chwal), a wedding cake, and, on occasion, champagne—is a ritual that does not demand that a person experience possession. It nevertheless involves a lifelong commitment to the spirit. One day a week is dedicated to the spirit spouse. Special colors sacred to the lwa must be worn on that day, and the devotee must sleep alone so that the spirit may appear in dreams.

6. "Taking the asson" as a path to gaining status as a priest or priestess is a ritual performed mainly in the south of Haiti and in Port-au-Prince. In the northern part of the country, such status is conferred by virtue of family position or reputation as a healer. The initiation rituals are costly for those who

take the asson. It may be partly as a result of economic factors that individuals sometimes claim to have received priestly training in dreams, visions, or periods of time spent "under the water."

7. Gerald F. Murray, "Women in Perdition: Ritual Fertility Control in Haiti," in *Culture, Natality and Family Planning,* ed. John F. Marshall and Steven Polgar (Chapel Hill: Carolina Population Center, University of North Carolina, 1976), 59–78. Murray points out that the socially useful part of this explanatory scheme is that, by being provided with the possibility of a pregnancy much longer than nine months, a woman can claim the father of her child to be almost anyone with whom she has ever had sexual relations. This in turn allows her to choose from among fathers the one who is most likely to be able to give meaningful support. Given the current social instability all over Haiti, finding men with the means and temperament to be responsible fathers is one of the major problems faced by women.

8. See Serge Larose, "The Meaning of Africa in Haitian Vodu," in *Symbols and Sentiments: Cross-Cultural Studies in Symbolism,* ed. Joan Lewis (New York: Academic Press, 1977), 85–116.

9. The ingredients for Vodou treatments are paid for by the client. Fees for the healer beyond the cost of materials are understood to be gifts, and theoretically it is up to the client to decide how much he or she will offer. In practice, however, the range of what is appropriate is usually well known to clients without their asking. It is worth noting that many of the most sought-after healers are not prosperous persons. They adhere strictly to the tradition that healing powers are not to be used for inordinate profit.

Chapter 5

1. See Anna Wexler's interview with Steve Quintana in this book (Chapter 6).

Chapter 6

1. Ethnic spirit guides considered to be among the "good" spirits in the pantheon of spiritualism. In Cuba, as George Brandon states, "spirit guides frequently embodied the popular stereotypic images of Cuban ethnic, racial, and professional groups. Not only did Cuban *espiritistas* in their mediumistic trance manifest spirit guides that resembled themselves, both physically and in temperament, but both black and white mediums manifested spirit guides who were *Africanos de nación*—Lucumi, Mandinga, Mina, and Congolese tribesmen who had suffered and died in slavery," in *Santería from Africa to the New World: The Dead Sell Memories* (Bloomington: Indiana University Press, 1993), 87.

2. Refers to a table covered with a white cloth around which mediums and other participants at spiritualist masses sit while spirits are contacted for help with problems afflicting members of the group. Usually a goblet of water, candles, and often flowers are placed on the table.

3. In Yoruba tradition, the "mounting" of initiates and priests by an Oricha refers to possession. The mounted individual is sometimes known as a "horse" in the pervasive equestrian metaphor (see J. Lorand Matory, *Sex and the Empire That Is No More: Gender and the Politics of Metaphor in Oyo Yoruba Religion,* Minneapolis: University of Minnesota Press, 1994). The use of the term "mount" here also includes spiritualist mediums.

Chapter 7

1. Joan Koss-Chioino, *Women as Healers, Women as Patients: Mental Health Care and Traditional Healing in Puerto Rico* (Boulder, Colo.: Westview Press, 1992); Julio Sánchez, *La religión de los orishas* (San Juan: Editorial Puertor-riqueña, 1987).

2. Ann Hohmann, Madeline Richeport, Bernadette Marriott, Glorisa Canino, Maritza Rubio-Stipec, and Héctor Bird, "Spiritism in Puerto Rico: Results of an Island-Wide Community Study," *British Journal of Psychiatry* 156 (1990): 328–35.

3. Vivian Garrison, "Doctor, *Espiritista*, or Psychiatrist? Health-Seeking Behavior in a Puerto Rican Neighborhood of New York City," *Medical Anthropology* 1:2 (1977): 65–191; Joan D. Koss, "The Therapist-Spiritist Training in Puerto Rico: An Experiment to Relate the Traditional Healing System to the Public Health System," *Social Science and Medicine* 14 (1980): 255–66; Mario Núñez Molina, "Preventive and Therapeutic Aspects of Puerto Rican Espiritismo," *Homines* 13 (1990): 267–76; Andrés Pérez y Mena, *Speaking with the Dead: Development of Afro-Latin Religion among Puerto Ricans in the United States* (New York: AMS Press, 1991).

4. Mario Núñez Molina, "Desarrollo del Médium: The Process of Becoming a Healer in Puerto Rican *Espiritismo*," Ph.D. diss., Harvard University, 1987.

5. Lydio Cruz Monclova, *Historia de Puerto Rico* (San Juan: Editorial Universitaria, 1952); Joan D. Koss, "Religion and Science Divinely Related: A Case History of Spiritism in Puerto Rico," *Caribbean Studies* 16:1 (1977): 22–43; Nestor Rodríguez, *Historia del Espiritismo en Puerto Rico* (San Juan: Author, 1978); and Teresa Yáñez, *El Espiritismo en Puerto Rico* (San Juan: Federación de Espiritistas en Puerto Rico, 1963).

6. Allan Kardec, *El libro de los espíritus* (Buenos Aires: Tipográfica Editora Argentina, 1978 [1857]); *El evangelio según el espiritismo* (Buenos Aires: Tipográfica Editora Argentina, 1978 [1864]); *El libro de los mediums* (Buenos Aires: Tipográfica Editora Argentina, 1977 [1859]).

7. See Nestor Rodríguez, *Historia del Espiritismo en Puerto Rico.*

8. See Yáñez's *El Espiritismo en Puerto Rico.*

9. See Cruz Monclova, *Historia de Puerto Rico.*

10. Cruz Monclova, 643.

11. Carlos Alvarado, "Psychical Research in Puerto Rico," *Parapsychology Review,* 10 (1979): 23–24.

12. See Ricardo Alegría, *La fiesta de Santiago en Loíza Aldea* (San Juan: Instituto de Cultura, 1954).

13. Alan Harwood, *Rx: Spiritist as Needed: A Study of a Puerto Rican Community Mental Health Resource* (New York: Wiley, 1977).

14. Vincent Crapanzano, *Tuhami: Portrait of a Moroccan* (Chicago: University of Chicago Press, 1980); Paul Rabinow, *Reflections on Fieldwork* (Berkeley and Los Angeles: University of California Press, 1977).

15. Shulamith Reinharz, *On Becoming a Social Scientist* (San Francisco: Jossey-Bass, 1984), 337.

16. Donald Polkinghorne, *Methodology of the Human Sciences* (Albany: State University of New York, 1983).

17. Hussein Fahim, ed., *Indigenous Anthropology in Non-Western Countries* (Durham: Carolina Academic Press, 1982).

18. Richard Katz, *The Straight Path: A Story of Healing and Transformation in Fiji* (Boston: Addison-Wesley, 1993).

19. Youngsoook Harvey, *Six Korean Women: The Socialization of Shamans* (New York: West, 1979), 199; Hohmann et al., "Spiritism in Puerto Rico."

20. Eric Fromm, *Psychoanalysis and Religion* (New York: Bantam, 1967).

21. Thomas Csordas, "Medical and Sacred Realities: Between Comparative Religion and Transcultural Psychiatry," *Culture, Medicine and Psychiatry* 9 (1985): 105.

22. Carl Rogers, *A Way of Being* (Boston: Houghton Mifflin, 1980).

23. Vivian Garrison, "Folk Healing Systems as Elements in the Community," in *Therapeutic Intervention: Healing Strategies for Human Systems* (New York: Human Science Press, 1982).

24. See Harwood.

25. Joan D. Koss, "Therapeutic Aspects of Puerto Rican Cult Practices," *Psychiatry* 38:2 (1975): 160–71.

26. Isaac Lubchansky, Gladys Egri, and Janet Stokes, "Puerto Rican Spiritualists View Mental Illness: The Faith Healer as a Paraprofessional," *American Journal of Psychiatry* 127:3 (1970): 313–21.

27. Melvin Delgado, "Accepting Faith Healers: Problems and Rewards," *Journal of Social Welfare* 6 (1979–80): 5–16.

28. See Garrison (1997, 1982).

29. See Núñez Molina, "Desarrollo del Médium."

30. Richard Katz and Mario Núñez Molina, "Researching 'Realities': A Method for Understanding Cultural Diversity," *The Community Psychologist* 19:2 (1986): 7–8.

31. Melvin Delgado, "Puerto Rican Spiritualism and the Social Work Profession," *Social Casework* 58 (1977): 451–58.

32. Moisés Gaviria and Ronald Wintrob, "Spiritist or Psychiatrist: Treatment of Mental Illness Among Puerto Ricans in Two Connecticut Towns," *Journal of Operational Psychiatry* 10 (1979): 40–46.

33. Beatrice Purdy, Renee Pellman, Sarah Flores, and Harvey Bluestone, "Mellaril or Medium, Stelzaine or Séance? A Study of Spiritism as It Affects

Communication, Diagnosis, and Treatment," in *On the Urban Scene,* ed. Morton Levitt and Ben Rubenstein (Detroit: Wayne State University Press, 1972), 65–79.

34. Pedro Ruiz and John Langrod, "The Role of Folk Healers in Community Mental Health Services," *Community Mental Health Journal* 12 (1976): 392–98.

35. Victor De La Cancela and Iris Zavala, "An Analysis of Culturalism in Latino Mental Health: Folk Medicine as a Case in Point," *Hispanic Journal of Behavioral Sciences* 5 (1983): 267.

36. José Figueroa, *The Cultural Dynamic of Puerto Rican Spiritism: Class, Nationality, and Religion in a Brooklyn Ghetto,* Ph.D. diss., City University of New York, 1981.

37. See Garrison (1977, 1982); and Ramona Salgado, *The Role of the Puerto Rican Spiritist in Helping Puerto Ricans with Problems of Family Relations,* Ph.D. diss., Columbia University, 1974.

38. Salgado, 203.

39. See Harwood, *Rx: Spiritist.*

40. Ibid.

41. Richard Katz, *Boiling Energy* (Cambridge: Harvard University Press, 1982).

Chapter 8

1. Susan Sontag, *Illness as Metaphor* (New York: Farrar, Straus and Giroux, 1977), 3.

2. For a more complete study of the wide variety of African-based religious customs in the Caribbean, see *Sacred Possessions: Vodou, Santería, Obeah, and the Caribbean,* ed. Margarite Fernández Olmos and Lizabeth Paravisini-Gebert (New Brunswick: Rutgers University Press, 1997).

3. Alvarez's second novel, *In the Time of the Butterflies,* celebrates the bravery of the martyred Mirabal sisters, who lost their lives under Trujillo (Chapel Hill, N.C.: Algonquin, 1994).

4. Julia Alvarez, *Something to Declare* (Chapel Hill, N.C.: Algonquin, 1998), 174.

5. Julia Alvarez, *How the García Girls Lost Their Accents* (New York: Penguin, 1992).

6. Julia Alvarez, *¡Yo!* (Chapel Hill, N.C.: Algonquin, 1997).

7. In this essay, I will periodically supplement examinations of the fictional Yolanda's experience with Alvarez's personal reflections in her collection of essays *Something to Declare.* While the novels cannot be read as purely autobiographical, or as dependably factual renditions of the Alvarez family's expatriation, the character Yolanda is, by Alvarez's own admission, enough of a composite of her creator to warrant such comparisons.

8. Julie Barak, "'Turning and Turning in the Widening Gyre': A Second Coming into Language in Julia Alvarez's *How the García Girls Lost Their Accents,*" *MELUS* 23 (Spring 1998): 160.

9. Alvarez, *¡Yo!*, 12.

10. Alvarez, *How the García Girls Lost Their Accents*, 231–32, and *Something to Declare*, 135–38.

11. Alvarez, *¡Yo!*, 24.

12. Ibid., 7.

13. Ibid., 300.

14. Ibid., 300.

15. Alvarez, *How the García Girls Lost Their Accents*, 198.

16. Ibid., 202.

17. Alvarez, *¡Yo!*, 28.

18. Ibid., 299.

19. Ibid., 307.

20. Ibid., 305.

21. Alvarez, *How the García Girls Lost Their Accents*, 290.

22. Ibid., 211.

23. Alvarez, *Something to Declare*, 109.

24. In a second instance of censorship in the first novel, the father tears up a speech (a loose plagiarism of Whitman's "Song of Myself") that the adolescent Yo has written, forbidding her to speak such self-congratulatory words in public. Though there is not space to examine the scene closely here, it is another instance of violation brought on by the father's haunting fears of political retribution for speaking aloud. Recognizing the root of her parent's oppression, Yo bitterly flings Trujillo's hated nickname "Chapita" at her father, as she weeps over her second unjust silencing (*How the García Girls Lost Their Accents*, 142–47).

25. By "first" and "second," I refer to the appearance of each episode in the book, an important distinction in shaping the reader's experience of mental illness in the novel. Because the novel moves backward through time, however, the chronological position of each breakdown is actually the opposite (historically, Yolanda's hospitalization occurs prior to Sandi's).

26. Joseph Breuer and Sigmund Freud, *Studies on Hysteria (1893–1895)*, trans. James Strachey (New York: Basic Books, 1957).

27. Alvarez, *How the García Girls Lost Their Accents*, 54.

28. Ibid., 55.

29. Alvarez, *Something to Declare*, 8.

30. Alvarez, *How the García Girls Lost Their Accents*, 55, 54.

31. Breuer and Freud, *Studies on Hysteria*, 25.

32. Alvarez, *How the García Girls Lost Their Accents*, 55.

33. Ibid., 53.

34. Ibid., 56.

35. Ibid., 60.

36. Ibid., 68.

37. Ibid., 75.

38. Ibid., 77.

39. Ibid., 80.

40. Ibid., 82.

41. Alvarez, *Something to Declare,* 58.

42. Alvarez, *How the García Girls Lost Their Accents,* 74, 80.

43. For a useful discussion of the talking cure as it is enacted in literary texts, including the psychoanalytic phenomena of transference, countertransference,
and resistance, see Jeffrey Berman's *The Talking Cure: Literary Representations
of Psychoanalysis* (New York: New York University Press, 1985).

44. In speaking of resistance in psychotherapy, Berman argues: "The psychobi-
ographer thus frees the word from any connotations of a conscious, insin-
cere, or fraudulent reluctance to tell the truth. There is resistance, then, in
the nature of all inquiry. Viewed in this way, resistance becomes the natural
reluctance to reveal or discover troubling human truths." The goal of therapy is, of course, to overcome resistance in order to uncover the real story,
whereas the goal of art might be construed as the creative use of facts as raw
material for weaving fictions.

45. Alvarez, *How the García Girls Lost Their Accents,* 85.

46. Thomas Szasz, "The Healing Word: Its Past, Present, and Future," *The Journal of Humanistic Psychology* 38, no. 2 (spring 1998): 8–20.

47. Alvarez, *How the García Girls Lost Their Accents,* 83.

48. Ibid., 84.

49. Ibid., 85.

50. List of "Commandments" in Alvarez, *Something to Declare,* 259–60.

51. Ibid., 123.

52. Alvarez, *¡Yo!,* 296.

53. See Joan Dayan, "Vodoun, or the Voice of the Gods," in Fernández Olmos
and Paravisini-Gebert, eds., *Sacred Possessions: Vodou, Santería, Obeah, and
the Caribbean,* 13–36.

54. Alvarez, *¡Yo!,* 218, 220.

55. Ibid., 219.

56. Dayan, 19.

57. Alvarez, *¡Yo!,* 200.

58. Ibid., 221.

59. Barak, "'Turning and Turning in the Widening Gyre,'" 162.

60. Alvarez, *¡Yo!,* 221. (My italics)

61. Ibid., 296.

62. Eugenio Matibag, "Ifá and Interpretation: An Afro-Caribbean Literary Practice," in Fernández Olmos and Paravisini-Gebert, eds., *Sacred Possessions:
Vodou, Santería, Obeah, and the Caribbean,* 153.

63. Alvarez, *¡Yo!,* 308–9.

64. While the obsessive return to this episode in previous narratives could be
seen as cathartic, a bringing to consciousness of an old injury to purge its
emotional power, this revised episode is fictional. It finally closes the recursive story by rewriting it, thus halting the cycle of repression and recovery.

65. Though, like psychotherapy, the Catholic confessional can offer relief for
mental suffering (see Szasz).

66. Matibag, "Ifá and Interpretation," 166.
67. Alvarez, *Something to Declare,* 11, 129.
68. Marny Requa, "Julia Alvarez: The Politics of Fiction," *Frontera* (5) online: www.fronteramag.com/issue5/Alvarez/
69. While it might be tempting to read this as a disturbingly colonial image—the patriarch as the sole controller of language—it must be remembered that it is the writer, Alvarez, who returns to this episode, in which to rewrite it and free her muse. In effect, she puts words in the mouth of her silencer and blesses *herself.*
70. In her daily writing rituals, Alvarez reveals more than a passing commitment to the syncretic spiritualism of her homeland: "I fill my writing bowl and say hello to my two old cemíes [stone and wooden Taino deities from the Dominican Republic] and make sure my Virgencita has flesh flowers, if it is summer, or a lit candle, in the winter" (*Something to Declare,* 285).
71. Requa, "Julia Alvarez: The Politics of Fiction."
72. Alvarez, *Something to Declare,* 173.

Chapter 9

1. See Edouard Glissant, *Caribbean Discourse: Selected Essays,* trans. J. Michael Dash (Charlottesville: University Press of Virginia, 1989), 146. Taken as a whole, Glissant's essays deal brilliantly and provocatively with the historical and cultural consequences of the plantation societies created by European expansion into the Americas and by the importation of enslaved Africans. His view of the "Caribbean" is broad. In concept, it reaches at least from Memphis, Tennessee, to Salvador, Bahia; from the poor white farmers in the work of William Faulkner to the practitioners of *candomble* in the novels of Jorge Amado; from the evangelical minister who uses African call-and-response patterns in *The Apostle,* directed by Robert Duvall, to the warrior Zumbi who rules a kingdom of escaped slaves in *Quilombo,* directed by Carlos Diegues. It includes, of course, the botánicas of Harlem and must now incorporate the salsa bands of West Africa, where the beats of Miami and Havana find new homes.
2. On the issue of Creole identities there is much recent writing. See Antonio Benítez Rojo, *The Repeating Island: The Caribbean and the Postmodern Perspective,* 2nd ed., trans. James E. Maraniss (Durham: Duke University Press, 1996); Jean Bernabé et al., *Éloge a la creolité/In Praise of Creoleness,* trans. M. B. Taleb-Khyar. (Baltimore: Johns Hopkins University Press, 1990); Chris Bongie, *Islands and Exiles: The Creole Identities of Post/Colonial Literature* (Stanford: Stanford University Press, 1998); J. Michael Dash, *The Other America: Caribbean Literature in a New World Context* (Charlottesville: University Press of Virginia, 1998); and Simon Gikanki, *Writing in Limbo: Modernism and Caribbean Literature* (Ithaca: Cornell University Press, 1992).
3. For the best summary of the debate about the baroque in the New World, see Carmen Bustillo, *Barroco y América Latina: Un itinerario inconcluso*

(Caracas: Monte Avila, 1996). For primary sources in the debate, see Alejo Carpentier, *Tientos y diferencias: ensayos* (Montevideo: Arca, 1967); Edouard Glissant, *Poetics of Relation*, trans. Betsy Wing (Ann Arbor: University of Michigan Press, 1997); José Lezama Lima, *La expresión americana* (La Habana: Editorial Cubanas, 1993); Severo Sarduy, *Barroco*, (Buenos Aires: Sudamerica, 1974); and Peter Wollen, "Baroque and Neo-Baroque in the Society of the Spectacle," *Point of Contact* 3:3 (April 1993): 8–21.

4. While no previous study emphasizes how Caribbean cinema has responded to modernity, there is a growing body of impressive scholarship about the films of the region. See Mbye B. Cham, ed., *Ex-Iles: Essays on Caribbean Cinema* (Trenton, N.J.: Africa World Press, 1992); Michael Chanan, *The Cuban Image* (London: British Film Institute, 1985); John King et al., eds. *Mediating Two Worlds: Cinematic Encounters in the Americas* (London: British Film Institute, 1993); Michael T. Martin, ed., *Cinemas of the Black Diaspora: Diversity, Dependence, and Oppositionality* (Detroit: Wayne State University Press, 1996); Michael T. Martin, ed., *New Latin American Cinema: Theory, Practices and Transcontinental Articulations* (Detroit: Wayne State University Press, 1997); and Ella Shohat and Robert Stam, *Unthinking Eurocentrism: Multiculturalism and the Media* (London: Routledge, 1994).

5. I follow two principles in selecting films for extended commentary. First, to my mind, they are of a first order of cultural and artistic importance. Second, they are available for rental or sales in the United States in English-subtitled versions. Two reliable vendors for the films are Facets Video (800–331–6197) and Movies Unlimited (800–523–0823). The remainder of the films under consideration are of equal merit but in many instances difficult to acquire or not in distribution.

6. See Roberto González Echevarría, *Alejo Carpentier: The Pilgrim at Home* (Ithaca: Cornell University press, 1977), 266.

7. For an excellent scholarly edition of the script and novel in English, see *Memories of Underdevelopment*, introduction by Michael Chanan (New Brunswick: Rutgers University Press, 1990).

Chapter 10

1. See Roy Armes, *Third World Filmmaking and the West* (Berkeley and Los Angeles: University of California Press, 1987); Manthia Diawara, *African Cinema* (Bloomington: Indiana University Press, 1992); John King, *Magical Reels: A History of Cinema in Latin America* (London: Verso, 1990); Jim Pines and Paul Willemen, eds., *Questions of Third Cinema* (London: BFI, 1989).

2. Antonio Benítez Rojo, *The Repeating Island: The Caribbean and the Postmodern Perspective* (Durham: Duke University Press, 1992).

3. Sidney W. Mintz, "The Caribbean as a Socio-Cultural Area," in *Cahiers d' Histoire Mondiale*, 9:4 (1966)

4. Benítez Rojo, op. cit., 81.

5. Nwachukwu Frank Ukadike, *Black African Cinema* (Berkeley: University of California Press, 1994), 166–245, 257–60.

6. Stuart Hall, "Cultural Identity and Cinematic Representation," *Framework,* 36 (1989): 68–81.

7. Ibid., 75–76.

8. Ibid., 80–81.

9. Jacques Roumain, *Masters of the Dew* (London: Heinemann, 1978).

10. Miguel Barnet, *Biography of a Runaway Slave* (Willimantic, Conn.: Curbstone Press, 1994).

11. Alejo Carpentier, *El reino de este mundo* (Barcelona: Seix Barral, 1991), 39–42.

12. Simone Schwarz-Bart, *The Bridge of Beyond* (London: Heinemann, 1982).

13. In Carpentier's *Guerra del tiempo* (Mexico City: Cía. General de Ediciones, 1966). See also Roberto González-Echevarría, *Alejo Carpentier: The Pilgrim at Home* (Austin: University of Texas Press, 1990), 131–33, 137.

14. Brian Goldfarb, "A Pedagogical Cinema: Development Theory, Colonialism, and Post-Liberation African Film," *Iris: A Journal of Theory on Image and Sound* 18 (spring 1995).

15. On this topic see Paul Stoller, *The Cinematic Griot* (Chicago: University of Chicago Press, 1992); and Manthia Diawara, "Popular Culture and Oral Traditions in African Film," *Film Quarterly* (spring 1988).

16. On the therapeutic power of music, and percussion specifically, see Luis Rafael Sánchez, *La guaracha del Macho Camacho* (Buenos Aires: Ediciones de la Flor, 1976), 20–22. See also Benítez Rojo, 71, and Andino Acevedo González, *¡Qué Tiempos Aquellos!* (San Juan: University of Puerto Rico Press, 1992), 87–88.

17. See Barnet's essay in *Sacred Possessions: Vodou, Santería, Obeah, and the Caribbean,* ed. Margarite Fernández Olmos and Lizabeth Paravisini-Gebert (New Brunswick: Rutgers University Press, 1997), 79–100.

18. See Mavis C. Campbell, *The Maroons of Jamaica, 1655–1796* (Granby, Mass.: Bergin and Garvey, 1988), 3, 44–47.

Chapter 11

1. Marlene Nourbese Philip, *She Tires Her Tongue, Her Silence Softly Speaks* (Charlottetown, Prince Edward Island: Ragweed Press, 1989), 97.

2. Alice Walker, *The Color Purple* (New York: Washington Square Press, 1983), 108.

3. Ibid., 175.

4. Ibid., 235.

5. Paule Marshall, *Praisesong for a Widow* (New York: E. P. Dutton, 1983), 204–5.

6. Ibid., 236.

7. Ibid., 160–61.

8. Philip, 96.

9. Marshall, 248–49.

10. Erna Brodber, *Myal* (London: New Beacon Books, 1988), 84.

11. Ibid. 67.

12. Ibid., 93.

13. Ibid., 107.

14. Ibid., 109.

15. Opal Palmer Adisa, *It Begins with Tears* (London: Heinemann, 1997), 216.

16. Ibid., 218.

17. Ibid., 222.

18. Ibid., 40.

19. Philip, 72.

Chapter 12

1. From a talk given at the presentation of *Da Haiti venne il sangue,* Italian translation of *Del rojo de tu sombra,* in Milan, on 16 February 1994.

Chapter 13

1. Caroline Ravello, "The Poet-Artist, Master," *Trinidad and Tobago Review* 20:12 (1998): 44.

2. A Yoruba word that means "the citing of one's origins." Oríkì are essentially genealogical songs of praise that may be vocal, in the form of a chant, or visual, in the form of sculpture (Rowland Abiodun, Henry J. Drewal, and John Pemberton III, eds., *The Yoruba Artist: New Theoretical Perspectives on African Arts,* London: Smithsonian Institution Press, 1994).

3. Alf Cadallo is a prominent artist who died in 1970.

4. Clarke sometimes uses "Eye" to replace the pronoun "I."

5. A Trinidadian expression used to describe wild mushrooms.

6. Ella Andall is a prominent singer and composer in Trinidad and a close friend of LeRoy Clarke. Andall, according to Clarke, resides in the house of Orisha.

7. Trinidadian expression meaning "flattery."

Contributors' Biographical Notes

ERNESTO ACEVEDO-MUÑOZ has recently completed his doctorate in film studies at the University of Colorado at Boulder.

OPAL PALMER ADISA, Jamaican born, is a literary critic, poet, novelist, and storyteller. She is the author of *It Begins with Tears* (1997), *Tamarind and Mango Women* (1992), *traveling women* (1989), *Bake-Face and Other Guava Stories* (1986), and *Pina, the Many-Eyed Fruit* (1995). Her poetry, stories, and essays have appeared in numerous anthologies.

KAREN MCCARTHY BROWN is the author of *Mama Lola: A Vodou Priestess in Brooklyn* (1991) and *Tracing the Spirit: Ethnographic Essays on Haitian Art* (1996), as well as numerous articles on spiritual and healing practices within Haitian Vodou, the result of her extensive fieldwork in Haiti and the Haitian diaspora community in Brooklyn. McCarthy Brown is on the faculties of the Graduate and Theological Schools of Drew University.

LYDIA CABRERA was born in Havana, Cuba, in 1900. A scholar and chronicler of Afro-Cuban culture, Cabrera's interest in the field developed in Paris in the 1920s, where she had gone to study religion and art. Her numerous works, in particular *El monte* (1954), are seminal studies for an understanding of Santería and the other African-based religious practices on the island. Cabrera died in Miami in 1991.

JERRY CARLSON is a professor in the Department of Media and Communication Arts of the City College (CUNY) and a producer for City University Television in New York City. He is the producer of *Charlando con Cervantes,* a forty-episode television series offering interviews with leading Latin American and Caribbean writers, artists, and filmmakers, and has curated retrospectives of Cuban, Mexican, Colombian, Argentine, and Venezuelan films for his regular television series *City Cinematheque.* In 1997 Carlson was inducted by the French government as a Chevalier de l'Ordre des Palmes Academiques.

KAREN CASTELLUCCI COX is an assistant professor of English at Bronx Community College of the City University of New York. Castellucci Cox's research interests include women's literature, short story theory, and narrative form; an essay, "Magic and Memory in the Contemporary Story Cycle: Gloria Naylor and Louise Erdich," appeared in *College English.*

LEROY CLARKE is an acclaimed Trinidadian poet and artist whose works have been described as "an elaborate/elaborated personal version of Trinidadian mythology; Clarke's Scriptures."

HÉCTOR DELGADO is the photographer of the Cuban Union of Artists and Writers (UNEAC) in Havana. His works—which document the cultural persistence of Afro-Cuban religions—have been exhibited in Canada, Mexico, and the United States, and have appeared in several books, including Miguel Barnet's *La Regla de Ocha* (1995) and our *Sacred Possessions: Vodou, Santería, Obeah, and the Caribbean* (1997).

BRIAN DU TOIT is Professor of Anthropology and African Studies at the University of Florida at Gainesville. He is the author of numerous books, among them *People of the Valley* (1974), *Drugs, Rituals, and Altered States of Consciousness* (1977), *Cannabis in Africa* (1980), *African Healing Strategies* (1985), *Dying and Menopause Among Indian South African Women* (1990), *Boer Settlers in the Southwest* (1995), and *The Boers in East Africa: Ethnicity and Identity* (1998).

HEIDI HOLDER studied art history at Brooklyn College where she was a Mellon Undergraduate Fellow. In the summer of 1997 Holder researched the life and work of Trinidadian artist LeRoy Clarke as part of a seminar hosted by the University of the West Indies in her native Trinidad.

MAYRA MONTERO is an award-winning novelist, short story writer, and journalist. Born in Cuba, Montero emigrated with her family to Puerto Rico, where she still lives today. Her novels and stories have been translated into many languages. Two novels—*In the Palm of Darkness* (1998) and *The Messenger* (1999)—were recently published in English to critical acclaim.

MARIO NÚÑEZ MOLINA teaches sociology at the Mayagüez campus of the University of Puerto Rico. He earned his doctorate from the Harvard Graduate School of Education with a dissertation on the medium as a healer in Puerto Rican Espiritismo. His work on the subject has appeared in various journals.

MARGARITE FERNÁNDEZ OLMOS is a professor of Spanish and Latin American Studies at Brooklyn College, CUNY. She has lectured extensively on contemporary Caribbean and Latin American literature as well as U.S. Latino literature, and has published essays in numerous journals and anthologies. She is the author of *La cuentística de Juan Bosch: Un análisis crítico-cultural* (1982), *Sobre la literatura puertorriqueña de aquí y de allá: aproximaciones feministas* (1989), and *Rudolfo Anaya: A Critical Companion* (1999). She coedited *Contemporary Women Authors of Latin America: New Translations* and *Introductory Essays* (1983) with Doris Meyer. Her other books include *El placer de la palabra: literatura erótica femenina de América Latina* (1991), *Pleasure in the Word: Erotic Writing by Latin American Women* (1993), *Remaking a Lost Harmony: Short Stories from the Hispanic Caribbean* (1995), and *Sacred Possessions: Vodou, Santería, Obeah, and the Caribbean* (1997), all coedited with Lizabeth Paravisini-Gebert, and *The Latino Reader: An American Literary Tradition from 1542 to the Present* (1997) and *U.S. Latino Literature: A Critical Guide for Students and Teacher* (2000), with Harold Augenbraum.

LIZABETH PARAVISINI-GEBERT is professor of Caribbean and Latin American literature at Vassar College. She coauthored *Caribbean Women Novelists: An Annotated Critical Bibliography* (1993) with Olga Torres Seda, and is the author of *Phyllis Shand Allfrey: A Caribbean Life* (1996) and of *Jamaica Kincaid: A Critical Companion* (1998). Her other books include *Ana Roqué's Luz y sombra* (1991), *Green Cane and Juicy Flotsam: Short Stories by Caribbean Women* (with Carmen Esteves, 1991), and three collections coedited with Margarite Fernández Olmos: *El placer de la palabra: literatura erótica femenina de América Latina* (1991), *Pleasure in the Word: Erotic Writing by Latin American Women* (1993), and *Remaking a Lost Harmony: Short Stories from the Hispanic Caribbean* (1995). She has just completed a study entitled *Obsolete Geographies: Race, Gender, and the Plantation in Caribbean Women's Fiction* and is working on a study of nineteenth-century geological exploration and the cultural history of the Caribbean.

ESTER REBECA SHAPIRO ROK is an associate professor of psychology at the University of Massachusetts at Boston and research associate at the Mauricio Gaston Institute for Latino Public Policy and Community Development. She is the author of *Grief as a Family Process: A Developmental Approach to Clinical Practice* (1994); coordinating editor of *Nuestros Cuerpos Nuestras Vidas* (1999), the Spanish language translation and cultural adaptation of *Our Bodies, Ourselves;* and coeditor with Murray Meisels of *Tradition and Innovation in Psychoanalytic Education* (1990). She has written professional articles on family development, culture and grief, resilience among urban immigrant adolescents and families, and multimethod program evaluation based on a sociocultural developmental model.

ANNA WEXLER is a writer and artist whose work has been shown in recent exhibits exploring the influence of the Afro-Caribbean religions on contemporary visual practice. She has published essays and interviews based on her doctoral dissertation (Harvard University, 1998), a study of spirit-mediated creativity in the artistry of the Haitian Vodou priest and flag maker Clotaire Bazile. Her current research centers on figural objects and magic in African Atlantic healing traditions.